Crossing the Line:
Black Major Leaguers, 1947–1959

Crossing the Line

BLACK MAJOR LEAGUERS,
1947–1959

By Larry Moffi and
Jonathan Kronstadt

University of Iowa Press
Iowa City

University of Iowa Press, Iowa City 52242
Copyright © 1994 by Larry Moffi and Jonathan Kronstadt
All rights reserved
Printed in the United States of America

International Standard Book Number 0-87745-529-5
Library of Congress Catalog Card Number 94-9056

Cover design by Richard Hendel

This edition is published by special arrangement with McFarland &
Company, Inc., Publishers, Jefferson, North Carolina.

Printed on acid-free paper

01   00   99   98   97   96   P   5   4   3   2   1

To
Harry Naiman
and
Tom Denson

Contents

1952

1953

1954

1955

1959

A c k n o w l e d g m e n t s

This is the only book of its kind, cataloguing all (known) black major leaguers from 1947 through 1959. We have placed players according to the year they broke into the major leagues. Within each year, players are listed alphabetically. Our intention was to give the reader a sense of the progression of these 13 years that the players, as a group, represent.

In our research, we relied on the following periodicals: *The Sporting News*, the *Pittsburgh Courier*, *Ebony* magazine, *Jet*, the *Chicago Herald American*, the *New York Age*, *New York Star*, *Sport* magazine, *Life* magazine, and *Look*.

We are also indebted to the authors of the following books, which we consulted regularly: *The Baseball Encyclopedia*, edited by Joseph L. Reichler; *The Encyclopedia of Baseball*, edited by David S. Neft and Richard M. Cohen; *The Baseball Chronology*, edited by James Charlton; *Total Baseball*, 2d ed., edited by John Thorn and Pete Palmer; *Only the Ball Was White*, by Robert Peterson; *Get That Nigger Off the Field*, by Art Rust, Jr.; *Baseball Has Done It*, by Jackie Robinson; *Baseball's Great Experiment—Jackie Robinson and His Legacy*, by Jules Tygiel; *The Boys of Summer*, by Roger Kahn; *Pride Versus Prejudice*, by Joseph Thomas Moore; *Glory Days with the Dodgers and Other Days with Others*, by John Roseboro; *Maybe I'll Pitch Forever*, by Satchel Paige; *Fenway: An Unexpurgated History of the Boston Red Sox*, by Peter Golenbock; *Bums*, by Peter Golenbock; *Extra Innings*, by Minnie Minoso; *Twenty Years Too Soon*, by Quincy Trouppe; *Aaron*, by Hank Aaron; *I Had a Hammer: The Hank Aaron Story*, by Hank Aaron and Lonnie Wheeler; *For the Love of the Game*, by Cynthia Wilber; *Tiger Stats*, by Fred T. Smith; *The Explosive Sixties*, by William Mead; *Speed*, by Steve Fiffer; *The Hurlers*, by Kevin Kerrane.

We also owe thanks to Milt Bolling, Minnie Minoso, Carl Erskine, and Vern Law for personal interviews; to Larry Doby and Bill White for public lectures; and to Bill Deane of the Baseball Hall of Fame Library and Dave Kelly of the Library of Congress.

Introduction

On April 15, 1947, a black baseball player named Jack Roosevelt Robinson opened the season at first base for the Brooklyn Dodgers against the Boston Braves at Ebbets Field in Brooklyn. Robinson went 0 for 3, with a sacrifice. Baseball would never be the same.

The story of Jackie Robinson breaking baseball's color line is one of the most dramatic and triumphant in sports history. With the eyes of a nation and the hopes of 14 million black Americans upon him, Robinson was brilliant, earning respect with his aggressive play and his determination. But while Robinson opened the door, the successful integration of baseball was also dependent upon the talent and character of the men who walked through it after him. This book is also about those men.

In July 1947, three months after Branch Rickey made Robinson baseball's first black player, Cleveland owner Bill Veeck signed Larry Doby to a contract, breaking the color line in the American League. A week later, an editorial in the *Sporting News* (*TSN*) proclaimed an end to racial problems in organized baseball. The "baseball bible" could not have been more wrong.

"Just so long as there was a Negro ball player in the National League — Jackie Robinson, with Brooklyn — and none in the American League, there was a Negro question in the majors," *TSN* stated. "Now that the Cleveland club has placed Larry Doby, a first baseman acquired from the Newark team of the Negro National League, on its roster, the race matter no longer is an official perplexity. It no longer exists insofar as Organized Baseball administration is concerned."

In fact, the "race matter," which was never "official," very much existed. Ever since the late 1800s, when a black catcher named Moses Fleetwood Walker played in the American Association — at the time considered a major league — there had never been an official ban on black players within the structure known as organized baseball. Segregation was so ingrained and so often unconsciously accepted by most Americans, particularly in the business world — and professional baseball has always been a business — that an "official" ban was practically redundant.

In 1901, John McGraw, managing the Baltimore Orioles of the American Association, tried to field a team that included a black second baseman,

1

Charlie Grant, who had previously played in an all-black league. McGraw tried to pass Grant off as a full-blooded American Indian, Cherokee, but the ruse caused so much commotion that the future Giants manager gave it up, and Grant never did play for the Orioles. The unwritten law was that effective.

For McGraw and for dozens of other managers, general managers, and team presidents who might have considered signing a black ballplayer, challenging an unwritten rule was not worth the aggravation. If you were white, and everyone in organized baseball was white, it was much easier to maintain the status quo.

Nearly 50 years passed before the Brooklyn Dodgers' Branch Rickey signed Robinson to a minor league contract with the Dodgers Class AAA affiliate, the Montreal Royals, in 1945. Surprisingly — maybe not surprisingly — the commissioner of baseball, A. B. "Happy" Chandler, supported Rickey's decision. "I have always said — and I repeat it now," said Chandler, "that Negro players are welcome in baseball. It is true that they have never been accepted, but that was because no one had the courage to sign them. Branch Rickey has made the initial step and there is nothing wrong with it. I sincerely hope Robinson makes good with Montreal. He is a fine young man, a fine American."

It was almost that simple. Until Rickey, no one did have the courage. And Robinson was a fine young man and a fine American. He was also an excellent ballplayer and an extraordinary human being. Among those who might have been called, from James "Cool Papa" Bell to Monte Irvin, Jackie Robinson was truly chosen.

Rickey had made Robinson his personal study for nearly a year. When he selected the former three-sport letterman at UCLA to integrate organized baseball, the success of the experiment was almost predictable. As much for his athletic ability, Rickey picked Robinson for his temperament, leadership qualities, intelligence, and maturity. "When I called Robinson to my office," said Rickey, recalling the day he signed Robinson to a Royals contract, "he had no idea I wanted him for a white team. I dramatized six situations I knew he would come up against in baseball. I called him names. I all but hit him. I had to test him."

Today, Jackie Robinson is legend. His life, like that of Dr. Martin Luther King, Jr., has come to symbolize a struggle for equality. Robinson has been the subject of movies, biographies, even a postage stamp. When filmmaker Spike Lee appears in his own movies wearing a baggy baseball shirt with *42* on the back, many in the audience immediately recognize the number as Jackie's.

Robinson began what author Jules Tygiel called "baseball's great experiment." On the field, he was subject to hateful racial slurs from both fans and opposing players; he was knocked down and brushed back by pitchers and spiked by base runners. When the Dodgers were on the road, he often roomed in "colored only" hotels or rooming houses in all-black neighborhoods.

But Robinson was also a unifying force. His teammates, and often members of the opposition, rallied around him. He packed the stands in Ebbets Field and on the road. Robinson's drive, daring, and stoicism made him the great player he became. In his time, he was an unparalleled competitor.

The pressure that Robinson lived with and the tension he endured in the first few seasons with the Dodgers probably took a few years off his life. But despite his winning the major leagues' first Rookie of the Year award, 1947 was just the beginning of the experiment.

Through the end of the 1953 season, only eight of the 16 major league teams had black players on their rosters. Not until Pumpsie Green pinch-ran for the Boston Red Sox on July 21, 1959, were all major league teams integrated. By then, Jackie Robinson, retired from baseball for more than two years, was personnel director at the Chock Full O' Nuts coffee company and restaurant chain.

More than 100 black ballplayers played in the major leagues between 1947 and 1959. Among them were some of the greatest names in baseball history: Satchel Paige, Roy Campanella, Monte Irvin, Willie Mays, Ernie Banks, Hank Aaron, Frank Robinson, Billy Williams, Roberto Clemente, Willie McCovey, Bob Gibson — each a Hall of Famer. Others, like Larry Doby, Minnie Minoso, Don Newcombe, Vic Power, Billy Bruton, Jim Gilliam, Brooks Lawrence, Curt Flood, Elston Howard, Orlando Cepeda, Leon Wagner, and Maury Wills, were unquestionably among the best of their time. Players like Joe Black, Sam Jethroe, Luke Easter, Sandy Amoros, and Hank Thompson will be remembered forever — for one season, one series, or one game. And there were those who are all but forgotten: Artie Wilson, Dan Bankhead, Jim Proctor, Don Eaddy, Charlie Peete . . .

Every black player who followed Robinson during the next 12 years experienced some form of racial discrimination. There were stories of players like Dave Hoskins, the first black player in the Texas League. Hoskins pitched just 140 innings in the major leagues but once took the mound after receiving three death threats on the same day and pitched Dallas to a 3–2 win over Shreveport. There were early stories of superstars like Aaron, who at the age of 18 was one of three black players to integrate the notorious South Atlantic, or "Sally," League, whose teams played in Georgia, Alabama, and Florida. Aaron also received death threats but decided that the best way to deal with racial hatred was by battering the league's earned run average (ERA).

Sometimes playing well was enough. Sometimes it made things worse. Brush-back pitches were an acceptable form of retribution against successful hitters in the 1940s and 1950s, and if you were black, you were already a popular target. Hit a home run, and the opposing pitcher suddenly had a justifiable cover for racially motivated head-hunting. Black players were regularly carried off the field after being beaned in the early days of integration. Denver's Curt

Roberts was actually hit by pitches four times in a single game. According to author Jules Tygiel, "Beanballs hospitalized one out of four black non-pitchers in Triple-A baseball in 1949."

Things were not much better in the majors. Midway through his first season with the Dodgers, Robinson had been hit by a pitch seven times, more than anyone else. "No question about it," Monte Irvin told Tygiel. "They threw at us like we were something good to eat." And when black players were not dodging beanballs or being harassed by fans, opponents, and sometimes their own teammates, they were suffering from the racial indignities of life off the playing field. Banned from team hotels and restaurants, they stayed in the homes of black families or in lousy hotels with no air conditioning. They sat on the bus or ate in the kitchen while their white teammates ate in restaurant dining rooms. "I had to go to the back door of the restaurant, like a beggar," wrote Curt Flood in his autobiography.

For the most part, however, black players were remarkably well accepted by their teammates, the opposition, and the fans who came to watch them play. Despite the threat of a strike by some St. Louis Cardinals players, Bill Veeck was essentially correct when in signing Larry Doby he said, "I am operating under the belief that [World War II] advanced us in regard to racial tolerance." Indeed, in 1948, when the Ku Klux Klan threatened to protest a Dodgers exhibition game in Atlanta, acting Atlanta mayor M. E. Thompson came out in support of the game and the participation of Robinson and Roy Campanella. "We are proud of Jackie Robinson here in Georgia," said Thompson, "not only as a ball player but as a gentleman." The Dodgers, with Robinson and Campanella, played before a capacity crowd and without incident. And while it was just a baseball game, it proved undeniably a fundamental point that Branch Rickey believed when he signed Robinson: "The public is not as concerned with a first baseman's pigmentation as it is with the power of his swing, the dexterity of his slide, the gracefulness of his fielding, or the speed of his legs."

Between 1947 and 1959, in city after city in the United States, black players proved Rickey right. Willie Mays proved it in New York, Minnie Minoso in Chicago, Larry Doby and Satchel Paige in Cleveland, Bob Thurman in Cincinnati, and Harry Simpson (playing beside Enos Slaughter, one of the players accused of instigating the strike in St. Louis), in Kansas City.

Black players were also proving themselves in the provinces. In 1950, Billy Bruton won the Northern League Rookie of the Year award. The following season, a 20-year-old outfielder named Percy Miller became the first black to play in the Carolina League. That year, seven of the eight Pacific Coast League teams had black players in their lineups, including Roy Welmaker, Gene Baker, Raoul Lopez, Frank Austin, Granville Gladstone, Sam Hairston, Bob Boyd, Sam Jones, and Bob Thurman. Two years later, Aaron won the Sally League batting title, hitting .362.

But there were trying times as well. It took a federal court to integrate the Southern Association. The judge in the case decreed that laws prohibiting integrated play in Birmingham, Alabama, were illegal. And in 1953, Jim Tugerson, a black player, filed a $50,000 damage suit against the Cotton States League and five club officials. Tugerson, who had been optioned to Knoxville earlier in the season to "preserve harmony" in the league, charged the defendants with conspiracy "to prevent him from carrying out his contract, following his lawful occupation of a baseball player, and enjoying the equal protection of the law in his privileges as a citizen of the United States of America."

Tugerson and his brother, Leander, both right-handed pitchers with the Indianapolis Clowns, were signed in 1952 by the Hot Springs (Arkansas) Bathers. Bathers management promised the Tugersons that they would play only in home games and in cities that did not object to their participation. When the Tugersons showed up at spring training, they were told that as a result of a special league meeting in Greenville, Mississippi, the Bathers had been barred from the league. The meeting took place five days after Mississippi's attorney general ruled that blacks could not play baseball with white players in the state. The ruling barred the Tugersons from playing in four league cities, all in Mississippi.

In defense of the ruling, league president Al Haraway claimed that the action was taken to preserve the league because the Hot Springs decision to play the blacks was against the will of other teams and would result in the "dissolution" of the league. Following the ruling, the Tugersons issued the following statement: "We hope this is not embarrassing to the city of Hot Springs, which has been so nice to us. We don't wish to keep the city from having baseball. But as long as the club wants us, we will stay here and fight."

A few days later, George Trautman, president of the national association of minor league teams, reinstated the Bathers in the league. In another secret meeting of team owners in Greenville, league officials agreed with Trautman's ruling. But one week after the team was readmitted, the Tugersons were optioned to Knoxville of the Mountain States League.

Team owners sometimes got caught in the middle of forces on both sides of the integration fight. Six years after Dallas owner Dick Burnett made Dave Hoskins the first black to play in the Texas League, he was forced to quit the league, caught in a financial vise between a boycott of black fans and the refusal of other league teams to challenge a Louisiana law banning mixed-race play.

In late July 1947, the St. Louis Browns signed Hank Thompson and Willard Brown to contracts, prompting yet another editorial in the *Sporting News*. The national baseball weekly criticized the Browns for resorting to promotional gimmickry. The purchase of the contracts of the two black ballplayers from the Kansas City Monarchs of the Negro American League was, *TSN* claimed, a poorly disguised attempt to sell more tickets. Neither Thompson nor Brown was of major league caliber, and, the editorial concluded, if St. Louis was serious about improving its team, management would have served its fans and its team better by signing any of the eminently more qualified white ballplayers from the higher levels of the minor leagues.

Bill Veeck, who in a few years would own the Browns, halfway agreed. But Veeck, in his inimitable way, argued that the reason there were not more qualified black ballplayers was that until now, black professionals were never able to set their sights as high as their white counterparts. But that was changing, Veeck announced. "As the years go by, we'll have an increasing number of colored boys in the majors."

Until Robinson took the field with the Montreal Royals in 1946, the highest level of professional ball a black player could aspire to was the segregated competition known as the "Negro leagues." Officially "founded" in 1920, the Negro leagues initially consisted of the Negro National League, joined in 1923 by the Eastern Colored League. From 1923 to 1927, the two leagues were composed of 14 teams whose schedules consisted of 50 to 89 games a year. At the end of each season, the first-place teams squared off in a Negro League World Series. In 1928, the Eastern Colored League disbanded, its teams reconfigured as the Negro American League in 1929 and later the Negro Southern League. World Series competition resumed between the Negro National League and the Negro American League in 1942 and continued through 1948.

In addition to the Negro leagues, many black players earned extra money and experience by signing on with teams in the Cuban, Panamanian, Dominican, Puerto Rican, and Mexican leagues, where they frequently played alongside white teammates without incident. But until the signing of Robinson, Negro league ball was the highest level a black player could experience in the United States.

In recent years, Negro league greats—Cool Papa Bell, Ray Dandridge, Smokey Joe Williams, Bullet Rogan, Mule Suttles, Josh Gibson, Willie Wells, Oscar Charleston, among others—have finally received long overdue recognition. Some, who were elected to the Baseball Hall of Fame, were among the greatest ballplayers of all time despite having been denied the opportunity to display their talents at baseball's highest level of competition. No doubt the names of many others would be familiar if the door to the majors had not been closed to them.

In comparison to the major and minor leagues, Negro league play was far from "organized." While the best players were well paid (Robinson actually took a pay cut when he went from the Kansas City Monarchs to the Montreal Royals), contracts between players and teams were practically nonexistent. Players jumped teams, and schedules were erratic. Most teams in larger cities rented the stadiums of major or minor league clubs, playing when the white team was on the road. In 1948, Robinson criticized the Negro leagues, saying that "Negro baseball needs housecleaning from bottom to top."

The standard by which Negro league ball was measured was known as "organized baseball." Organized ball meant the major leagues' 16 teams, divided into the American and National leagues, and the vast network of minor league teams in the United States, Canada, and Cuba that fed them. Most leagues were small-scale replicas of the two major leagues. They played their schedules to completion year after year, paid their players regularly, and often staged interleague postseason championships.

In one sense, the term "organized" merely reflected the contractual agreements between players and management. Teams owned the contracts of each ballplayer, and contracts were sold as property, with prices determined by the perceived value of the player and the needs of the purchasing team. When a contract changed ownership, all profit from the sale remained with the seller.

When organized baseball was at its height following World War II, minor league baseball consisted of 366 teams divided into 52 leagues of various levels, ranging from Class AAA to Class D. On any given summer day, there were as many as 9,000 or 10,000 players, all white, under contract to a team in organized ball.

Organized baseball meant white baseball. Negro league baseball meant baseball outside "the organization." Much like the 1954 Supreme Court case *Brown v. Board of Education*, Negro league ball was an example of the inequity of the "separate but equal" doctrine. Not surprisingly, arguments from both white players and white management resembled the logic of those opposed to integrated schools.

A white player who signed with a Class D team as a teenager might have his contract bought and sold six or seven times before he reached the major leagues. The competition for a spot on any team in any league was cutthroat, and the likelihood of a player reaching the majors was a long shot at best.

In 1948, the *Sporting News* anonymously quoted a white all-star: "I do not object to playing alongside a Negro. However, the Negroes have their own league. Is it going to open up to white players, as the majors opened up to Negroes?

"Another thing. The Negroes holler 'discrimination.' Well, Robinson moved right into the National League after only one year in the AAA minors, and Doby gets a job in the American League without previous schooling in white baseball.

"I fought my way through the minors for five years. I rode buses all night for three of those five years, so that I could get a chance in the majors.

"If we are to have Negroes in the majors, let them go through the long preparation the white player is forced to undergo. Let us not discriminate against the white player because he is white."

Seven years later, Red Sox manager Pinky Higgins, who had far less at stake than any ballplayer, was more to the point. "There'll be no niggers on this ballclub as long as I have anything to say about it."

The tack of major league club owners was much more genteel and diplomatic. It was also highly transparent. When protestors marched outside Yankee Stadium accusing the Yankees of Jim Crowism, Yankee owner Dan Topping, in defense of one of the most inept player assessments of all time, said, "Our scouting reports rate [Vic] Power a good hitter, but a poor fielder." St. Louis Cardinals owner Fred M. Saigh barely veiled his lack of interest in pursuing black prospects in an article in *Ebony* magazine: "The Cardinal organization has always been interested in securing baseball players that might have capabilities of ultimately playing with the St. Louis Cardinals."

Branch Rickey went so far as to cite a conspiracy among club owners to keep Jackie Robinson and other black players from participating in organized ball. "After I signed Robinson, but before he had played a game," Rickey claimed, "a joint major league meeting adopted unanimously a report prepared that 'however well intentioned, the use of Negro players would hazard the physical properties of baseball.'"

The Yankees' Larry MacPhail as much as called Rickey a liar. Rickey's motivation in signing Robinson, according to MacPhail, came not from his conscience but his wallet. As MacPhail reminded the public, Rickey had scouts all over the country looking for players, black or white, and would sign them for a song. According to MacPhail, the agenda of organized baseball was to compensate the Negro league teams adequately in the purchase of contracts of their players. It was not in the best interests of either organized ball or the Negro leagues, MacPhail argued, for teams in organized ball to "raid" the Negro leagues.

Basically, the argument was the slogan of the times: "We" and "they" are just not ready. What MacPhail neglected to say, however, was that money was also in the best interests of the Yankees, who earned approximately $100,000 in rent from Negro league tenants in Yankee Stadium and stadiums in Kansas City, Newark, and Norfolk.

Rickey was nobody's fool. He knew that black Americans, who had a share in the post–World War II economic boom, were a largely untapped market for organized baseball and that integrating the game was the best way to get more blacks through the turnstiles. He was right. For example, on July 14, 1948, an exhibition game between the Dodgers and the Indians drew a crowd of 64,877 fans, 26,000 of whom were black. One of every six blacks in Cleveland was at the game. Black players were big box office in the minors as well. Attendance throughout baseball was dropping in the early 1950s, and integration saved some teams from bankruptcy. Hoskins drew record crowds wherever he pitched in 1952, crowds so big that he became known as "the savior of the Texas League." In Aaron's first season in the Sally League, attendance at Jacksonville rose 135 percent.

Even black sportswriters acknowledged profit as a legitimate motivation for signing black ballplayers. In January 1949, C. Wendell Smith of the

Pittsburgh Courier wrote, "There is likely to be a considerable increase in the top minor leagues. . . . As in the majors, good Negro players in the minors have box office appeal. Branch Rickey found that out at St. Paul and Montreal, especially on the road. [In 1948 the Dodgers, showcasing Robinson and Campanella, reportedly earned more than $75,000 on a "back to Brooklyn" barnstorming trip following spring training.]

"The attendance angle is an important factor in the entire picture of the Negro player's future. The good American dollar is still the world's best medium of exchange and there isn't an owner in baseball who is so haughty that he'll turn it down because it comes to him via low classification minor league channels."

In a matter of just a few years, $100,000 in rent seemed like pocket change compared to the potential that Smith — and Rickey, Bill Veeck, and the New York Giants' Horace Stoneham — realized. Ultimately, "acquisition of Negro players became a matter of financial wisdom, if nothing else, for the Yankees," wrote Dan Daniel. And so it was for virtually every team in the minor and major leagues.

But the signing of Robinson signaled the death knell of the Negro leagues. In 1947, the attendance at Newark Eagles games was just 57,119, down from 120,923 the year before. Team owners got pennies on the dollar or nothing at all when their players were signed by major league clubs. Ernie Banks brought $20,000 to the Kansas City Monarchs when his contract was sold to the Chicago Cubs, but that was the highest price ever paid for a Negro league player. More typical was the case of Sam Jethroe, who was sold by Cleveland Buckeyes owner Ernie Wright to the Dodgers for $5,000. Two years later, Jethroe was sold to the Braves for more than $100,000. With revenues declining, many teams were forced to sell their best players for whatever they could get just to stay in business.

In 1953 the Indianapolis Clowns signed a woman, Toni Stone, to a $12,000 contract to play second base, then denied the signing was a publicity stunt. But the deed was done, and while the Negro American League lasted until 1960, Negro league baseball was really finished the day Robinson appeared in a Dodger uniform.

While in many respects the "time was right" in post–World War II America for black players to gain acceptance into organized ball, their ascent to the major leagues was hardly coincidental. Change became the only constant in American society. And baseball reflected the difference as accurately as any aspect of American life.

On June 19, 1946, baseball, including Commissioner Chandler, celebrated its centennial with a game in Hoboken, New Jersey, where the first game at present regulation distances was played 100 years before. Meanwhile, the great baseball names of the century were giving way to many of the black players who would break their records. Babe Ruth, Lou Gehrig, Ty Cobb,

Connie Mack, Shoeless Joe Jackson, and Hack Wilson died. Joe DiMaggio, Hank Greenberg, and Bob Feller retired.

The Braves moved from Boston to Milwaukee, the Athletics from Philadelphia to Kansas City. And the St. Louis Browns gave up trying to compete with the Anheuser-Busch–owned Cardinals and became the Baltimore Orioles. The Dodgers and Giants moved to the West Coast, opening the 1958 season not in the ballparks that had been their home fields for decades — Ebbets Field and the Polo Grounds — but in a converted football stadium that seated nearly 100,000 and a minor league park that was formerly home to the San Francisco Seals of the Pacific Coast League.

Television, which in 1948 brought the World Series live to nearly eight million people, was doing to the minor leagues what the major leagues had done to the Negro leagues. North Carolina, home to 45 minor league teams in 1950, had only nine by 1954. In 1956, the Cincinnati Reds announced plans to air-condition the dugouts at Crosley Field.

In 1958, Commissioner Ford Frick implored an antitrust Senate hearing to control television's coverage of baseball in order to save the game. Frick went on to say that baseball could not continue to lavish on players unrealistic bonuses of $100,000 just for the privilege of signing them. Jackie Robinson, retired for less than a year, testified before the hearing and argued that players ought to have a say in choosing baseball's commissioner. By 1959, airplanes had replaced trains as the primary mode of transportation between cities, at least in the National League.

Amid so much exciting, complex, and often difficult change, 116 black baseball players did what no one of their race had done before, what no one of the white race thought to insist on. They came to the big leagues from sharecropping towns in northern Florida and the steel mills of Pennsylvania; from Mobile, Alabama, and McClymonds High School in Oakland, California. They came from Panama, Puerto Rico, and Cuba.

As skilled as any major leaguer must be, the majority of these players were, like their white counterparts, average ballplayers. Few possessed the boyish charm or all-around skill of a Willie Mays; few were as outspoken as Robinson. Yet each served. And each endured difficulties that, for some, diminished the potential of their own careers while taking much of the pressure off their brethren whose greater baseball skills won them eternal fame.

To a man, they opened eyes and allayed fears. As a group, from Jackie Robinson and Hank Aaron to Milt Smith and Jim Proctor, they are the most influential players in the history of baseball, the thread and weave of one of the most significant lessons in the education of a nation.

1947

Daniel Robert "Dan" Bankhead

Pitcher. Batted right. Threw right. 6'1", 184 lbs. Born 5/30/20, Empire, Alabama.

Branch Rickey needed pitching, and Jackie Robinson needed a room-mate. And besides, Rickey wanted to see for himself what all the fuss was about. So on August 23, 1947, he left the pennant race behind and flew to Memphis to watch Dan Bankhead pitch. He must have been impressed because three days later Bankhead took the mound in a Dodger uniform, becoming the major leagues' first black pitcher.

Bankhead had already been looked over by Dodger scouts George Sisler and Clyde Sukeforth, and his advance notices included such comparisons as "the next Satchel Paige" and "the colored Bob Feller." Bankhead never lived up to those expectations, but little about his career was ordinary.

The Bankhead family were wall-to-wall ballplayers. Dan's father was a star first baseman in the Cotton Belt League until the day he saw a man die after being hit by a flying bat. Dan's oldest brother, Sam, was one of the finest short-stops in the Negro leagues for nearly 20 years and in 1951 became the first black manager in organized baseball with Farnham, Quebec, in the Provincial League. His brother Fred was an infielder and Dan's teammate with the Memphis Red Sox, while two other brothers, Garnett and Joe, had short careers in the Negro leagues.

Dan broke into professional baseball as a shortstop with the 1940 Birmingham Black Barons and was a fine hitter throughout his career. But he moved to the mound and went 6-1 for the Barons in 1941 before spending nearly four years in the marines, where he organized an all-black baseball team. Bankhead returned to the Memphis Red Sox in 1946, was voted to the All-Star team for the second of three times, and was the winning pitcher in both All-Star games that season. A year later, with Branch Rickey looking on, Bankhead struck out 11 of his former Birmingham teammates. Rickey reportedly paid $15,000 for Bankhead's contract, the highest price paid for a black player's contract in 1947.

Rickey's Dodgers were in first place but dangerously short on pitching, so Bankhead was not afforded the luxury of a year or two in the minors. "I can't help myself," Rickey said. "We need pitchers and we need them badly. I know this boy has the physical equipment to help this club.... The only question is whether he will be able to understand the tremendous pressure under which he will work."

Bankhead's major league debut was nightmarish — on the mound at least. Pitching in relief, Bankhead was tagged for eight runs and 10 hits in just three innings. "I was scared as hell," he said. "When I stepped on the mound, I was perspiring all over and tight as a drum. I wound up to throw to the first batter and I thought I'd never get unwound." Still, he did something no other National League pitcher had ever done. He homered in his first major league at-bat. It would also be his last major league homer.

Bankhead appeared in just three more games that season, the highlight being four scoreless innings on Jackie Robinson Day at Ebbets Field. His confidence appeared shot, so Rickey decided to send him down to Class B Nashua to start the 1948 season. Well, Bankhead may not have proven himself in the majors yet, but he had too much stuff for Class B hitters to handle. With a good fastball, an array of breaking pitches, and a herky-jerky delivery, Bankhead became the league's first-ever 20-game winner, tossed a no-hitter, and struck out 240 in 202 innings before ending the season with four consecutive victories with Class AAA St. Paul.

In 1949 he became known as "the wild man of the International League" as he led the league in strikeouts and walks with Montreal but went 20-6 and led the Royals to the pennant. He had a brilliant winter league season, winning 10 games, hitting seven home runs, and clinching the Puerto Rican League pennant for Caguas with a five-hit shutout. The 1950 preseason speculation had Bankhead being offered for sale by Rickey, but the reported $100,000 price tag was too steep.

Instead, Bankhead opened the season as reliever and spot starter and won his first four decisions. After shutting out the Cardinals on three hits in June, he earned the number three spot in the Dodger rotation behind Don Newcombe and Preacher Roe. Rickey called him "the best pitcher in the big leagues right now."

But in July Bankhead developed a stiff shoulder, and an exam revealed that a dislocation when he was 17 had calcified. The shoulder injury was one explanation for Bankhead's quick fall from a starting spot to the minor leagues. Others speculated that Bankhead was too timid to make it in the majors, an explanation Rickey himself had fueled. Bankhead had his own explanation — financial pressure brought on by an inability to find an apartment in Brooklyn that would accept children. He and his family stayed at an expensive hotel suite, which ate up most of his salary. "Nobody with an apartment would let me bring in my kids," he said. "Nobody wanted them. But I did."

After a dismal start in 1951, Bankhead was shipped to Montreal where he pitched until being sold by the Royals to the Escogido Lions of the Dominican Republic League in the summer of 1952. In August, Bankhead was player-manager for the Lions when he was at the center of a nasty incident. He slid in hard on Estrellas Elephants catcher Luis Rosario, and on his way back to the dugout, Rosario fired a ball at Bankhead and missed. Bankhead whirled, spotted Rosario's mask, picked it up, and hit him on the head with it, opening a gash that needed three stitches and sparking a melee on the field. When the dust settled, Bankhead was out cold and on his way to jail. A few weeks later he was fired.

Bankhead suffered as a result of what historian Jules Tygiel called a new stereotype of black athletes spawned from the "high standards established by baseball's racial pioneers . . . a pitcher of blazing speed, tinged with a touch of wildness." Like many of baseball's first black players, he was thrown into white baseball with the physical tools to succeed but little or no emotional support.

Statistics: Dan Bankhead

YR	Team	W	L	PCT	G	IP	H	BB	SO	ERA	SV
1947	BKN-N	0	0	—	4	10	15	8	6	7.20	1
1950	BKN	9	4	.692	41	129.1	119	88	96	5.50	3
1951	BKN	0	1	.000	7	14	27	14	9	15.43	0
Totals											
3 Years		9	5	.643	52	153.1	161	110	111	6.52	4

Willard Jessie Brown

**Outfield. Batted right. Threw left. 5'11½", 200 lbs.
Born 6/26/11, Shreveport, Louisiana.**

Tommy Lasorda called Willard "Home Run" Brown the greatest hitter never to play in the major leagues. Well, sort of.

Brown did have "a cup of coffee" with the dreadful St. Louis Browns in 1947, but that was not the same Willard Brown who terrorized Negro league pitching for 13 years. With the possible exception of Josh Gibson, Brown was the most dangerous hitter ever to play in Negro league baseball. A shortstop early in his career, he was discovered by Kansas City Monarchs owner J. L. Wilkinson and eventually moved to center field. He won seven home run titles and was known as "The Big Bomb." He hit .355 in the Negro leagues, seventh best all-time, and was a five-time all-star. He hit .313 in three Negro

League World Series and regularly tore up big-league pitching in exhibition games.

But by the time the Browns purchased his contract in July 1947—along with Kansas City Monarchs teammate Hank Thompson—Brown was 36. St. Louis general manager Bill DeWitt was desperate; his Browns were 27½ games out of first place, and things had gotten so bad that on July 14 only 478 fans paid their way into Sportsman's Park to see the team play. St. Louis had a large black population, and DeWitt was counting on Brown and Thompson to lead the team out of the cellar and the red. They did neither.

Brown reportedly was thrilled at the chance to play in the majors, but his mood changed quickly when he and Thompson were greeted with icy silence by their new teammates, one of whom threatened to quit the team if they were kept on. A local sportswriter reported, "The gloom that pervaded the dressing room and the bench of the Browns was thick enough to make one gasp for air."

It didn't get better. Brown grounded into two bases-loaded double plays in his first game in the majors. He put on power shows in batting practice but failed to produce during games. And while the addition of Brown and Thompson helped the team draw big crowds on the road, it had no effect on home attendance. The pair were subject to a barrage of racial slurs, brush-back pitches galore, and no support from their teammates. One month and one home run after signing with St. Louis, Brown was released. He had hit .179, and his lone home run, the first hit by a black player in the American League, was inside the park.

Brown was not unhappy at leaving St. Louis. He had tired of the racism and isolation and believed he had taken a step down in caliber of teammates. "The Browns couldn't beat the Monarchs no kind of way, only if we was all asleep," he said. "That's the truth. They didn't have nothing. I said, 'Major league team?' They got to be kidding."

Brown rejoined the Monarchs and picked up where he had left off, hitting .336. In 1948 he had the best season of his career, hitting .374 with 18 home runs, 20 doubles, and 13 stolen bases—all career highs—in 66 games. And he was 37. As successful as he was with the Monarchs, Brown was even more of a hit with Santurce of the Puerto Rican winter league. Nicknamed "El Hombre" (The Man), he won three batting and three home-run titles in five years, including what was perhaps the most awesome triple crown in baseball history. In the winter of 1947-48, Brown hit .432 with 27 homers and 86 RBIs in just 60 games.

Brown continued to play in the minor leagues well into the 1950s, including a stint in the Texas League where Brown received a cruel reminder of baseball's painfully slow road to true integration. In 1957, three years after *Brown v. Board of Education*, Brown was barred by Louisiana law from playing in Shreveport, his hometown.

Statistics: Willard Brown

Year	Team	Games	AB	Runs	Hits	2B	3B	HR	RBI	BA
1947	STL-A	21	67	4	12	3	0	1	6	179

Lawrence Eugene "Larry" Doby

Outfield. Batted left. Threw right. 6'1", 180 lbs. Born
12/13/23, Camden, South Carolina.

At a joint press conference and team meeting on July 5, 1947, Cleveland
Indians president Bill Veeck announced the signing of Larry Doby to an
Indians contract, making Doby the first black player in American League
history. Veeck predicted that the 23-year-old infielder would "become a bigger
star than any guy in this room." Fifteen months later, Doby and his legendary
teammate Satchel Paige became the first black players to play on a world championship team as the Indians defeated the Boston Braves four games to two in
the 1948 World Series.

Doby's performance in the 1948 series and throughout the pennant race
made Veeck look like a sage: Doby's .318 series batting average was highest
among Cleveland regulars, and his home run in Game 4 was the margin of victory in a 2–1 win; in 121 regular season games, he hit .301 with 14 home runs.
He hit nearly .400 during the Indian stretch drive to the pennant, and over
the course of the season he had made a successful transition from the infield
to the outfield.

Still, Doby's accomplishments are not what most fans remember about
1948. Bigger were the dead-heat pennant race and Cleveland's playoff win over
Boston; player-manager Lou Boudreau's .355 average; the pitching of Gene
Bearden, Bob Lemon, and Bob Feller; and Veeck's promotions, which helped
bring a major league record 2,260,627 fans into Cleveland's Municipal
Stadium.

Being overshadowed seemed to be Larry Doby's lot during his 13-year
major league career. As a center fielder with speed and power, Doby's competition for fame at that position was three future Hall of Famers who played in
New York: Duke Snider, Willie Mays, and Mickey Mantle.

Though his statistics would never compare with those of "Willie, Mickey,
and The Duke," Doby was never unappreciated, particularly in Cleveland. His
tape-measure home runs were legendary. He once hit a 470-foot homer to
dead-center field at Yankee Stadium. In 1949, his 500-foot shot cleared the
bleachers at Washington's Griffith Stadium. When the ball landed on the roof
of a house, an irate mother called the Senators' front office complaining to
officials: "You'll have to stop it. Someone from your stadium just threw a ball

onto our house and woke up my children, and now I can't get them back to sleep."

In 1950, when he hit .326 with 25 home runs and 102 RBIs, Doby was voted Man of the Year by Cleveland sportswriters. A member of six consecutive American League All-Star teams, his pinch-hit home run in the 1954 All-Star game made Doby the first black to homer in the midseason talent show.

Doby entered the major leagues with none of the fanfare heralding social change — nor the elaborate preparation — that accompanied Jackie Robinson's signing by Branch Rickey. Until the Indians signed Satchel Paige in 1948, Doby had no roommate on the road. Still, for Doby's first game, Veeck hired two plainclothes police to be sure that black fans in Chicago did not overwhelm his new player. Veeck's public advice to Doby that day in July was simple. "Just remember," Veeck told Doby, "they play with a little white ball and a stick of wood up here just like they did in your league."

"Your league" was the Negro National League, where Doby played second base from 1943 to 1946, leading the Newark Eagles to a Negro World Series championship win over the Kansas City Monarchs in his final season. As the first player to make the jump directly to the major leagues from the Negro leagues, Doby soon earned overdue respect for players of both Negro leagues.

Following the 1947 season, Doby signed a contract with the Paterson Panthers of the American Basketball League, becoming the first black to play in the league. Thirty-two years later, he was named director of community relations with the New Jersey Nets of the National Basketball Association, a position he held through the 1980s.

As biographer Joseph Thomas Moore points out, "Doby neither enlarged his myth nor subordinated himself to a cause." Yet he was fully conscious of his special place in the American League, and his social consciousness tended toward the practical. As black fans began switching allegiance from the Negro leagues to the integrating majors, Doby suggested that American and National League teams support their Negro league counterparts as they did minor league teams. He also offered that "some of the younger white players . . . get their seasoning in the Negro leagues" as a way to "boost the gate."

A photograph taken in the Cleveland locker room following the fourth game of the 1948 World Series symbolizes what Moore called the "fusion and unity" with which Doby has lived his life. Doby's homer had just won Game 4 2–1 over the Braves. Winning pitcher Steve Gromek, jubilant, is hugging Doby. Both men are grinning ear to ear. They are literally cheek to cheek, with the flesh of one face indistinguishable from that of the other.

Returning home from Cleveland following the series, 10,000 of Doby's fellow Paterson, New Jersey, citizens, white and black, paraded him to the steps of his former high school, East Side High. There, Doby told an additional 3,000 people, including Paterson mayor Michael U. DeVita, "I'm not much of a speaker, but I know how to say thanks."

Doby pursued his career with dignity and a quiet intensity that made him popular among his teammates and Cleveland's working-class fans. Yet his low profile did not make him immune to the prejudice all black players felt off the field. "Not many people realize this," Doby remarked 30 years after he broke in with Cleveland, "but I was segregated in spring training for ten out of thirteen years, right through the spring of 1959."

Doby's sports career began to blossom in 1938 when he moved from Camden, South Carolina, to Paterson, where he lettered in baseball, basketball, football, and track at East Side. Under the alias "Larry Walker" during the spring prior to his high school graduation, Doby played in his first professional baseball game with the Newark Eagles at Yankee Stadium. Five summers later, the same Larry Walker, now using his real name, was hitting .458 with 14 home runs and 35 RBIs with Newark when Veeck bought his contract from Effa Manley, the Eagles' owner.

In 1978 Larry Doby was named manager of the Chicago White Sox, the second black to be named field manager of a major league team. Again it was Veeck who hired him, and again it was a Robinson—this time, Frank—who preceded him.

Statistics: Larry Doby

Year	Team	Games	AB	Runs	Hits	2B	3B	HR	RBI	BA
1947	CLE-A	29	32	3	5	1	0	0	3	.156
1948	CLE	121	439	83	132	23	9	14	66	.301
1949	CLE	147	547	106	153	25	3	24	85	.280
1950	CLE	142	503	110	164	25	5	25	102	.326
1951	CLE	134	447	84	132	27	5	20	69	.295
1952	CLE	140	519	104*	143	26	8	32*	111*	.276
1953	CLE	149	513	92	135	18	5	29	102	.263
1954	CLE	153	577	94	157	18	4	32*	126*	.272
1955	CLE	131	491	91	143	17	5	26	75	.291
1956	CHI-A	140	504	89	135	22	3	24	102	.268
1957	CHI	119	416	57	120	27	2	14	79	.288
1958	CLE	89	247	41	70	10	1	13	45	.283
1959	DET-A/									
	CHI-A	39	113	6	26	4	2	0	12	.230
Totals										
13 Years		1533	5348	960	1515	243	52	253	969	.283
World Series										
1948	CLE-A	6	22	1	7	1	0	1	2	.318
1954	CLE	4	16	0	2	0	0	0	0	.125
Totals										
2 Years		10	38	1	9	1	0	1	2	.237

*League leader.

Jack Roosevelt "Jackie" Robinson

Infield. Batted right. Threw right. 5'11", 195 lbs. Hall
of Fame, 1962. Born 1/31/19, Cairo, Georgia. Died
10/24/72, Stamford, Connecticut.

Probably no player in the history of sports had such an immediate and lasting effect on the game he played as Jackie Robinson. Not even Babe Ruth's influence was as dramatic. No doubt someone else would have broken the "color line" sooner or later, but the fact that it was Robinson seems almost predestined. On the field, he was a star; off the field, he was an icon.

Following the separation of his parents, Robinson's mother moved her five children from their home in Cairo, Georgia, to Pasadena, California, where they were the first blacks on Pepper Street. Robinson went on to star as a halfback at UCLA, where he became the first athlete in the university's history to letter in four sports in a single year. By the time he was introduced to Branch Rickey, who signed him to a Montreal Royals contract in the fall of 1945, Jackie Robinson was a man of talent and experience who had earned his college degree, served as an army officer, played professional football in Los Angeles, coached in Texas, and played nearly a full season with the Kansas City Monarchs of the Negro American League.

Shortly after Robinson announced his retirement from baseball in 1957, his brother Mack, who had finished second to Jesse Owens in the 200-meter dash at the 1936 Olympics, commented, "My brother had that intangible, something called color. Besides, he was great. You could always depend on him to come through in the clutch." These were important qualities to Branch Rickey when he considered signing Robinson 12 years earlier. But there was another side to the athlete and the man Rickey had seen. Whereas Mack Robinson claimed that "in retrospect, it seems nothing short of remarkable that Jackie was able to wear the cloak of humility until he had become more or less accepted as a major league player," Rickey saw in Robinson an inner strength that would carry him through the difficult time ahead, that would allow him to accept Rickey's challenge "to have the courage not to fight back" against the insults, the spikings, the brush-back pitches, the locked hotels—all of which, because of his race, awaited him.

The public's reaction to Robinson's signing was mixed, though curiously enough, the most accurate assessment of his challenge—and his ultimate acceptance—came from a southern writer, W. N. Cox, who wrote in the Norfolk *Virginian Pilot*: "The mainspring of this question is the Negro player's ability to deliver on the line in competition. I guarantee that if Jack Robinson hits homers and plays a whale of a game in Montreal that the fans soon will lose sight of his color."

But there were those, particularly blacks, who would never lose sight of "his color." In the black press, the response was primarily, and predictably, elation. One black writer called the signing of Robinson "the most democratic step in the last 25 years." However, there was more introspective, more deeply personal and psychological consequence, which Ludlow Werner, editor of the *New York Age*, expressed. "I'm happy over the event," wrote Werner, "but I'm sorry for Jackie. He will be haunted by the expectations of his race. To 15,000,000 Negroes he will symbolize not only their prowess in baseball but their ability to rise to an opportunity. Unlike white players, he can never afford an off-day or an off-night. His private life will be watched, too, because white Americans will judge the Negro race by everything he does. And Lord help him with his fellow Negroes if he should fail them."

This was Robinson's burden, which he accepted and which Rickey too acknowledged. "Surely God was with me when I picked Jackie," Rickey once said. "I don't think any other man in the Negro race or any other race could have done what he did those first two or three years. He really did understand the responsibility he carried. Then he had the intelligence of knowing how to handle himself. Above all, he had what the boys call guts, real guts."

From that very first season in 1946, when he won the International League batting title with a .349 average and led the Montreal Royals to a Little World Series championship, Robinson displayed nothing less than guts and passion on the field. He was one of the most aggressive base runners in the history of baseball. Despite recurring football injuries, Robinson stole home a record 19 times in his 10-year major league career. In 1949 alone, he stole home five times.

During his first five seasons, Robinson was the biggest single drawing card in the National League. He was named major league Rookie of the Year in 1947 (the first major-leaguer so honored) and National League Most Valuable Player in 1949, the first National League second baseman to win that honor since Frankie Frisch in 1931. In six consecutive All-Star games (1949–1954) Robinson hit .333. In the field, he played first, second, third, and the outfield with equal skill. In 1950 he set a new National League record for double plays by a second baseman — 133. In leading the Dodgers to six National League pennants, he had a .311 lifetime batting average. He was elected to the Hall of Fame in his first year of eligibility.

In 1946, Montreal general manager Mel Jones said of Robinson: "He can run faster than 75 percent of the players in the majors today. He can bunt better than 90 percent of them. He has good hands, a trigger quick baseball mind and an accurate and ample arm. And what makes him look like a big timer is that he never makes any play around second base look hard, not even the difficult ones. What can't he do but eat in the dining room of the Waldorf Astoria?"

And in time, Robinson would change that too.

Following two seasons of "that restraint Mr. Rickey taught me to use, to turn the other cheek," Robinson became baseball's most public figure since Babe Ruth and the game's most socially conscious player ever. As one writer said, Robinson "was born with a big mouth, a rattlesnake temper and one hell of a desire to win," which was not confined to the ballfield. With a history of speaking out against racial intolerance — as a lieutenant in the army, Robinson challenged the military's racial decree that barred blacks from riding a bus to the base exchange — Robinson began to speak out whenever it seemed appropriate, and he defended his right to do so. "You call me insolent," he once said to a New Orleans reporter. "I'll admit I have not been subservient, but would you use the same adjective to describe a white ballplayer — say Ted Williams? . . . Am I insolent, or am I merely insolent for a Negro who has courage enough to speak against injustices such as yours and people like you?"

On television in 1952, he called the management of the New York Yankees racist because they had not yet brought up a black player. He spoke before a Senate subcommittee charging that Paul Robeson was not speaking for American blacks when Robeson said in a speech in Paris that blacks would not fight against Russia. He spoke in Canada, saying that "all of the nations of the world are looking to us now, to see what we're going to do about our own problems. We've got to train our kids to be decent citizens and to live free from hate." He challenged the financial integrity of the Negro baseball leagues. He challenged the social conscience of major league owners, arguing that owners let in kids for free on nights when games would not sell out.

Robinson grew openly critical of the South and the advances it had not made, suggesting that blacks boycott games as a way of getting organized baseball to respond to its obligation fully to integrate both on the field and in the stands. He spoke of the necessity of education, of a day when many more ballplayers would have a college education. "In order to eliminate all or most of the problems we have facing us today," Robinson said, "education of Negroes and whites is the only solution. We can't say that people today are educated enough on these problems. In most instances the whites are afraid of the things that are going to happen. Therefore, education is just as imperative to them as it is to us."

Robinson's public persona was evident in many areas. In 1950 he starred with Ruby Dee in the movie *The Jackie Robinson Story*, the screenplay of which was partially written by Branch Rickey. He published his autobiography during his career, as well as another book, *Baseball Has Done It*, interviews with some of the first black players to break the color barrier. He edited a magazine for blacks, *Our Sports*, and was one of the first ballplayers to host his own television show, the focus of which was high school students from the New York metropolitan area. In 1965 he became the first black to announce baseball games for a major national network.

On the field, Robinson's passion inspired his teammates and the opposition to play with a competitiveness that made baseball in the late 1940s and 1950s one of the most exciting eras ever. Ben Chapman, a southerner, vowed he would not give Robinson an inch, that his Phillies would ride him the way they rode any other player, that they would dust him off the way Chapman had been dusted off as a rookie, and that he was certain that Robinson would not want it any other way.

"If Robinson has the stuff," Chapman declared, "he will be accepted in baseball the same as the Sullivans, the Lombardies, the Schultzes, the Grodzickies. All that I expect him to do is prove it. Baseball is big enough for everybody who has the stuff, but let's not carry anyone around on a cushion." Robinson, as his career attests, concurred.

"Of course there are still some players and umpires who resent me and the others of my race, and who don't give us a fair break," Robinson said in 1949. "But for everyone like that there are many more like Eddie Stanky of the Giants, who tries to beat you, tries to take you out of the play, and yet expects you to do the same thing to him."

And Robinson did. In February 1956, Robinson knocked down Giants second baseman Davey Williams on a play at first base. "It wasn't Williams I was after. It was [Giants pitcher Sal] Maglie. He had been throwing at us and someone on our bench, looking at me, said, 'We got to do something about it.' Well, whenever there's something like that to be done the players expect me to do it. I went up to the batter's circle and our batboy said, 'Let someone else do it for a change.' I didn't agree with him.

"I dropped a bunt down the first base line, figuring Maglie would come over to field it. He didn't. Williams covered first and I got him. If Maglie had covered first base, I would have done my best to drive him into right field."

Robinson's effect on others in the game is baseball lore. There was the famous moment in a game in Boston when Dodger shortstop Pee Wee Reese approached Robinson at second base and put his arm around his teammate's shoulder, a gesture of solidarity before the loudly intolerant Braves fans.

A. B. "Happy" Chandler, the commissioner of baseball who intervened on Robinson's behalf and in support of Rickey's signing of the first black player in organized ball, said, years after the fact, "I never regretted my decision to let Robinson play, but it probably cost me my job."

Following his first game in the majors, Robinson said, "Give me five years of this and that will be enough. If I can make enough money to build my own little place and give my boy a good education, everything will be all right. I realize I have been given a great opportunity, and I believe I can make it." By the end of the 1951 season, he had. He was a 32-year-old gray-haired veteran. Already apparent, as *Ebony* magazine reported, was the fact that "the game will never be able to make up to Robinson for those first couple of years.

Money, fame and position won't repay him for the way he had to claw his way through that human jungle all by himself."

But Robinson was far from done. He played five more years with Brooklyn, including the team's only world championship season, 1955. Following the 1956 season, Robinson retired, refusing a December trade to the rival New York Giants. Instead, he accepted a position as personnel director with the Chock Full O' Nuts coffee and restaurant chain. (Of the company's 1,000 employees, 750 were black.) Robinson's last hit in the majors was a line drive over the head of New York's Enos Slaughter that won Game 6 of the 1956 World Series.

When Robinson died of a heart attack in 1972, Leonard Koppett wrote, "What is so hard to remember now (and completely unknown to younger people) is the devastating fact that until Jackie Robinson, there was no pressure whatever from the 'decent' people to break the color line that all accepted. . . .

"On the vast middle-class, middle-road, ordinary, friendly, decent backbone of America, Robinson had the vitally important effect of making them aware of what they had been able to ignore.

". . . So when all is said and done, as much as Robinson meant directly to his own people—as an example and inspiration and pioneer—he meant even more to the white society. He did more than any other single human being could do to focus their attention on the inequities of a system in which lilywhite baseball was only one small symptom."

Twenty-five years after becoming the first black to play in the World Series, an arthritic and nearly blind Jackie Robinson made his last public appearance, throwing out the first ball in Game 2 of the 1972 series at Cincinnati's Riverfront Stadium. A few months earlier, when the Los Angeles Dodgers honored him with a ceremony retiring his number, Robinson told the crowd at Dodger Stadium (where he never played), "I couldn't care less if someone out there is wearing No. 42. I get more of a thrill knowing there are people in baseball who believe in advancement because of ability."

A month or so after he died, when National League official batting statistics were released, the top seven hitters were black.

Statistics: Jackie Robinson

Year	Team	Games	AB	Runs	Hits	2B	3B	HR	RBI	BA
1947	BKN-N	151	590	125	175	31	5	12	48	.297
1948	BKN	147	574	108	170	38	8	12	85	.296
1949	BKN	156	593	122	203	38	12	16	124	.342*
1950	BKN	144	518	99	170	39	4	14	81	.328
1951	BKN	153	548	106	185	33	7	19	88	.338
1952	BKN	149	510	104	157	17	3	19	75	.308
1953	BKN	136	484	109	159	34	7	12	95	.329
1954	BKN	124	386	62	120	22	4	15	59	.311

Year	Team	Games	AB	Runs	Hits	2B	3B	HR	RBI	BA
1955	BKN	105	317	51	81	6	2	8	36	.256
1956	BKN	117	357	61	98	15	2	10	43	.275
Totals										
10 Years		1382	4877	947	1518	273	54	137	734	.311
World Series										
1947	BKN-N	7	27	3	7	2	0	0	3	.259
1949	BKN	5	16	2	3	1	0	0	2	.188
1952	BKN	7	23	4	4	0	0	1	2	.174
1953	BKN	6	25	3	8	2	0	0	2	.320
1955	BKN	6	22	5	4	1	1	0	1	.182
1956	BKN	7	24	5	6	1	0	1	2	.250
Totals										
6 Years		38	137	22	32	7	1	2	12	.234

League leader.

Henry Curtis "Hank" Thompson

Third base, outfield. Batted left. Threw right. 5'9", 174 lbs. Born 12/8/25, Oklahoma City, Oklahoma. Died 9/30/69, Fresno, California.

Hank Thompson was the first black to play for two major league teams (St. Louis Browns, New York Giants) and the first to play in both the American and National leagues. When the St. Louis Browns signed Thompson and Willard Brown in July 1947, they became the first black teammates to appear in the same major league lineup, Thompson at second base and Brown in right field. Four years later, in the 1951 World Series, Thompson, replacing an injured Don Mueller in right field, joined Willie Mays in center and Monte Irvin in left to form the first all-black outfield in major league history.

What distinguished Hank Thompson's major league career was not so much what he accomplished but the potential that eluded him. "I became a baseball has-been at thirty-two," Thompson remarked just a few years before he died. "It was awful. I couldn't move around third base. Balls were going by me that I should have had. I was disgracing baseball and I still kept boozing it up."

Thompson was 21 when the Browns signed him from the roster of the Kansas City Monarchs. The *Sporting News* accused St. Louis of promotional gimmickry and questioned the qualifications of both Thompson and Brown. The baseball weekly argued that the Browns, recognizing the fan appeal of Jackie

Robinson and Larry Doby, were merely trying to put fans into the seats of Sportsman's Park. But while Thompson hardly set the league afire in 1947, there was no question that he belonged in the majors.

Thompson played all of 1948 with the Monarchs and in the Cuban winter league, where he caught the attention of the New York Giants. Early in 1949, New York signed Thompson, Monte Irvin, and pitcher Ford "Speedball" Smith, a University of Arizona grad and an air force lieutenant who went 10-5 against Negro league competition in 1948. While Smith never reached the majors, Thompson and Irvin became the core of New York's 1951 and 1954 pennant-winning teams.

Following a quiet but respectable 1949 season, Thompson came into his own in 1950 when he led the Giants with 91 runs batted in, 20 home runs, and a batting average of .289. But it was in the field where Thompson seemed destined for greatness. Breaking Pie Traynor's National League record for double plays started by a third baseman, 43, Thompson was hailed as the best all-around player in the league at third.

In 1951 someone asked Giants manager Leo Durocher to name an all-star team of players he had managed. "On the basis of the one full year of play he gave me," Durocher said, "I'd have to pick Henry Thompson. He was the best third baseman in the league last year and the best I've ever had playing for me." At the time, however, Thompson was in the minors with Ottawa, trying to work out the kinks of an ankle injury.

When he was recalled to the Giants in August, third base belonged to the other "Tom-Tom" twin, Bobby Thompson, who hit .358 from July 20 to his historic playoff winning homer against the Dodgers on October 3. Hank was moved to the outfield, hitting all eight of his home runs during the Giants' "Miracle of Coogan's Bluff" pennant run.

Thompson opened the 1952 season in left field, replacing Irvin, who had broken an ankle during spring training. When Willie Mays entered the army at the end of June, Durocher, making the most of Thompson's speed, moved his "all-star" third baseman to center. And while no one could replace Willie Mays in center field, Thompson's versatility did not go unappreciated. "It would be shuddersome," wrote Arch Murray in midseason, "to think where the Giants would be now without Henry." By the end of the season through 1955, Thompson was Durocher's full-time third baseman, fielding the position like no Giant before him.

At the plate, Thompson's most dramatic year was 1954. Twice he drove in seven or more runs in a game—a two-homer, four-hit afternoon against the Dodgers, and a three-homer, four-hit, eight-RBI game against the Cardinals.

While Willie Mays's famous catch off the bat of Vic Wertz and Dusty Rhodes's clutch hitting are what fans remember most about the 1954 World Series, Thompson was easily the all-around best in those four games. In addition to batting .364, he set a record for a four-game series by walking seven times. At third, Thompson handled 16 chances without an error, and when he turned a sure hit off the bat of Al Smith into a double play in the third inning of Game 4, the Indians were totally demoralized.

On July 27, 1957, hitting .240 with the Class AAA Minneapolis Millers, Thompson retired. "This game has been good to me, but it's a young man's game," he said. "I'm going home to California."

Unfortunately, there were other stops along the way. In 1959 he pleaded guilty to hitting Ruth Bowen, press agent of Dinah Washington and The Ink Spots among others, and the wife of Ink Spots singer Billy Bowen. At the time, Thompson was managing a chain of candy stores in Brooklyn. Later he would serve time in Texas for holding up a liquor store and in New York for holding up a bar.

Thompson spent the two years before his death of a heart attack working with teenagers on the playgrounds of Fresno, California. "I try to help the youngsters by pointing to my life," he said. "I tell them how easily and quickly a man can fall from the limelight and get into trouble if he isn't careful. I tell them how easy it is to go the other way."

"Quiet and soft-spoken," wrote Major Robinson in the Pittsburgh *Courier*, "Hank's attitude belied the turmoil that churned within him."

Statistics: Hank Thompson

Year	Team	Games	AB	Runs	Hits	2B	3B	HR	RBI	BA
1947	STL-A	27	78	10	20	1	1	0	5	.256
1949	NY-N	75	275	51	77	10	4	9	34	.280
1950	NY	148	512	82	148	17	6	20	91	.289
1951	NY	87	264	37	62	8	4	8	33	.235
1952	NY	128	423	67	110	13	9	17	67	.260
1953	NY	114	388	80	117	15	8	24	74	.302
1954	NY	136	448	76	118	18	1	26	86	.263
1955	NY	135	432	65	106	13	1	17	63	.245
1956	NY	83	183	24	43	9	0	8	29	.235
Totals										
9 Years		933	3003	492	801	104	34	129	482	.267
World Series										
1951	NY-N	5	14	2	2	0	0	0	0	.143
1954	NY	4	11	6	4	1	0	0	2	.364
Totals										
2 Years		9	25	8	6	1	0	0	2	.240

1948

Roy Campanella

Catcher. Batted right. Threw right. 5'9½", 190 lbs. Hall of Fame, 1969. Born 11/19/21, Philadelphia, Pennsylvania. Died 6/26/93, Los Angeles, California.

Roy Campanella is a character in nearly every movie ever made. He is the one so full of life, the gifted but gentle and unassuming soul who you know from the first scene is destined for tragedy. In many ways, Campanella was the backbone of the great Brooklyn Dodger teams of the late 1940s and 1950s. Three times named the league's Most Valuable Player, he caught at least 100 games for nine straight seasons, and the Dodgers were National League champions five times in that span. The first black catcher in the majors, he handled a nearly all-white pitching staff and earned their respect with his toughness, his knowledge of hitters, and his steady play behind the plate.

Campanella played ice to Jackie Robinson's fire on those Dodger teams. Robinson burned with the passion of a man keenly aware of his role as a racial pioneer. "Campy" was just glad to be playing. They were never close and had several well-publicized feuds over the years, but Campanella acknowledged the debt he owed Robinson. "Jackie made things easy for us," he said. Because of him, "I'm just another guy playing baseball."

But he was a powerful force everywhere he played. In his uniform he appeared almost roly-poly, but underneath it was all muscle. "His thighs bulged with muscle and his belly was swollen, but firm," wrote Roger Kahn. "He was a little sumo wrestler of a man, a giant scaled down rather than a midget fleshed out."

Campanella was the son of a white Italian mother and a black father in the Nicetown section of Philadelphia. A star athlete in football and baseball, he went to integrated schools and played on integrated teams. He began his professional baseball career in 1937 at age 15, earning $25 a weekend playing for the Bacharach Giants, a local semipro team. At 16 he was playing full time for the Baltimore Elite Giants of the Negro National League and going to catching school with the Giants' Bizz Mackey, the finest defensive catcher of his era.

27

Campanella earned the starting job with the Giants in 1939 and led them to playoff wins over the Newark Eagles and Homestead Grays, driving in seven runs in four games. In 1940 began a string of six straight .300-plus seasons—five with the Giants sandwiched around a season in the Mexican League. During these years Campy played his demanding position on an even more demanding schedule—year-round baseball, traveling from city to city, often daily. "Rarely were we in the same city two days in a row," he said. "Mostly we played by day and traveled by night; sometimes we played both day and night and usually in two different cities." He once caught four games in one day—first a day doubleheader in Cincinnati, then a twi-nighter in Middletown, Ohio. During his career with Baltimore, Campanella even managed twice to nudge all-time great Josh Gibson off the Negro league all-star team.

After leading the league in RBIs in 1945, Campanella appeared in a black-white all-star game in mid–October at Brooklyn's Ebbets Field. One of his teammates was a 19-year-old pitcher named Don Newcombe. Later that week, Campanella met with Branch Rickey for four hours. Campanella later called Rickey "the talkingest man I ever did see."

Dodger scouts loved what they saw in Campanella—size, speed, power—and Rickey asked him if he wanted to play in the Dodger organization. Campanella assumed, incorrectly, that he was being offered a spot on the Brooklyn Brown Dodgers, a member club of a new Negro league Rickey was about to start. He was already earning one of the highest salaries in the Negro leagues and had a wife and three kids to support. The prospect of starting out in a new league with little security was not very appealing, so he declined the offer but promised not to sign with another team without consulting the Dodgers.

About a week later, Campanella and Robinson were staying at the same hotel in Harlem before they left on a barnstorming tour in South America. Robinson, whose signing was one day away from becoming public, knew that Campanella had met with Rickey and invited his teammate to his room to play cards. Robinson asked him about the meeting, and when Campy told him what had happened, Robinson asked, "Did Mr. Rickey tell you that he wanted you for the Brown Dodgers?" It suddenly struck Campanella that Rickey had never mentioned a particular team. Robinson then disclosed that he had signed to play with Montreal of the International League, the previously all-white International League.

Campanella was stunned. He worried that he had blown a shot, perhaps his only shot, at playing in the major leagues. But before he left, he sent Rickey a telegram with his address in South America. After a long, anxious winter, Campanella got a telegram from Rickey asking him to report to Brooklyn by March 10. "Very important," it read. "When that telegram from the Dodger organization arrived, that guy was the happiest person in the hotel," recalled Quincy Trouppe, one of Campanella's barnstorming teammates. "Campanella was just living to get a chance with the Dodgers. It was all he thought about and talked about."

Rickey's plan was to assign Campanella and Newcombe to the same farm team and have them room together and work their way through the system together. The problem was that they had not decided where to send them by the time they arrived in Brooklyn. Most of the Dodger higher minor league teams were located in the South, and the pair were too talented and experienced to play in a lower league. So with Campanella looking on, one of Rickey's assistants called around to Dodger farm teams trying to find them a home. It was not easy. Fortunately, two solid baseball men — future club president Buzzy Bavasi and future Hall-of-Fame manager Walter Alston — were running the Dodger Class B team in Nashua, New Hampshire. All Bavasi cared about was winning. "If they can play better than what we have," he said, "then we don't care what color they are."

At first, Campanella thought he heard Finch say Nashville, not Nashua, and was stunned. But this misunderstanding was quickly cleared up, and he and Newcombe were on their way to New England. Campy, Newcombe, and their wives were the only blacks in Nashua, but they were welcomed by most of the locals. "These people are wonderful," Campanella said. "Newcombe and I go any place we want to, do anything we please, and are treated like long lost sons."

It did not hurt that the pair quickly became league stars. In his debut, Campanella had three hits, including a 440-foot home run, the first of 14 he hit that season in a league marked by faraway fences. His 14 homers not only led the league but made his father into a farmer. Jack Fallgren, a Nashua poultry farmer, offered 100 baby chicks for every home run hit by the local team. At the end of the season, Campy collected his 1,400 chicks and shipped them to his father, who started a farm on the outskirts of Philadelphia. When Fallgren decided to quit farming, Campanella bought the rest of his stock and expanded.

Campanella also became Alston's coach on the field. At 25, he was older than most of the other players, so Alston told him, "If I'm ever thrown out of a game, I want you to run things." In June, Campanella got his chance when Alston was ejected in the sixth inning with Nashua trailing Lawrence by three. Baseball's first black manager sent his roommate up to pinch-hit. Newcombe responded with a game-tying homer, and Nashua went on to win.

Campanella hit .290 that season with 96 RBIs, and he and Newcombe led Nashua to the New England League title, sparking playoff wins over Pawtucket and Lynn. Their season had been remarkably free of racial incidents. Campy's only serious confrontation came when Manchester's Sal Yvars threw a handful of dirt in his face while he was catching. "Try that again and I'll beat you to a pulp," Campanella fired back, and that was the end of it. More intense was the confrontation between Bavasi and the general manager of Nashua's rival,

Lynn. After a key Nashua win late in the season, Lynn's GM approached Bavasi. "If it wasn't for them niggers, you wouldn't have beat us," he said. Bavasi assaulted the man, and the pair had to be separated.

In 1947 Campanella was promoted to Montreal and had another fine season. Paul Richards, then manager of Buffalo, said, "Campanella is the best catcher in the business — major or minor leagues. If [Rickey] doesn't bring that guy up, he may as well go out of the emancipation business."

Rickey's initial plan called for Campy to integrate the American Association with St. Paul in 1948, but Dodger manager Leo Durocher wanted him as his catcher. The pair feuded, and Rickey allowed Campy to start the season with Brooklyn but told Durocher he could be used only as an outfielder, all but assuring an early-season demotion. In mid–May, after seeing little action, Campanella was sent to St. Paul where he quickly dissipated any racial tensions with an explosion at the plate. He hit eight home runs in his first seven games, then went on to hit .325 with 13 homers and 33 RBIs in 35 games before being recalled to Brooklyn.

By the time he reached the Dodgers on July 2, the defending National League champions were mired in the second division. Campy had three hits in each of his first three games, and celebrated July 4 with two home runs in a 13–12 win over the Giants. The Dodgers' second-half surge led them to third place, and according to author Jules Tygiel, "By using Campanella as a pawn in the integration campaign, [Rickey] probably cost the Dodgers the 1948 pennant."

No such mistake was made in 1949, as Campy was firmly entrenched behind the plate, Newcombe was in the rotation, and another relative newcomer, future Hall of Famer Duke Snider, was in center field. The Dodgers battled St. Louis all season long for the top spot and clinched the pennant on the final day of the season with a 9–7, 10-inning win over Philadelphia. Campy was named to his first of eight straight All-Star teams, and in the World Series, which the Dodgers lost to the Yankees in five games, he stunned shortstop Phil Rizzuto by picking him off third base. "What an arm that guy has!" Rizzuto said.

Over the next several years Campy established himself as the finest catcher in baseball. He won his first MVP award in 1951, then another in 1953 when he set a major league record for most homers by a catcher in a season with 40. He also had the most public racial confrontation of his career that season. Milwaukee pitcher Lew Burdette, a West Virginia native known for knockdown pitches, dusted Campanella twice in the same at-bat. Campanella glowered at him. "Nigger, get up and hit," Burdette replied. Campanella charged the mound, and a free-for-all ensued.

In 1955 Campanella won his third MVP award, and the Dodgers finally beat the Yankees, Campy hitting key home runs in Games 3 and 4. But the years behind the plate had taken their toll. He had beaten back injuries before, once returning in 1950 just 11 days after suffering a compound dislocation of his glove thumb, then suffering blisters on both corneas after a water heater blew up in his face in 1951. But in 1956, bone chips in the heel of his left hand helped bring his batting average down nearly 100 points, and in 1957 he caught only 100 games.

Still, with the Dodgers slated to move into the Los Angeles Coliseum — and its 295-foot left field porch — in 1958, there was reason to believe Campanella could have a renaissance as a hitter. But all that came to an end on the evening of January 28, 1958. Campanella was driving from his liquor store in Harlem to his home on Long Island when his car skidded on a patch of ice and slammed head-on into a telephone pole. His neck was broken, and he was paralyzed from the chest down.

After initial hope of some recovery, it became clear that Campanella would never walk, much less play baseball, again. And his hard times continued. In February 1959, just one day before he was to return to spring training with the Dodgers as a special coach, his 15-year-old son David was arrested in connection with a burglary of a drugstore. But Campanella was an eternal optimist. An attendant at the hospital where Campanella spent months after the accident said, "I don't know how he did it. There was a stream of people in and out of his room all day long. He met and talked with all of them as though they were doing him a favor by stopping. He gave them a bigger lift, lots of times, than they gave him."

On May 7, 1959, fans showed their appreciation. A crowd of 93,103, the largest in baseball history, jammed the Coliseum to watch the Dodgers play an exhibition game against the Yankees and to pay tribute to Campanella. Campanella continued to work hard for decades after the accident, committing much of his time to community service in Los Angeles. In 1969 he was inducted into the Baseball Hall of Fame.

It is easy — and fairly accurate — to paint Campanella as something less than a crusader for civil rights in baseball. He was too busy being grateful for and taking advantage of his opportunities. But he took his share of stands on the issues. For years, the Chase Hotel in St. Louis refused to allow black players to stay there, but in 1954 hotel management relented somewhat, agreeing to allow blacks to stay but banning them from the swimming pool and dining room. Robinson grudgingly accepted the concessions, but Campanella refused. "If they didn't want us before, they won't get my business now," he said.

But for the most part Campanella avoided controversy and confrontations because they got in the way of what he wanted to do most — play ball. "I try never to hurt anybody, and I stay clear of arguments," he said. "I figure there's good in everybody I meet, and I look for it." And if people wanted to paint him as naive and childlike, that seemed okay with him. After all, he said, "to play this game good, a lot of you's got to be little boy."

Statistics: Roy Campanella

Year	Team	Games	AB	Runs	Hits	2B	3B	HR	RBI	BA
1948	BKN-N	83	279	32	72	11	3	9	45	.258
1949	BKN	130	436	65	125	22	2	22	82	.287
1950	BKN	126	437	70	123	19	3	31	89	.281
1951	BKN	143	505	90	164	33	1	33	108	.325
1952	BKN	128	468	73	126	18	1	22	97	.269
1953	BKN	144	519	103	162	26	3	41	142*	.312
1954	BKN	111	397	43	82	14	3	19	51	.207
1955	BKN	123	446	81	142	20	1	32	107	.318
1956	BKN	124	388	39	85	6	1	20	73	.219
1957	BKN	103	330	31	80	9	0	13	62	.242
Totals										
10 Years		1215	4205	627	1161	178	18	242	856	.276
World Series										
1949	BKN-N	5	15	2	4	1	0	1	2	.267
1952	BKN	7	28	0	6	0	0	0	1	.214
1953	BKN	6	22	6	6	0	0	1	2	.273
1955	BKN	7	27	4	7	3	0	2	4	.259
1956	BKN	7	22	2	4	1	0	0	3	.182
Totals										
5 Years		32	114	14	27	5	0	4	12	.237

*League leader.

Leroy Robert "Satchel" Paige

Pitcher. Threw right. Batted right. 6'3", 185 lbs. Born 7/7/06, Mobile, Alabama. Died 6/5/82, Kansas City, Missouri. Hall of Fame, 1971.

The Cleveland Indians were in the thick of the American League pennant race that afternoon on July 9, 1948, when Tribe manager Lou Boudreau sent the call to the bull pen in relief of starter Bob Lemon. And as a tall skinny black pitcher made the long walk in from right field, 35,000 Cleveland fans rose to their feet, welcoming the rookie's first major league appearance with thunderous applause.

Home plate umpire Bill McGowan, showing uncommon restraint and in deference to history in the making, stood to the side as photographers rushed the mound to shoot Satchel Paige taking his warmup pitches. St. Louis Browns first baseman Chuck Stevens stepped into the batter's box and promptly singled. Then the rookie settled down, giving up no runs and two hits in two innings of work, the kind of relief pitching that Boudreau and team president Bill Veeck knew Cleveland had to have for the Indians to contend for the pennant.

But by the time Boudreau decided to pinch-hit for the rookie in the bottom of the sixth, Cleveland's fans knew full well that they had witnessed more than solid relief pitching; indeed, more than history. Pitching to just seven batters, Satchel Paige had brought legend to life.

"Sometimes he wound his arm in six revolutions, sometimes only in two," according to Cleveland sportswriter Ed McCauley. "He threw overhand, side-arm and underhand. He threw a blooper and he threw his famous 'hesitation pitch,' an amazing delivery on which he practically completes his follow-through before he releases the ball."

A week later, on July 15, Paige won his first major league game in relief against Connie Mack's Athletics before a crowd of 37,684 in Philadelphia. In between, he pitched two hitless innings against the Dodgers in an exhibition game that attracted 64,877 fans in Cleveland. On August 3, in his first major league start, Paige drew a crowd of 72,434 to Cleveland Stadium. In his next home start, a night game against Chicago, more than 78,000 fans showed up. Wherever he appeared that first season in the majors, Paige pitched to a sellout crowd.

Satchel Paige was to pitching what Babe Ruth was to hitting. Unrivaled as a gate attraction, each man was a consummate showman whose on-field performance equaled any exaggerated billing and hyperbole that preceded him. Ironically, the summer Ruth died, 1948, was Paige's rookie season in the majors. Tragically, according to some records, Paige was only one year younger than the Babe during that rookie season. Paige's "exact age," wrote the *New York Star*'s Tom Meany, "is one of the mysteries of our time." But whether the legendary Satchel was 39, 42, or 52 when he became the first black to pitch in the American League is irrelevant. So too is the fact that by any account, Paige was the oldest rookie in major league history. What matters is that in 1948, in 72⅔ innings Paige won six games, lost one, and recorded a 2.48 ERA, statistics that represented a major contribution to Cleveland's pennant-winning season. Indeed, those numbers refute a vindictive editorial that appeared in the *Sporting News* following Veeck's announced signing of the veteran Negro league pitcher.

"Veeck has gone too far in his quest of publicity," *TSN* stated in part, "and he has done his league's position absolutely no good insofar as public reaction is concerned. . . . It would have done Cleveland and the American League no good in the court of public opinion if, at 50, Paige were as Caucasian as, let us say, Bob Feller.

"To bring in a pitching 'rookie' of Paige's age casts a reflection on the entire scheme of operation in the major leagues."

Not only did the editorial underestimate Veeck's integrity, but it obviously had little regard for Paige's ability, his competitiveness, and his work ethic. "Mr. Veeck signed me because he thought I could help his club, and the only way I can help is to get those batters out," Paige said when he was signed. "That's all I'm thinking about out there. I know some of my friends would like to see me get cute, the way I used to do in some of the exhibition games. They'll never see it. Not in this league.... This is the chance of a lifetime."

When Paige beat the Chicago White Sox 1–0 on August 21, Veeck wired the *Sporting News*: "Paige pitching — no runs, three hits. Definitely in line for THE SPORTING NEWS Rookie of the Year award. Regards. Bill Veeck."

But as Robert Peterson wrote in his history of the Negro leagues and black ballplayers, *Only the Ball Was White*, "The essence of Satchel Paige cannot be captured by dry statistics, and besides, most of the available figures are somewhat elusive, like the man himself."

Though all accounts are estimates, by the time he reached the majors, Paige had probably pitched in 2,500 games, winning 2,000. From 1929 through 1958, he played both summer and winter ball, and in one year he is reported to have pitched in 153 games. He estimated having pitched 300 shutouts and 55 no-hitters against semipro and Negro league opponents. During his entire professional career, he pitched for no fewer than 250 teams.

Satchel Paige possessed a fastball — he called it his "bee ball," because it hummed, his "trouble ball," or his "Long Tom" — and pinpoint control that was surpassed only by his appeal, which according to Peterson "transcended race." "More fabulous tales have been told of Satchel's pitching ability than of any pitcher in Organized Ball," wrote Tom Meany.

Dizzy Dean said that Paige was the best pitcher he had ever seen. "Satch has instincts," said Dean. "He can look at a man and tell whether he is a low-ball or high-ball hitter." In 1934, when Dean won 30 games for the Cardinals and was named National League Most Valuable Player, Paige beat Dean's major league all-star team 1–0 in 13 innings. For Bill Veeck, it was "the best game I've ever seen."

In the fall of 1947, Paige beat a Bob Feller all-star team 8–0, striking out 16. He once struck out Rogers Hornsby five times in a row. The first time he faced Joe DiMaggio, he struck him out on three straight fastballs. In 1935, when he was the phenom of the Pacific Coast League, Joe DiMaggio, after picking up a scratch single against Paige, said, "Now I know I'll hit in the majors — I finally got a single off Satchel Paige."

In 1934, Paige started 29 games in a 30-day stretch for a racially mixed team in North Dakota; the team won 104 of 105 games, and Paige pitched in each of them. He played for the original House of David team managed by Grover Cleveland Alexander. In three days in 1934, Paige is reported to have no-hit the Homestead Grays, pitched and won for the House of David, then driven 1,000 miles to Chicago and pitched in the Negro league East-West game, which he won 1–0 in extra innings. He once struck out 60 batters in winning four consecutive games. In a game against the Baltimore Black Sox in Yankee Stadium, he struck out 18 batters. It is no wonder that in 1952 Ed Fitzgerald, making a case for Paige's Hall-of-Fame credentials in *Sport Magazine*, wrote, "If Satchel Paige isn't a famous baseball figure, then Babe Ruth was an unknown."

Paige was the seventh of 11 children born to Lula and John Paige. His father earned a meager living as a gardener. Young Leroy acquired the nickname "Satchel" while working as a railroad redcap in Mobile. "When I got three or four suitcases in my arms, about all you could see was those suitcases." Arrested for stealing toys as a youngster, he was sent to a reform school for black youths in Mt. Meigs, Alabama, where he learned to play baseball. He started pitching in the semipro leagues in 1927 in Chattanooga, Tennessee. In 1928 he signed with the Birmingham Black Barons.

In time, Paige would pitch for virtually every team in the Negro American and Negro National leagues. He pitched in Canada, Mexico, South America, and Japan. In 1937, he teamed with legends Josh Gibson and Cool Papa Bell on a team organized by Santo Domingo dictator Rafael Trujillo. In 1938, Satchel "jumped" his contract and signed with the Mexican League, a move that resulted in his being banned for life from the Negro American and Negro National leagues. The edict was rescinded as soon as Paige returned to the States.

Following a respectable season with Cleveland in 1949, Paige joined the Negro American League Chicago American Giants. By then, his presence was in such demand that he would pitch as many as 21 innings a week, broken up into three-inning stints.

When Veeck bought the St. Louis Browns in 1951, he immediately signed Paige to a contract. By July of the following season, Paige had appeared in one-third of the Browns games, winning six, losing three, saving nine, and compiling a 2.25 ERA. Those numbers prompted Casey Stengel to name him to the pitching staff of the American League All-Star team, of which Paige said, "This completes everything in baseball for me."

Off the field, Paige, who at one time had publicly doubted the success of integration in baseball and had recommended an all-black major league team, was a reserved man with myriad interests. He was a collector of antiques, a musician, a photographer, and a one-time pilot. In 1968 he ran, unsuccessfully, for the Missouri legislature. Unlike Jackie Robinson, who was vocal in his fight against racism, Satchel Paige was quietly principled, refusing to play in any town that denied him or his teammates room or board. And he was loyal. In 1956 he turned down offers to pitch for three major league teams to honor his contract with Bill Veeck's Class AAA Miami Marlins.

Paige pitched in his final major league game at age 59. On September 25,

1965, Paige made his first big-league appearance in 12 years, going three innings, striking out one, and giving up just one hit, a single to 26-year-old Carl Yastrzemski.

The author of two books, including the famous *Maybe I'll Pitch Forever*, published in 1961, Satchel Paige was as much a poet and philosopher as a pitcher. When asked by a reporter to describe the solution to his longevity and his success, Paige answered:

> "Avoid fried meats, which angry up the blood.
> "If your stomach disputes you, lie down and pacify it with cool thoughts.
> "Keep the juices flowing by jangling gently as you move.
> "Go very light on the vices, such as carrying on in society — the society ramble ain't restful.
> "And don't look back. Something might be gaining on you."

Statistics: Satchel Paige

Year	Team	W	L	PCT	G	IP	H	BB	SO	ERA	SV
1948	CLE-A	6	1	.857	21	72.2	61	25	45	2.48	1
1949	CLE	4	7	.364	31	83	70	33	54	3.04	5
1951	STL-A	3	4	.429	23	62	67	29	48	4.79	5
1952	STL	12	10	.545	46	138	116	57	91	3.07	10
1953	STL	3	9	.250	57	117.1	114	39	51	3.53	11
1965	KC-A	0	0	0	1	3	1	0	1	0.00	0
Totals											
6 Years		28	31	.475	179	476	429	183	290	3.29	32
World Series											
1948	CLE-A	0	0	0	1	.2	0	0	0	0.00	0

1 9 4 9

"Luscious" Luke Easter

**First base. Batted left. Threw right. 6'4½", 240 lbs.
Born 8/4/15, Jonestown, Mississippi. Died 3/29/79,
Euclid, Ohio.**

Luke Easter was the biggest thing to hit the West Coast since celluloid.
Wherever the towering first baseman went in 1949, huge crowds followed. In
the first 10 games he played for San Diego, crowds averaged over 34,000; and
this was the minor leagues. In San Francisco, 5,000 fans were turned away from
Seals Stadium, and another 1,000 climbed on top of cars to get a look at the
Pacific Coast League's new box-office star. Ballparks opened their gates earlier
than usual so fans could watch Easter take batting practice. They came to see
a man who could hit a baseball about as far as anyone who ever tried.

Sacramento manager Del Baker, whose playing career lasted 22 years,
said, "For sheer ability to knock the ball great distances, I've never seen
anybody better than Easter." Hollywood manager Fred Haney was more concerned with the balls Easter hit that stayed in the park. "I wish they'd get him
out of here before he kills every infielder in the Coast League," he said.

In his first 15 games in the PCL, Easter hit .436 with five home runs and
23 runs batted in. By July 1, he had dipped to .363, but he had 25 homers
and 92 RBIs in just 80 games. And as it turned out, Easter had been playing
with a broken kneecap he suffered in spring training until the pain became
unbearable, forcing him to undergo surgery.

Easter's impact as a gate attraction was not lost on owners of other PCL
teams. By May, Oakland had signed its first black player, and later that year
Portland and Los Angeles followed suit. The *Sporting News* reported that his
injury cost owners $200,000 in gate receipts. Easter's popularity came largely
from his unbridled hitting power but was enhanced by his demeanor. Jules
Tygiel wrote that at 6'4" and 240 pounds, Easter "was a figure of Bunyanesque
proportions . . . yet he charmed people with his gentle manner and humor."
He once drew a suspension while playing in the minors for tossing baseballs
to young fans in the stands. He had a penchant for pinstripe suits and big

diamond rings. Newspapers wrote editorials praising him, and his words to San Diego owner Paul Starr before the season proved prophetic. "Mister Starr, everybody likes me when I hit that ball," was Easter's response to Starr's warning that he would likely be booed because of his race.

Integration in the PCL went quickly and smoothly, and Easter deserves much of the credit. "History cannot ignore the fact that Big Luke was an important contributor to the cause of integration," Doc Young wrote in *Jet*. "His most important donation was proof that when an athlete hits home runs and plays a Titanic game, fans quickly lose sight of his color."

But as Easter found out later that season, fans are nothing if not fickle. Six weeks after knee surgery he was sold to the Cleveland Indians, with whom San Diego had a working agreement. He struggled in his late-season stint in the majors, and as a result was "the most booed player in the history of Cleveland Stadium," according to the *Sporting News*. And he was often depicted by sportswriters as slow-witted or having what the Pittsburgh *Courier* called a "Stepin Fetchit manner." Even the *Sporting News* was guilty, reporting Easter's comment to Starr as "Mistuh, when ah hits dat home run ball, everybody likes me." He also was thrown at so many times in his rookie season in the PCL that the league president issued a memo warning pitchers.

Easter got off to a slow start in 1950 but soon righted himself and became wildly popular with Cleveland fans, and with Larry Doby he gave Cleveland the most powerful black duo in baseball.

Easter grew up in St. Louis' South Side, played schoolyard softball, and left school after the eighth grade to work for a paint company. In 1941, one day before he was to enter the army, he went to Memphis to see a softball game along with a few friends, one of whom was future big leaguer Sam Jethroe. On the way home, Jethroe fell asleep at the wheel and crashed the car, killing one passenger and leaving Easter with two broken legs. Thirteen months in the army and a few jobs later, Easter found himself hanging around Chicago's Washington Park hoping to get a chance to play for one of the city's all-black teams. He homered the first time he got up, and a spectator named Ben Lindts offered him $18 a week to play on his traveling team. The team was so bad, "we changed our name most every day so we could book games," Easter said, but his hitting exploits got around.

He played with the Cincinnati Crescents in 1946, then jumped to the Homestead Grays in 1947 where he filled the power void left by the retirement of Josh Gibson. Veeck had heard about Easter from his friend Abe Saperstein, owner of the Cincinnati Crescents and the Harlem Globetrotters, and flew to Puerto Rico to sign Easter while he was playing winter ball after the 1948 Negro National League season.

Easter had three outstanding seasons with the Tribe, averaging 29 home runs and 100 RBIs. His memorable home runs included a 477-foot shot into the second deck in right field at Cleveland Stadium, the longest ever hit there. But he was 34 by the time he reached the majors, and after knee and ankle injuries limited his playing time in 1953, he returned to the minors, where he continued to terrorize pitchers for another decade.

In 1957 he led the International League with 40 home runs, including a 500-foot blast over the scoreboard at Offerman Stadium in Buffalo. It was the first ball to clear the scoreboard in the stadium's 33-year history. Easter continued to play in the minors until 1949, his final years as a crowd favorite with the Rochester Red Wings.

For Easter, hitting was unscientific. "It's a gift," he said. "It's like a fella feels he can play the piano. I know I can hit. I feel it inside."

Easter's life ended tragically when he was gunned down during a 1979 bank robbery while working as a messenger.

Statistics: Luke Easter

Year	Team	Games	AB	Runs	Hits	2B	3B	HR	RBI	BA
1949	CLE-A	21	45	6	10	3	0	0	2	.222
1950	CLE	141	540	96	151	20	4	28	107	.280
1951	CLE	128	486	65	131	12	5	27	103	.270
1952	CLE	127	437	63	115	10	3	31	97	.263
1953	CLE	68	211	26	64	9	0	7	31	.303
1954	CLE	6	6	0	1	0	0	0	0	.167
Totals										
6 Years		491	1725	256	472	54	12	93	340	.274

Monford Merrill "Monte" Irvin

Outfield. Batted right. Threw right. 6'1", 195 lbs. Hall of Fame, 1973. Born 2/25/19, Columbus, Alabama.

If Monte Irvin's army unit had had a baseball team, Jackie Robinson might have become just another Hall of Famer. When Irvin went to France in 1943 with an all-black engineering unit, he was a four-time Negro league all-star and acknowledged by many to be the leading candidate to break baseball's color line. When he got back in 1945, Dodger president Branch Rickey approached him, ostensibly to join Rickey's new Negro league team. But Irvin declined, feeling he needed to get back in shape playing winter ball in Puerto Rico. Had he known Rickey was ready to integrate the majors, he might have made a different choice.

Still, Irvin was a towering talent whose combined career in the Negro and major leagues earned him election to the Hall of Fame in 1973. Irvin was born in Columbus, Alabama, in 1919, but his family moved to New Jersey when he was eight. He was a brilliant athlete at East Orange High School, where he collected 16 letters and all-state honors in four sports. He began his professional baseball career with the Newark Eagles and quickly proved to be a dominant player, hitting .422 in 1940 and .396 in 1941.

After his army stint, Irvin returned to win Most Valuable Player honors in the 1945-46 Puerto Rican winter league, then led the Eagles to a Negro league championship, hitting .389 and leading the league in RBIs. In the World Series against the Kansas City Monarchs that year, Irvin hit .462 with three home runs, and scored the winning run in Game 7. Rickey owned the rights to Irvin but did not want to pay Eagles owner Effa Manley the $5,000 it would take to make Irvin a Brooklyn Dodger. So Irvin continued to star away from the majors, leading the Negro National League in home runs and RBIs in 1947.

Finally, in 1949 Rickey gave up his claim, and the rival New York Giants bought Irvin's contract. He was 30. Irvin hit .373 with Jersey City in the International League before being called to the majors in late July along with Hank Thompson, and the pair simultaneously became the Giants' first black players. Giants manager Leo Durocher, hardly known for his gentility, was the key to a relatively easy transition for Irvin and Thompson. "He couldn't have been nicer," Irvin said. "He welcomed us very warmly and introduced us around. Then he talked to us privately. 'Fellows,' he said, 'it's no different from what you've been doing everywhere else. Just go out and play your game and you'll be all right.'"

Irvin played sparingly that season and started the 1950 campaign back in the minors. But after hitting .510 with 10 homers in 18 games, he was back in New York where he played 110 games at first base and the outfield, hitting .299 with 15 home runs. In 1951 he gained star status as the most prolific run producer on the most memorable Giants team ever, the one that wiped out a 13½-game Dodger lead and then beat Brooklyn in a best-of-three-games playoff, capped by Bobby Thomson's pennant-winning home run. Irvin hit .312 with 24 homers and a league-leading 121 RBIs that season. He homered off Ralpha Branca in game one of the playoff, helping the Giants to a 3–1 win. Even at 32 Irvin could still win games with his speed. He stole 12 bases, finished second in the league with 11 triples, and stole home against the Yankees in the World Series. The Giants lost the series in six games, but Irvin led both teams with 11 hits and a .458 average.

A broken ankle in an exhibition game cut short Irvin's 1952 season. He rebounded in 1953 to hit .329 with 21 homers and 97 RBIs despite reinjuring the ankle in August, and in 1954 played a key role in the Giants' world championship season. But Irvin never fully recovered from the injury and was demoted to the minors midway through the 1955 season. He resurfaced for a final season in 1956 with the Cubs and hit .271 with 15 homers.

Irvin returned to baseball in 1967 as a scout for the New York Mets and later became a public relations representative for the commissioner's office. He was elected to the Hall of Fame in 1973 and later became a member of the Hall of Fame Committee on Negro Leagues, and a member of the Veterans Committee.

Irvin missed his chance to break baseball's color line, but he did establish himself as one of the most feared power hitters of his generation. And he did something no one before him had ever done: He hit a ball into the center-field stands at the Polo Grounds 487 feet from home plate.

Statistics: Monte Irvin

Year	Team	Games	AB	Runs	Hits	2B	3B	HR	RBI	BA
1949	NY-N	36	76	7	17	3	2	0	7	.224
1950	NY	110	374	61	112	19	5	15	66	.299
1951	NY	151	558	94	174	19	11	24	121*	.312
1952	NY	46	126	10	39	2	1	4	21	.310
1953	NY	124	444	72	146	21	5	21	97	.329
1954	NY	135	432	62	113	13	3	19	64	.262
1955	NY	51	150	16	38	7	1	1	17	.253
1956	CHI-N	111	339	44	92	13	3	15	50	.271
Totals										
8 Years		764	2499	366	731	97	31	99	443	.293
World Series										
1951	NY-N	6	24	4	11	0	1	0	2	.458
1954	NY	4	9	1	2	1	0	0	2	.222
Totals										
2 Years		10	33	5	13	1	1	0	4	.394

League leader.

Saturnino Orestes Arrieta Armas "Minnie" Minoso

**Outfield. Batted right. Threw right. 5'10", 175 lbs.
Born 11/29/22, El Perico, Cuba.**

What Willie Mays was to the National League, Minnie Minoso was to the American. With reckless speed on the bases and a seemingly innate all-around sense of the game, both men captured the imagination of fans and players throughout their rookie season, 1951.

"He literally lives the game," said Paul Richards, Minoso's first manager with the White Sox. "I doubt if he ever knew or cared about anything else. He's learned about money now, but I doubt if that will make any difference in the exemplary life he leads. He does everything well on the field. He can run, throw, hit, think, and he can play any position. You can put him anywhere on the field and forget about him.

"He hit a homer the first time at bat for the Sox, and he hit a home run the last time he batted. He was better in between."

Saturnino Orestes Arrieta Armas Minoso grew up picking sugarcane, but he was born to play baseball. At 14, Minoso convinced his father that his destiny lay on a baseball diamond, not a sugarcane field. He quit school and with a $100 grubstake from his father, left his home for the ballfields of Havana. Ten years later, while Minoso was playing with the New York Cuban Giants of the Negro National League, Bill Veeck of the Cleveland Indians signed him to a minor league contract. Minoso was called up to the Indians at the end of the 1949 season and wound up playing in the majors in five decades. Only a ruling by A. Bartlett Giamatti, the late commissioner of baseball, kept him from competing in a sixth.

Following the 1950 season with the Indians Class AAA farm club in San Diego—he hit .339 with 20 home runs, 30 stolen bases, 40 doubles, 130 runs and 115 RBIs—Minoso was traded to the Chicago White Sox at the beginning of the 1951 season. Cleveland, loaded with hitting, was looking for another starting pitcher; in exchange for Minoso, the Indians received future Hall of Fame pitcher Early Wynn. Minoso was in tears when manager Lopez broke the news of the trade to him on a train between cities. He thought his career was over. He simply could not imagine why any team would trade a player of his caliber.

"I had no idea how long it would take me before I would be able to capture the hearts of the White Sox fans," Minoso said in his autobiography, *Extra Innings*. But in his first at-bat for Chicago, the first black player ever to wear a White Sox uniform hit a 450-foot home run to dead-center field off Yankee Vic Raschi. The hearts of White Sox fans, and fans throughout baseball, have been his ever since.

Minoso tore up American League pitching in 1950. In his first 12 games with Chicago, Minoso hit 11 triples. And when he was not legging out triples and doubles, Minoso was stealing bases as no American Leaguer had since Ty Cobb. White Sox fans, incited by Minoso's base-running skills, soon nicknamed him "Minnie the Moocher," and whenever he reached base, Comiskey Park would rock with the rhythmic chant "Go, Minnie, go!" According to Veeck, a game without Minoso in the lineup was "just another ball game. I don't believe there is a player in the game today who can give you the thrill he can."

Minoso hit .360 against Cleveland's Early Wynn, Mike Garcia, Bob Lemon, and Bob Feller, who combined to win 81 games in 1950. By season's end, he had registered one of the greatest rookie years in baseball history. In 146 games and 530 at-bats, Minoso hit .326. Of his 173 hits, 34 were doubles, and 10 were home runs; his 14 triples led the league. He scored 112 runs, drove in 76, and stole a league-leading 31 bases. He played 82 games in the outfield, 68 at third, one at short, and one at first.

Minoso's immediate popularity in Chicago translated into record-breaking attendance—1,328,000 fans—for the White Sox in 1951. As an expression of thanks, the team honored him late in the season with a Minnie Minoso Day, a gesture unprecedented for a rookie. He was given a brand new Packard automobile and a deed to a lot in Chicago.

Despite his numbers, Minoso came in second in Rookie of the Year balloting to Yankee infielder Gil McDougald, who finished lower than Minoso in every category except home runs. But Minoso's statistics—a .298 career batting average, eight seasons .300 or better, three consecutive seasons leading the American League in stolen bases, and nearly 2,000 hits in professional baseball—tell only part of his story. Minnie Minoso was baseball itself, and anyone who saw him play can vouch for that. Minoso claimed that his "baseball philosophy is two things. One, if you think you're great, you're through. Two, if you don't feel like you give your best, you're through."

Batting from a crouch, crowding the plate, and swinging with his full torso, Minoso was a frequent target of brush-back pitches. But rather than charge the mound after being hit, Minoso would retrieve the ball and toss it back to the pitcher with a smile. "It was accident every time," said Minoso. "I been hit in head eight times. But I rather die than stop playing."

In one 1955 game against the Yankees, he almost did. Struck above the left eye by a Bob Grim fastball, Minoso suffered a hairline fracture of the skull. While he was expected to recover, the general feeling around the league was that Minoso would come out of his convalescence "gun shy" at the plate. Instead, he returned to the lineup fearless and with no less determination to play the game the only way he knew. Following that injury, Minoso hit safely in 23 straight games during which he compiled a .430 batting average.

On September 7, 1956, Minoso was hit by a Bob Lemon pitch, the twenty-second time he had been hit that year, breaking Jake Stahl's 48-year-old major league record. "Why, that guy crouches so far over the plate," Casey Stengel once said of Minoso, "that you can't throw an inside strike to him without hitting him. I tell my fellows to throw 'em inside there with plenty of mustard on the pitch. But that don't scare Minnie."

Evidently nothing scared Minnie. He seemed impervious to the challenges of age and the racial insults he endured early in his career. In downplaying any racism he encountered, Minoso let his flair for the game win over anyone who challenged racial equality. On April 7, 1952, Minoso and Hector Rodriguez became the first blacks to play on the same ballfield as whites in the history of New Orleans as the White Sox played the Pittsburgh Pirates in an exhibition game at Pelican Park. The next day, Hap Glaudi wrote in the *Item*, "A throng of 9,502 paid to see this new era in baseball make a tardy appearance. [The game] will assist tremendously in erasing the impression which some organizations give our people that there is something wrong with the way God distributes his color."

In 1956, Minoso hit .354 over a two-month span despite the pain of a severely injured groin muscle. The year before, one day after learning he had broken a toe, he refused to come out of the lineup and doubled his first time up.

Thirty years later, in an old-timers game, Minoso lined a shot off the right-center-field fence of Buffalo's rickety War Memorial Stadium. Running full-steam — which even at the age of 62, was a fair clip — Minoso rounded first and continued on past second, hook-sliding ahead of the relay into third with a triple.

"I am a professional," Minoso said in his autobiography. "I wear the uniform I love. We all have to die. What better way to die than in the uniform I love."

Statistics: *Minnie Minoso*

Year	Team	Games	AB	Runs	Hits	2B	3B	HR	RBI	BA
1949	CLE-A	9	16	2	3	0	0	1	1	.188
1951	CLE/									
	CHI-A	146	530	112	173	34	14*	10	76	.326
1952	CHI	147	569	96	160	24	9	13	61	.281
1953	CHI	157	556	104	174	24	8	15	104	.313
1954	CHI	153	568	119	182	29	18*	19	116	.320
1955	CHI	139	517	79	149	26	7	10	70	.288
1956	CHI	151	545	106	172	29	11*	21	88	.316
1957	CHI	153	568	96	176	36*	5	12	103	.310
1958	CLE-A	149	556	94	168	25	2	24	80	.302
1959	CLE	148	570	92	172	32	0	21	92	.302
1960	CHI-A	154	591	89	184*	32	4	20	105	.311
1961	CHI	152	540	91	151	28	3	14	82	.280
1962	STL-N	39	97	14	19	5	0	1	10	.196
1963	WAS-A	109	315	38	72	12	2	4	30	.229
1964	CHI-A	30	31	4	7	0	0	1	5	.226
1976	CHI	3	8	1	0	0	0	0	0	.125
1980	CHI	2	0	0	0	0	0	0	0	.000
Totals										
17 Years		1841	6577	1137	1962	336	83	186	1023	.298

*League leader.

Donald "Don" Newcombe

Pitcher. Threw right. Batted left. 6'4", 230 lbs. Born 6/14/26, Madison, New Jersey.

Game 1 of the 1949 World Series was classic: Yankee veteran Allie Reynolds versus the Brooklyn Dodgers rookie phenom Don Newcombe. Both pitchers had won 17 games for their respective pennant winners. Reynolds, part American Indian, was one of the toughest pitchers in the major leagues, averaging 15 wins a year since 1943. But Newcombe, the first black to pitch for a National League team in the World Series and the National League Rookie of the Year, pitched with the same composure that Reynolds was known for.

Coming up to the Dodgers from the Class AAA Montreal Royals in late May, Newcombe had completed 19 of 31 starts, led the league with five shutouts, and finished only three strikeouts behind league-leading Warren Spahn. Newcombe's ERA was 3.17, slight indeed for a pitcher who earned his keep in cozy Ebbets Field.

Each pitcher was overwhelming that October 5 afternoon, treating a Yankee Stadium crowd of 66,224 to one of the best-pitched games in World Series history. Through eight full innings, neither team scored. Brooklyn had managed just two base hits off Reynolds, and the 6'4" Newcombe scattered five hits, striking out 11, and walking none. But when the Yankees' 36-year-old first baseman, Tommy Henrich, led off the bottom of the ninth, the rookie rudely learned that Henrich's nickname was well deserved. "Old Reliable" drove a Newcombe mistake over the right-field fence, and the Yankees were one game up in the series. That was as close as Newcombe ever came to winning a World Series game.

In four more series starts (1949, 1955, and 1956), Newcombe's ERA ballooned. And despite winning 20 or more games three times, including a league-leading 27 in 1956, he was tagged as the kind of pitcher who "can't win the big one." It was an undeserved label, but it was a convenient excuse for fans and the press. It was also one that Newcombe took to heart.

That the Dodgers even won the 1949 pennant was attributable in large part to Newcombe's presence. He pitched three consecutive shutouts and ran up 31 consecutive scoreless innings. He pitched his way onto the All-Star team, one of four black players (Jackie Robinson, Roy Campanella, and Larry Doby being the others) to make the squad. On September 21, Brooklyn manager Burt Shotton called on "Newk" to open against the Cardinals in what was billed as the series to decide the National League pennant. And it was the rookie once again on the final day of the season against the Phillies (he had pitched the second game of a doubleheader against Boston just three days before) in a showdown game that clinched the pennant.

And 1949 was not a fluke season. Newcombe led the team in wins and innings pitched in five of his seven years in Brooklyn. His twenty-seventh win of 1956 came on the final day of the season against Pittsburgh and clinched another Brooklyn pennant.

In addition to his pitching skills, a moving fastball and a wicked curve, Newcombe was one of the best-hitting pitchers ever and one of the Dodgers' most dependable pinch-hitters. His career batting average was .271; of his 15 lifetime home runs, seven were hit in 1955. His .628 slugging average is a major league record for pitchers.

Despite his talent, Don Newcombe almost missed his calling. At age 16, with a burning desire to drive trucks for a living, Newcombe lied about his age and joined the army. But on the day of his scheduled induction he was nowhere to be found. Luck was on his side: He had landed a tractor-trailer gig and had driven from New Jersey to Memphis, where with no transportation home, he was for all practical purposes AWOL from an army unit he had never joined. When the military police contacted the enlistee's father, the elder Newcombe was shocked. Obviously he had no idea his son had joined up. As proof, he produced the birth certificate of his peripatetic son. The army relinquished rights to a soldier, and baseball gained a pitcher.

Following high school, Newcombe was signed by Effa Manley's Negro National League Newark Eagles, winning 14 games and losing four in 1945. There he was "discovered" by Brooklyn's Branch Rickey, who wanted to send Newcombe and a newly signed catcher named Roy Campanella to the Dodger Class C affiliate in Danville, Illinois. But when the league president refused permission for teams to sign black players, Rickey sent the first black battery in organized baseball to Nashua, New Hampshire, where general manager Buzzi Bavasi and field manager Walter Alston recognized that Rickey was offering them their ticket to the majors.

Newcombe won 14 and lost four in 1946, and in 1947 he led the New England League with 19 wins (against six losses) and 186 strikeouts. Promoted to Montreal in 1948, Newk won 17 games, losing only six.

Newcombe began the 1949 season in Montreal, but when Brooklyn's pitching faltered, he was called up in mid–May. Dodger manager Burt Shotton, elderly and sick and the last manager (other than Connie Mack) to manage in streetclothes, started the rookie against the Cardinals in St. Louis, a city that until 1957 had barred Newcombe (and all blacks) from rooming in hotels with their white teammates.

The rookie was shelled. Recalling the game in Jackie Robinson's *Baseball Has Done It*, Newcombe said, "As I came back to the dugout I expected him to hand me a train ticket back to Montreal. Instead, he came running to me, shook my hand and said, 'Big fellow, don't you worry. I'm starting you in Cincinnati on Sunday.' He did, and I threw a shutout.

"I was twenty-one, a Negro and worried sick about making good. His words made the big difference between losing my confidence and becoming a winner.... Burt Shotton made me a member of the team."

Newcombe missed all of the 1952 and 1953 seasons, putting in a "second" stint in the army. (His final appearance before entering the service was against the Giants in the third game of the 1951 playoffs; he was relieved by Ralph Branca, who gave up Bobby Thomson's famous pennant-winning home run.) He returned to the Dodgers in 1954, 20 pounds lighter but somewhat rusty from the lack of pitching. Following his second 20-win season in 1955, Newk was named National League Most Valuable Player in 1956 when he also became the first recipient of the Cy Young Award.

Like many of Brooklyn's "Boys of Summer," Newcombe never adjusted to Los Angeles. With his best years behind him, Newcombe was traded to Cincinnati where he learned that Reds general manager Gabe Paul had been trying for two years to acquire him. He made an impressive comeback in 1959 but retired after suffering chronic arm problems in 1960. He later played in the Japanese leagues, the first of many former major-leaguers to do so, before returning to the Dodger organization where as a recovered alcoholic, he worked in community relations for a number of years.

Statistics: Don Newcombe

Year	Team	W	L	PCT	G	IP	H	BB	SO	ERA	SV
1949	BKN-N	17	8	.680	38	244.1	223	73	149	3.17	1
1950	BKN	19	11	.633	40	267.1	258	75	130	3.70	3
1951	BKN	20	9	.690	40	272	235	91	164*	3.28	0
1954	BKN	9	8	.529	29	144.1	158	49	82	4.55	0
1955	BKN	20	5	.800*	34	233.2	222	38	143	3.20	0
1956	BKN	27*	7	.794*	38	268	219	46	139	3.06	0
1957	BKN	11	12	.478	28	198.2	199	33	90	3.49	0
1958	LA-N/										
	CIN-N	7	13	.350	31	167.2	212	36	69	4.67	1
1959	CIN	13	8	.619	30	222	216	27	100	3.16	1
1960	CIN/										
	CLE-A	6	9	.400	36	136.2	160	22	63	4.48	1
Totals											
10 Years		149	90	.623	344	2154.2	2102	490	1129	3.56	7
World Series											
1949	BKN-N	0	2	.000	2	11.2	10	3	11	3.09	0
1955	BKN	0	1	.000	1	5.2	8	2	4	9.53	0
1956	BKN	0	1	.000	2	4.2	11	3	4	21.21	0
Totals											
3 Years		0	4	.000	5	22	29	8	19	8.59	0

*League leader.

1950

Samuel "Sam" Jethroe

Outfield. Batted both. Threw right. 6'1", 178 lbs. Born 1/20/22, East St. Louis, Illinois.

Sam Jethroe could flat-out fly, and he had the nicknames to prove it — "The Jet," "The Mercury Man," "Larceny Legs," and "The Colored Comet," among others.

No one ever questioned Jethroe's speed, but throughout his all too brief major league career sportswriters, management, and even his teammates questioned almost everything else about him. He came to the big leagues carrying a high price tag and even higher expectations, and although he led the majors in stolen bases his rookie and sophomore years, he never lived up to his advance billing.

First there was his fielding. He had a tendency to misjudge fly balls, and while his speed bailed him out often, he still led National League outfielders in errors in each of his three full seasons in the majors. Then there was his arm. Although he was twice runner-up in assists in the NL to the legendary arm of Dodger right fielder Carl Furillo, writers constantly harped that he could not throw. One Boston writer went so far as to print that "Jethroe can carry the ball back to the infield faster than he can throw it." He could not bunt well enough, they said. He did not hustle, they said. And almost everybody was convinced he lied about his age.

But despite all the questions and disappointments, Jethroe brought a spark to the game wherever he played. Growing up in East St. Louis, Jethroe honed his base-stealing techniques on local sandlots playing for semipro teams. In 1942 he signed with the Cleveland Buckeyes of the Negro American League, and by 1944 he was a full-fledged star, hitting .353 to win the batting title and playing in his first of three East-West all-star games. In 1945 Jethroe had his finest Negro league season, hitting .393 with 10 triples and 21 stolen bases as the Buckeyes won both halves of the NAL season, then swept the vaunted Homestead Grays in the Negro World Series.

That season, Jethroe was one of three Negro league stars to travel with sportswriter Wendell Smith to Boston for a tryout with the Red Sox. Smith had contacted a Boston councilman who was pressuring both the Red Sox and Braves to integrate, and Red Sox management agreed to the tryout, but apparently only to get the councilman off its back. Manager Joe Cronin was not even there. "It was kind of a dull day," Jethroe said. "There wasn't anything spectacular about it; no fans in the stands, just a few newspaper reporters and a coach or two."

In 1948, the emergence of Larry Doby as a star for the Cleveland Indians emptied the seats during Cleveland Buckeyes games and the coffers of owner Ernie Wright, so in July Wright sold Jethroe to the Dodgers for $5,000. It would turn out to be one of the best financial decisions Branch Rickey made. The Dodgers had scouted Jethroe in winter baseball in Cuba and liked what they saw.

Jethroe was assigned to Montreal in the Class AAA International League and took the league by storm, hitting .322 with 11 triples and 18 stolen bases in 76 games. He even impressed league president Frank Shaughnessy. "Sam doesn't run," Shaughnessy said. "He skates." The *Sporting News* described him as "an ebony ghost, drifting wraithlike all over center pasture for amazing catches."

The following season Jethroe earned another nickname — "the man who made Montreal forget Jackie Robinson." It was a monster year — .326, 207 hits, 151 runs scored, 83 RBIs, and a new league record with 89 steals. He capped the season with two game-winning home runs in the Junior World Series against Buffalo. His speed so unnerved Buffalo manager Paul Richards that Richards came up with a bizarre but effective strategy. Seven times during the season Richards intentionally walked the Montreal pitcher to put a roadblock ahead of Jethroe. "He can't hurt us with his speed if he's got the pitcher ahead of him," Richards reasoned.

In the off-season, Rickey decided that with Duke Snider firmly ensconced in center field, the Dodgers did not need Jethroe, so he began shopping him around. Rickey also believed he had reached the saturation point for blacks on the Dodgers and saw an opportunity to help integrate another team. He also saw dollar signs. The Braves spent $100,000 for Jethroe, but general manager John Quinn figured to get a good return on the investment. Quinn called Jethroe "the greatest attraction in the history of the International League." Montreal writer Lloyd McGowen went even further. "The Braves have not only acquired a first-class baseball artisan, but a sure-fire attraction to make the turnstiles hum a merry tune," McGowen wrote. "If Jethroe can't catch a plane in the majors, I'll quit scribbling about the pastime and start driving a hack."

Jethroe had mixed feelings about playing for the Braves. He was happy to be playing for manager Billy Southworth, one of his boyhood heroes, but was still uneasy about Boston from the disappointing 1945 tryout with the Red Sox. Still, Jethroe was confident he would hit and steal bases because he always had.

"The bases sure aren't any farther apart" in the majors, he said. But he came to spring training with a sore arm and got off to a rocky start. Jethroe broke the color line in St. Petersburg, Florida, without incident despite a law prohibiting integrated play. But the press was brutal. One columnist called Jethroe one of Rickey's "gold-brick specialties." "I'd have gone stone crazy if I hadn't stopped buying papers," he said.

Jethroe, now the first black to play major league baseball in Boston, continued slumping a few weeks into the first few weeks of the regular season. But support poured in; he got phone calls from boxers Joe Louis and Sugar Ray Robinson. Then Southworth moved him into the leadoff spot where he had hit for most of his career, and Jethroe took off. He reached base eight times in his first 10 tries at leadoff. In his first 47 games, he stole six bases; in the next 27 games, he stole 18.

But on July 9 he suffered a bone bruise sliding after his third stolen base of the game. He missed a few games, and when he came back, he seemed to have lost something. In the second half of the season he hit just .258, and scored half as many runs, and stole half as many bases as he did before the All-Star break. Everyone had a theory. Some of his teammates claimed he was dogging it, but others, including Phillies owner Bob Carpenter, said the loneliness and stress of being the only black player on the team were taking their toll. "From what I hear, Jethroe is very lonely," Carpenter said. "The Braves should have taken [black pitcher] Dan Bankhead when the Dodgers offered him to them." Braves management denied there was a problem. "We don't consider a roommate for Jethroe to be a vital problem," a spokesman said. "We told Sam to come to us any time with problems, or if he got at all lonely. He never said a word about it." All in all, a pretty tough season for a 28-year-old who was named NL Rookie of the Year.

Jethroe's woes continued in the off-season when he slipped on an icy driveway and broke a bone in his throwing hand. He got off to another slow start in 1951, and after dropping a routine fly ball to help lose a game in St. Louis, he locked himself in his compartment on the train and refused to eat or talk to anyone, including his new roommate, Luis Marquez. When the train reached New York, Jethroe told writers, "I'm ready to quit." But Southworth talked him out of it, and someone suggested his hitting and fielding woes might be eyesight-related. Armed with new glasses, Jethroe hit .330 the second half of the season and became the gate attraction the Braves had paid for. "Base stealing is a lost art, and that's why Jethroe is doing so much to stimulate interest," Southworth said. "He is drawing fans who come out to the game to see him steal a base or two."

Jethroe's base-stealing technique was fairly simple: Outrun the ball. He took relatively short leads and did not dart back and forth like Jackie Robinson, whom he supplanted as the league's top base stealer. But the Braves had another speedy center fielder in the pipeline, Billy Bruton, and after a subpar season in 1952, Jethroe opened the 1953 season back with Toledo of the American Association. He had a fine year, including becoming the first player ever to hit a ball over the 472-foot left-field fence at Toledo's Swayne Field, but in December he was traded to Pittsburgh. He appeared in two games for the Pirates in 1954, then was optioned to Toronto where he played for five years before retiring.

Sam Jethroe never had the success in the major leagues he had everywhere else he played, but he had ridden the tough road of a pioneer. "Jackie [Robinson] may have broken the barrier to playing, but I knew when I arrived there was more required for me to do than a white player," he said. "It was still a hard thing to go through."

Statistics: Sam Jethroe

Year	Team	Games	AB	Runs	Hits	2B	3B	HB	RBI	BA
1950	BOS-N	141	582	100	159	28	8	18	58	.273
1951	BOS	148	572	101	160	29	10	18	65	.280
1952	BOS	151	608	79	141	23	7	13	58	.232
1954	PIT-N	2	1	0	0	0	0	0	0	.000
Totals										
4 Years		442	1763	280	460	80	25	49	181	.261

1951

Robert Richard "Bob" Boyd

First base. Batted left. Threw left. 5'10", 170 lbs. Born 10/1/26, Potts Camp, Mississippi.

In his prime, Bob Boyd put up some awesome numbers. But like many of his peers in baseball's early days of integration, his prime was over before he got a decent shot.

When he finally did spend a full season in the majors and off the bench, Boyd made the most of it. In 1957 he became the first Baltimore Oriole with more than 400 at-bats to hit over .300, and the franchise made it to the .500 mark for the first time since 1945. But by this time, Boyd was 30. Three years later, he lost his starting job to a man seven years his junior.

Boyd spent most of his youth in New Albany, Mississippi. But his mother died while he was in high school, so he moved to Memphis to live with his father, who was a fine player in his youth. After three years in the army, he was back in Memphis working in a warehouse when he and his brother Jimmy tried out for the Memphis Red Sox of the Negro American League. Boyd stroked line drives to all fields that day, and he was signed on the spot and sent to Birmingham of the Negro Southern League. He hit .372 for Birmingham in 1946, then spent the next four years destroying NAL pitching, hitting .339, .375, .376, and .356. Once, in a game at Chicago's Comiskey Park, he became just the third player ever—Ted Williams and Larry Doby were the others—to reach the left-field stands.

Scouted by former Negro league pitching star John Donaldson, Boyd was signed by the Chicago White Sox midway through the 1950 season, along with Sam Hairston of the Indianapolis Clowns. He left Memphis that day for Colorado Springs of the Western League, went straight from the airport to the ballpark, and homered in his first at-bat. Hitting .373 with 39 RBIs in 42 games for Colorado earned him a ticket to spring training with the White Sox in 1951. Manager Paul Richards was impressed with his glove and his speed but questioned whether he had hit enough to stick.

Richards would be the prime decision-maker in Boyd's up-and-down major league career. It was Richards who kept him shuttling back and forth between the majors and minors with the White Sox, then Richards who drafted him back to the majors after he had taken the reins in Baltimore. Boyd respected Richards as a manager but suffered from his prejudice. "He never broke his word . . . but he didn't like blacks," Boyd said. "I was in enough team meetings where he would talk about the black players on the team . . . and he wouldn't say very nice things about them."

Boyd also suffered from a logjam at first base on the White Sox. When he first signed, the Sox had power-hitting Eddie Robinson at first. Then before the 1953 season they traded Robinson for AL batting champ Ferris Fain, also a first baseman, despite the fact that Boyd had won the batting title in 1952 for Chicago's top farm team, then hit .374 to lead the Puerto Rican winter league. Then there was some lousy luck. In 1953 Richards tried Boyd in left field, and he broke his elbow on a throw to second base, ending his season. He was plagued throughout his career by an ulcer the size of a quarter, and doctors finally found it a year after Boyd had left the majors for the last time.

But in 1954, after being sent back to the minors for the third time in three years, the frustration began to take its toll on the cheerful, soft-spoken Boyd. "When they sent me back to Houston again, I almost didn't report," he said. "I told them I was going back to the Negro league." But Boyd reconsidered, hit .321 that season, and went nowhere. Boyd took the disappointment in stride, but Doc Young of *Jet* magazine had had enough. "Boyd's case is typical of several Negro players who linger in organizations which, for one reason or another, are either unable or unwilling to give them breaks," he wrote. "In Boyd's case, it is unlikely that the Sox will allow him to beat out Fain . . . just as they never let him threaten slow poke Eddie Robinson. Still, they won't sell him."

Years later, Boyd allowed that he probably got a raw deal. "Looking back, I really feel that the early black ballplayers had to do a little better than the white players to make it to the majors," he said. "Back then, they picked black players carefully. The White Sox kept me in the minors for the entire 1955 season, and I began to wonder again if I'd ever get a real shot with them." He did not, but one winter morning in Havana Boyd's wife woke him to read in the *Havana Post* that he had been drafted by the Orioles.

In Baltimore, Boyd got his nickname, "Rope," after pitching coach Lum Harris watched him stroke line drive after line drive in spring training. He played part-time in 1956 but was the regular first baseman in 1957 and finished fourth in the AL batting race behind Ted Williams, Mickey Mantle, and Gene Woodling. In 1958 he had seven straight hits in a doubleheader against Cleveland and led the AL in night-game hitting, .367 in 56 games. "I'm laying out those ropes because I'm playing regularly," Boyd said. "Shucks, I like to be in the lineup every day. Man, I come to play."

Boyd had, for him, a subpar season in 1959 with Baltimore. Teams expected more power from their first basemen than Boyd could offer, so in 1960 he gave way to rookie Jim Gentile. But Boyd took it in stride and hit .304 in 56 pinch-hitting appearances. "I figured this was the year to bounce back, but if I have to do it as a pinch-hitter, that's okay too."

Boyd was traded twice in 1961, his final season in the majors. He continued to play minor league and semipro ball well into his forties, driving and playing for the Dreamliner Bus Company of Wichita. He spent a few years as a scout for the Orioles, and later he organized autograph shows in Wichita and Kansas City featuring major league players.

Statistics: Bob Boyd

Year	Team	Games	AB	Runs	Hits	2B	3B	HR	RBI	BA
1951	CHI-A	12	18	3	3	0	1	0	4	.167
1953	CHI	55	165	20	49	6	2	3	23	.297
1954	CHI	29	56	10	10	3	0	0	5	.179
1956	BAL-A	70	225	28	70	8	3	2	11	.311
1957	BAL	141	485	73	154	16	8	4	34	.318
1958	BAL	125	401	58	124	21	5	7	36	.309
1959	BAL	128	415	42	110	20	2	3	41	.265
1960	BAL	71	82	9	26	5	2	0	9	.317
1961	KC-A/									
	MIL-N	62	89	10	21	2	0	0	12	.236
Totals										
9 Years		693	1936	253	567	81	23	19	175	.293

Samuel "Sam" Hairston

**Catcher. Batted right. Threw right. 5'10½", 187 lbs.
Born 8/29/45, Crawford, Mississippi.**

Sam Hairston's major league career consisted of exactly five official at-bats, but he lived a dream of fathers everywhere: He signed his son to a major league contract.

Hairston had two sons in the majors, but it was as a scout for the Chicago White Sox in 1970 that he signed his son Jerry, who went on to play 14 years in the majors. Hairston's other major league son, John, lasted only four at-bats.

Hairston began his professional career in 1945 as a catcher with the Cincinnati Clowns of the Negro American League. He followed the team to Indianapolis in 1946 and stayed until August 1950 when the White Sox made him their first American-born black player on the strength of his .465 batting average. "We are looking for good young players in building the White Sox for the future," said general manager Frank Lane upon signing Hairston. "Whether they are white or black makes no difference."

Hairston had his five at-bats in 1951, but in the off-season the White Sox traded him for Sherm Lollar, who held down the catching spot for the next 12 years. So Hairston spent most of the rest of his career with Colorado Springs of the Western League, where he became a star. In 1952 he hit .316 and came within four points of winning the league batting title. The next season he was named the league's Most Valuable Player, hitting .445 in his final 121 trips to the plate. After spending 1954 with Charleston, Hairston returned to Colorado Springs where his season featured a .350 average, a batting title, and a night in his honor. He was honored not only for his play but his work fighting juvenile delinquency in the community. Before the game, Hairston was presented with a new Pontiac, luggage, a television and radio, and a significant amount of cash. His wife and three small sons were on hand as he went three for four in the game that followed.

Statistics: Sam Hairston

Year	Team	Games	AB	Runs	Hits	2B	3B	HR	RBI	BA
1951	CHI-A	4	5	1	2	1	0	0	1	.400

Samuel "Sam" Jones

Pitcher. Batted right. Threw right. 6'4", 192 lbs. Born 12/14/25, Stewartsville, Ohio.

If not for a bobble and a small tornado, Sam Jones might have been a lot more famous.

Jones already had one no-hitter to his credit when he took the mound for the San Francisco Giants on June 30, 1959, against the first-place Dodgers. With two outs in the bottom of the eighth, Jim Gilliam hit a grounder to shortstop Andre Rodgers who bobbled the ball and then threw too late to first. Official scorer Charlie Park of the *Los Angeles Mirror* ruled it a hit, and Jones had to settle for a one-hit, 10-strikeout win.

Three months later, in the thick of a three-team pennant race, Jones, already a 20-game winner, faced his former teammates, the St. Louis Cardinals. Through seven innings Jones was nearly perfect, allowing no hits, walking two, and striking out five. Then the heavens opened and sent down wind and rain that made for "two wet, miserable and frightening hours," according to one sportswriter. Another no-hitter lost. Three career no-hitters would have put Jones in a class with Bob Feller. Only Sandy Koufax and Nolan Ryan have more than three.

Jones always had great stuff—a good fastball and a stunning curve. "You've never seen a curveball until you've seen Sam Jones' curveball," said Hobie Landrith, who caught Jones with the Giants. "If you were a right-handed hitter, that ball started out a good four feet behind you." Jones once threw a 3-2 curve that Dodger shortstop Pee Wee Reese thought was going to hit him, so he hit the deck. The ball broke neatly across the plate for strike three. Reese dusted himself off and came back to the dugout, grumbling, "In all my years playing baseball, I've never struck out sitting down."

Reese had good reason to fear being hit by Jones. Not only was he wild— he led the National League four times in walks—but most hitters believed he had a mean streak. Don Drysdale recalled a knockdown duel between Jones and Don Newcombe of the Dodgers. "Batters on either side were falling like duckpins," he said. Jones claimed that it was wildness, pure and simple. "When I was having trouble with my control, there were a lot of guys who were afraid to bat against me," he said late in his career. "I was fast and I was wild and the players knew it. What a lot of people never realized was that I was always worried I might permanently hurt someone. I didn't want it to happen. . . . I just don't believe in the beanball."

Jones began his career in 1946 with the Homestead Grays of the Negro National League, then led the Cleveland Buckeyes to the Negro World Series in 1947. Buckeye manager Wilbur Hayes tried several times to get the crosstown Indians interested in Jones and finally succeeded. "[Jones] was very fast, but not only that, he had several different deliveries, and each time the ball did something," said Indians general manager Hank Greenberg. "He was doing things fellows in the majors hadn't learned."

Jones was assigned to Wilkes-Barre where he won 17 games in 1950 and led the team to the Eastern League title. He spent most of 1951 with San Diego and led the Pacific Coast League in innings pitched, strikeouts and complete games. He was called up to Cleveland near the end of the season, and in his first start allowed just four hits in eight innings in a 2–1 loss.

Jones pitched all winter in Panama, going over 400 innings for the year, and came to spring training in 1952 with a dead arm. "An arm's a funny thing," he said. "One day it's perfect, the next day you can't lift it." Jones was also trying to crack what was arguably the best starting rotation in history—Bob Feller, Early Wynn, Bob Lemon, and Mike Garcia. He pitched poorly in 14 games with the Indians in 1952, then spent the next couple of years knocking around the minors. His break came when the Indians traded him to the Cubs in November 1954.

Jones had a great winter season, going 14-4 with a 1.75 ERA for Santurce in Puerto Rico, then had a roller-coaster ride of a rookie year in Chicago. He led the team with 14 wins and led the league with 20 losses. His 198 strikeouts were the most by an NL rookie since Grover Cleveland Alexander's 227 in 1911. And on May 12 he no-hit the Pirates. Jones walked seven, including the first three hitters in the ninth inning. But then he struck out Dick Groat, Roberto Clemente, and Frank Thomas to become the first Cub to pitch a no-hitter in 40 years.

Jones was traded after the 1956 season to the Cardinals, making Stan Musial a happy man. "I've always had trouble hitting against him," said the seven-time NL batting champ. "I'm glad he's on our side." Jones had two solid seasons with the Cards, including a team-record 225 strikeouts in 1958. Then he was traded to the Giants, where in 1959 he was the best pitcher in baseball.

He made his Giants debut April 11 and beat his old mates the Cardinals 5–2. On May 13 he had a no-hitter until the Phillies' Willie Jones singled with two outs in the seventh; he settled for a two-hit shutout and 12 strikeouts. On September 12 he beat the Phillies 9–1 for his twentieth win, putting the Giants back in first place. He lost a heartbreaking 2–0 decision to Milwaukee's Lew Burdette on September 16, and 10 days later kept the Giants' pennant hopes alive with his seven-inning no-hitter. But the Dodgers eliminated the Giants one day later. After the season, Jones told manager Bill Rigney, "I wish I could have done more for you." "What more could he do?" Rigney said. "He must have thrown 3,000 pitches this year."

On April 12, 1960, Jones pitched the first game ever at Candlestick Park, and before Vice President Richard Nixon and a capacity crowd, he tossed a three-hitter in a 3–1 win. He won another 17 games for San Francisco that season, coming within four outs of another no-hitter, then slumped in 1961. In March of the following year, doctors found a low-grade malignancy in four knotty tissues removed from the neck, and Jones had to undergo radiation treatments. He won just four major league games after that.

Despite his brilliant stuff, Jones won just one more game than he lost in the majors. But he was the first black pitcher to win an ERA title and the first to throw a no-hitter. He was a two-time NL all-star, and his career average of 7.54 strikeouts per nine innings tops those of Steve Carlton, Tom Seaver, and Bob Gibson.

And he always came to play. "Every time Sam goes to the mound," Rigney said, "he gives you a good day's work."

Statistics: Sam Jones

Year	Team	W	L	PCT	G	IP	H	BB	SO	ERA	SV
1951	CLE-A	0	1	.000	2	8.2	4	5	4	2.08	0
1952	CLE	2	3	.400	14	36	38	37	28	7.25	1
1955	CHI-N	14	20*	.412	36	241.2	175	185*	198*	4.10	0
1956	CHI	9	14	.391	33	188.2	155	115*	176*	3.91	0
1957	STL-N	12	9	.571	28	182.2	164	71	154	3.60	0

Year	Team	W	L	PCT	G	IP	H	BB	SO	ERA	SV
1958	STL	14	13	.519	35	250	204	107*	225*	2.88	0
1959	SF-N	21*	15	.583	50	270.2	232	109*	209	2.83*	4
1960	SF	18	14	.563	39	234	200	91	190	3.19	0
1961	SF	8	8	.500	37	128.1	134	57	105	4.49	1
1962	DET-A	2	4	.333	30	81.1	77	35	73	3.65	1
1963	STL-N	2	0	1.000	11	11	15	5	8	9.00	2
1964	BAL-A	0	0	.000	7	10.1	5	5	6	2.61	0
Totals											
12 Years		102	101	.502	322	1643.1	1403	822	1376	3.59	9

League leader.

Luis Angel Marquez

Outfield. Batted right. Threw right. 5'10", 174 lbs.
Born 10/28/25, Aguadilla, Puerto Rico. Died 3/1/88.

In 1950, the Boston Braves "drafted" outfielder Luis Marquez, making him the first black player drafted by a major league club. The next year, Marquez led the Class AAA Pacific Coast League with 241 hits and 38 stolen bases. As the Braves headed south to their 1951 spring-training camp, Marquez was tabbed as the next Sam Jethroe. Known as "Canena" in Puerto Rico and "Heater" in the States, Marquez was an exceptional fielder with speed to match that of Jethroe, and his .311 batting average with Portland in 1950 was proof enough for the Braves that Marquez could hit. Unfortunately for Boston, and Marquez, Heater could not hit major league pitching.

Marquez's entry into organized ball was anything but organized and clouded in controversy. From 1945 to 1948, he played for the Negro National League's New York Black Yankees, Homestead Grays, and Baltimore Elite Giants. With the demise of the NNL following the 1948 season, players from the league's six teams were drafted by teams in the Negro American League. Simultaneously, major league teams began signing the out-of-work Negro American Leaguers. Ensuing signings revealed the disorganization that plagued Negro league teams. Claimed by the Baltimore Elite Giants of the recently defunct NNL, Marquez actually played the 1948 season for the Homestead Grays. Nevertheless, when the New York Yankees signed Marquez, his contract was purchased from Baltimore.

Compounding matters, the Yankees also claimed to have signed black infielder Artie Wilson, whom Bill Veeck had signed to a Cleveland Indians contract that winter. Ruling that Cleveland and New York had interfered with the negotiating rights of each other, baseball commissioner Happy Chandler ordered Cleveland and New York to swap Wilson for Marquez.

Boston sent Marquez back to the minors for the 1952 and 1953 seasons. Signed by the Chicago Cubs, Marquez made the Cubs roster in spring training of the 1954 season. In June, Marquez was traded to the Pittsburgh Pirates for outfielder Hal Rice.

Statistics: Luis Marquez

Year	Team	Games	AB	Runs	Hits	2B	3B	HR	RBI	BA
1951	BOS-N	68	122	19	24	5	1	0	11	.197
1954	CHI-N/									
	PIT-N	31	21	5	2	0	0	0	0	.095
Totals										
2 Years		99	143	24	26	5	1	0	11	.182

Willie Howard Mays

Outfield. Batted right. Threw right. 5'11", 180 lbs. Born 5/6/31, Westfield, Alabama. Hall of Fame, 1979.

While Jackie Robinson won the respect of baseball fans, black and white, Willie Mays won their hearts. His irrepressible love for the game infected anyone who saw him play. Even fans of the Giants' archrival, the Brooklyn Dodgers, had to admit that Willie Mays was something special. From the streets of Harlem, where he played stickball with kids who were both neighbors and fans, to the Giants' home field, the Polo Grounds, Mays exuded excitement in every aspect of the game: hitting, running, fielding, and throwing, which he did as well as, or better than, anyone of his era. "Maybe I was born to play ball," he once said. "Maybe I truly was."

Mays' batting statistics are among the most impressive of anyone who played in the major leagues. One of just five major-leaguers ever to hit 50 or more home runs in two seasons, he ranks third on the all-time list (behind Hank Aaron and Babe Ruth) in home runs, ninth in total hits, fifth in total runs scored, seventh in total runs batted in, and tenth in career slugging average. The first major-leaguer to hit 50 home runs and steal 20 bases in the same season and the first National Leaguer to hit 30 homers and steal 30 bases in a season, Mays hit four home runs in one game in 1961 and is one of a handful of players to hit three in a game twice. In 1954 he equaled a major league record by hitting home runs in six consecutive games. For four consecutive seasons, 1956–1959, Mays led the National League in stolen bases. The 1951 National League Rookie of the Year, he was named NL Most Valuable Player in 1954 and 1965.

But for all of his accomplishments as a hitter and base stealer, Mays was even more impressive in the field. No one played center field better than Willie Mays. With his trademark "basket catches" and flying cap, Mays set the major league record for most outfield putouts in a career, 7,095. Combining speed with a powerful and accurate arm, Mays made the impossible plays look routine, including the most famous catch in baseball history.

With the scored tied 2–2 in the top of the eighth inning of Game 1 of the 1954 World Series, Cleveland's Vic Wertz drove a Don Liddle fastball into right-center field. In any ballpark but the Polo Grounds, the drive would have been a home run; with any other center fielder, Wertz would have had his second triple of the day. But Mays was running at the crack of the bat and outran the ball. Approximately 450 feet from home plate he made an over-the-shoulder catch, whirled, and in one motion threw back to the infield to hold the runners. Dusty Rhodes's home run in the tenth won it for the Giants, who swept the Indians in four games.

"I think the throw was the remarkable thing, because the ball did get back there in a hurry, and I was a good 450 feet out when I caught it," Mays told Art Rust, Jr., in his *Get That Nigger Off the Field*. "The catch wasn't that difficult. Any ball you go a long way for is exciting to the fans in the stands. They're not looking at you when you get the jump on it. . . . At that moment, they're looking at the hitter. I'd gotten the good jump . . . had plenty of running room and the ball stayed up on me."

Throughout his career, Mays consistently made plays that were just as difficult if not more so. There was the game in 1951 when he threw out Dodger Billy Cox, who had tagged up and tried to score the winning run from third on a twisting fly ball to right-center. Catching the ball on the dead run, Mays spun 270 degrees and threw a strike on the fly to catcher Wes Westrum, who tagged—and shocked—the sliding Cox. In 1948, playing for the Birmingham Black Barons, Mays caught up to a line drive in dead-center field and threw out a stunned Larry Doby, who had tagged up at third.

As Gary Schumaker said, "Willie catches the triples."

Mays learned baseball from his father, a semipro player who worked in the steel mills of Birmingham, Alabama. But he probably got a good dose of his athleticism from his mother, who excelled in basketball.

At the age of 17, Mays hit .312 for the Birmingham Black Barons of the Negro American League. The following year, 1949, he hit .311. The Giants discovered Mays by accident in 1950 when they were looking for a power-hitting first baseman to sign a minor league contract. Assigned to Trenton, Mays hit .353 in 81 games and was promoted to the Class AAA Minneapolis Millers at the beginning of the 1951 season. After a month and a half, he was destroying International League pitching with a .477 batting average.

When the Giants called up Mays in late May 1951, team owner Horace Stoneham bought full-page ads in Minneapolis newspapers apologizing to

Millers fans for taking Mays away from them. Barely 20, Mays's influence on his teammates was immediate as the Giants made their long steady climb from sixth place to the "Miracle of Coogan's Bluff" playoff with the Dodgers. From a personal standpoint, however, Mays's entry into the majors, an unheroic one hit in his first 26 at-bats, has become baseball legend. Dejected and in tears, Mays went to manager Leo Durocher and asked to be sent back to the minor leagues.

Durocher, of course, would not hear of such a thing. "Son," he said, "you're not going anywhere but here. Just keep swinging because you're my center fielder, even if you don't get a hit for the rest of the season." Mays, and the Giants, came to life, causing Durocher to crow, "In two years, Mays is going to be the greatest ever to lace on a pair of spiked shoes."

Actually, in two years Mays was just three months out of the army. Inducted just 34 games into the 1952 season, Mays received a hardship discharge (he was the primary support of 11 dependents) in March 1954. With his discharge papers in hand, Mays flew all night to the Giants' spring-training camp in Phoenix. Rather than check into his room, Mays took a cab to the ballpark, suited up for an intrasquad game, and homered in his very first at-bat. "There's the pennant!" bragged Giants vice president Chub Feeney.

In 1954 Mays established his reputation for hitting in the clutch and wearing out the opposition's best pitchers. The Dodgers, in particular, suffered the wrath of Mays's bat. In the six years following his army discharge, Mays hit .392 against the Dodgers, including 56 home runs and 127 RBIs in 507 at-bats. In Dodger ballparks alone, he hit .417 with 37 home runs in 269 at-bats.

From the moment he saw Mays, sportswriter Grantland Rice called him "the kid everybody likes." But to fans Mays was known as "Say Hey," for his penchant for beginning sentences with, "Say, hey," when he had forgotten the name of the person he was addressing.

Rooming with Monte Irvin, Mays began to apply intellect to his talent, becoming a serious student of the game under Irvin's tutelage. By the end of the 1957 season, Mays was well on his way to fulfilling everyone's expectations, even those of actress Tallulah Bankhead, who said, "There have been two geniuses, Willie Mays and Willie Shakespeare." The most demanding group, however, were the fans of San Francisco, where the Giants moved at the end of the 1957 season.

As the first black player around which an entire franchise had been built, Mays encountered both racism and skepticism in San Francisco. When he tried to buy a home in the city's exclusive St. Francis Wood section, his original offer was turned down because of his race. Throughout the fall and winter, Mays was hot copy for San Francisco reporters. Before seeing him play, fans began comparing him to Joe DiMaggio, a San Francisco native. By February 1958, before he had played a single game in Seals Stadium, the home of Willie and Marghurite Mays had become a tourist attraction along San Francisco's Gray

Line bus tour, which may have prompted a cab driver to say, "There's too much emphasis on Mays. He isn't going to impress this town. After all, this is the town where the DiMaggios started. Real fans remember them."

Going into the 1958 season, Mays was voted the most exciting player in the majors by 12 of the *Sporting News'* 16 beat writers, making San Franciscans' expectations of the 27-year-old Mays even greater. "Mays attacks a ball game," wrote Joe King, "any game, one that doesn't count as well as one that figures importantly in the standings — as if history for ages to come depended on that score when the final out is made. . . .

"He is one of the few players of high quality who can 'get across' to the fans. He vibrates with urgency."

Which was precisely how Mays opened the 1958 season. He hit .412 for the first month. While San Francisco fans could never appreciate Mays's fielding skills in quite the same way as New York fans — the 484-foot center field of the Polo Grounds, unlike Seals Stadium or Candlestick Park, was conducive to Mays's uncanny abilities — they did enjoy Mays at his slugging best. Finally, by 1969, when the *Sporting News* again voted him player of the decade, Mays had won over, albeit grudgingly, the most aloof San Francisco fan. That same season, on September 22, Mays, batting for rookie George Foster, hit his 600th career home run.

Traded to the New York Mets for Charlie Williams early in the 1972 season, Mays homered in his first at-bat against his former team. On September 26, 1973, before a sellout crowd at New York's Shea Stadium, Mays stood at home plate and announced his retirement. "Willie," he said, "say good-bye to America."

Statistics: *Willie Mays*

Year	Team	Games	AB	Runs	Hits	2B	3B	HR	RBI	BA
1951	NY-N	121	464	59	127	22	5	20	68	.274
1952	NY	34	127	17	30	2	4	4	23	.236
1954	NY	151	565	119	195	33	13*	41	110	.345*
1955	NY	152	580	123	185	18	13*	51*	127	.319
1956	NY	152	578	101	171	27	8	36	84	.296
1957	NY	152	585	112	195	26	20*	35	97	.333
1958	SF-N	152	600	121*	208	33	11	29	96	.347
1959	SF	151	575	125	180	43	5	34	104	.313
1960	SF	153	595	107	190*	29	12	29	103	.319
1961	SF	154	572	129*	176	32	3	40	123	.308
1962	SF	162	621	130	189	36	5	49*	141	.304
1963	SF	157	596	115	187	32	7	38	103	.314
1964	SF	157	578	121	171	21	9	47*	111	.296
1965	SF	157	558	118	177	21	3	52*	112	.317
1966	SF	152	552	99	159	29	4	37	103	.288
1967	SF	141	486	83	128	22	2	22	70	.263

Year	Team	Games	AB	Runs	Hits	2B	3B	HR	RBI	BA
1968	SF	148	498	84	144	20	5	23	79	.289
1969	SF	117	403	64	114	17	3	13	58	.283
1970	SF	139	478	94	139	15	2	28	83	.291
1971	SF	136	417	82	113	24	5	18	61	.271
1972	SF/									
	NY-N	88	244	35	61	11	1	8	22	.250
1973	NY	66	209	24	44	10	0	6	25	.211
Totals										
22 Years		2992	10,881	2062	3283	523	140	660	1903	.302

League Championship Series

1971	SF-N	4	15	1	4	2	0	1	3	.267
1973	NY-N	1	3	1	1	0	0	0	1	.333
Totals										
2 Years		5	18	2	5	2	0	1	4	.278

World Series

1951	NY-N	6	22	1	4	0	0	0	1	.182
1954	NY	4	14	4	4	1	0	0	3	.286
1962	SF-N	7	28	3	7	2	0	0	1	.250
1973	NY	3	7	1	2	0	0	0	1	.286
Totals										
4 Years		20	71	9	17	3	0	0	6	.239

League leader.

Rafael "Ray" Noble

Catcher. Batted right. Threw right. 5'11", 210 lbs. Born 3/15/22, Central Hatillo, Cuba.

The second black catcher in major league history, Ray Noble (pronounced "no-blay") was the first rookie to make the New York Giants roster in 1951. Used primarily as a replacement for starting catcher Wes Westrum, Noble was one of a number of black ballplayers — including Junior Gilliam, Bennie Taylor, Vibert Clarke, Pat Scantlebury, Connie Johnson, and Hector Lopez — who made their way through the winter Caribbean and Panamanian leagues to the minor leagues and often the majors in the early 1950s.

From 1947 to 1950 Noble caught with the New York Cuban Giants. Signed by Horace Stoneham early in the 1950 season, Noble finished out the year with San Diego, hitting .316 with 14 home runs and 76 RBIs.

Noble was involved in one of the most vicious and overtly racial fights in baseball history. In a San Francisco Bay rivalry between the Oakland Oaks and the San Francisco Seals, Seals pitcher Bill Boemler, a white man, had repeatedly thrown at Noble and Piper Davis, also black. Two weeks after hitting Davis on the elbow and sidelining the Oakland outfielder for a week, Boemler knocked Davis down again on two successive pitches. Davis then doubled and on the very next play bowled into Boemler, who was covering the plate.

According to accounts, Boemler's attempted tag was more of a punch, violently delivered to the face of Davis, who came up swinging. Players and fans rushed the playing field, and Noble "knocked down San Francisco players as though they were ten pins." According to Davis, "Noble was hitting everything white coming towards him."

The incident sparked threats of retaliation against Noble and Davis from a group of San Franciscans that went by the name "Group of 19." The FBI and local police investigated the incident, and the remainder of the schedule was played without altercation.

Noble's contract was purchased from the Giants by the Cuban Sugar Kings during the 1953 season. He finished his career in the Cuban League in the late 1950s.

Statistics: Ray Noble

Year	Team	Games	AB	Runs	Hits	2B	3B	HR	RBI	BA
1951	NY-N	55	141	16	33	6	0	5	26	.234
1952	NY	6	5	0	0	0	0	0	0	.000
1953	NY	46	97	15	20	0	1	4	14	.206
Totals										
3 Years		107	243	31	53	6	1	9	40	.218
World Series										
1951	NY	2	2	0	0	0	0	0	0	.000

Harry Leon Simpson

Outfield, first base. Batted left. Threw right. 6'1", 180 lbs. Born 12/3/25, Atlanta, Georgia. Died 4/3/79, Akron, Ohio.

Few black players during the early years of integration were given a second chance to make good in the majors. Initial failure was terminal. For Harry Simpson, however, failure kept him in the majors.

In 1951, Cleveland Indians general manager Hank Greenberg, convinced that Simpson was the better of two players, traded Minnie Minoso to the

Chicago White Sox. Minoso was hitting .429 at the time of the trade (after eight games) and finished the season with a .326 average; he led the league with 14 triples and was named the *Sporting News* American League Rookie of the Year. Simpson suffered a long season burdened with the unrealistic expectations of management, fans, and himself. His batting stance changed almost constantly, and he was shifted back and forth from the outfield, his natural position, and first base. As Doc Young wrote in the Pittsburgh *Courier*, Simpson "should have been playing minor league ball for experience." Instead, he lost the confidence that had earned him the nickname "The Tan Ted Williams" just one year before.

Simpson was originally signed by Goose Curry of the Negro National League Philadelphia Stars in 1948. A converted pitcher, Simpson was platooned by Curry, playing only against right-handed pitchers. The following year, during winter ball, Dodger catcher Roy Campanella observed that Simpson hit equally well against right- and left-handed pitchers, and he wrote Curry advising him that Simpson was too good a hitter to be platooned.

After three seasons with Philadelphia, Simpson was discovered in 1948 by Eddie Gottlieb, head coach of the National Basketball Association Philadelphia Warriors. Gottlieb, who had played minor league ball prior to entering basketball, knew talent and was adamant about his good judgment. "He has a 50–50 chance to be a second Williams," Gottlieb said of Simpson. "He is built like Ted, is faster and can field much better. I am not going to say that he will hit better than Ted, but he has a chance."

On Gottlieb's recommendation, eight major league scouts gave Simpson a tryout, and all eight turned him down. Finally, after repeated letters to the Cleveland Indians and at the suggestion of Harlem Globetrotters owner Abe Saperstein, Cleveland agreed to give Simpson a look in spring training if Gottlieb would pay expenses and transportation to Arizona. Gottlieb paid, and in his first intrasquad game for the Indians Simpson hit two home runs, a single, and a double. Greenberg signed him in a heartbeat.

Simpson was optioned to Wilkes-Barre in the Eastern League where he hit .305 for the season, leading the league with 31 home runs and 120 RBIs. His powerful wrists produced tape-measure home runs, including two that traveled more than 500 feet and an inside-the-park shot in Scranton that measured 475 feet. Promoted to Class AAA San Diego in 1950, Simpson hit .323 and led the league with 156 RBIs. His 225 hits included 41 doubles, 19 triples, and 33 home runs.

"I don't believe there's a pitcher alive who can consistently throw the ball by me," Simpson proclaimed at one point during that season. But after three years in Cleveland, all he could say was "I'm dead weight here."

Traded to the Athletics in 1955, Simpson found new life in Kansas City where manager Lou Boudreau encouraged him to hit from any stance that made him feel comfortable. Without the pressure that plagued him in

Cleveland, Simpson began to relax, hitting with power to all fields again. And the Athletics began to edge their way out of the cellar. Simpson finished the 1955 season with the third highest batting average among KC regulars. Chosen by Casey Stengel for the 1956 American League All-Star team, Simpson led Kansas City with 105 RBIs that year despite a season-ending injury in September.

"Until I was sold to the Athletics," Simpson said, "I'll admit I was a badly confused player, and there were a lot of times when I doubted my ability. But I kept hoping that I would get the chance to play regularly, to play the way I felt was best suited to my ability.

"And then the chance came. I can't say how well I have succeeded, but I do know that I have tried....

"I have hustled for the Athletics and I am going to go on hustling. I may not be the greatest ball player in the world, but there ain't nobody who will try any harder."

Though usually soft-spoken, Simpson was critical of any ballplayer, black players in particular, who did not hustle on the field. "The important thing as I see it," he told the *Sporting News* in 1956, "is that I, as a Negro, have been given a great privilege and I just wish all members of my race felt the same deep gratitude as I do.

"Here I am making more money than a great percentage of the men of my race. Here I am on a ball club where I've been given every chance in the world to make good. What more could I possibly want?...

"I live as good as anybody possibly could. I get a good salary. I've got a good job. Baseball has given this to me. Where else could I have gotten all this? In what other profession could I have been given the same chance?"

Statistics: Harry Simpson

Year	Team	Games	AB	Runs	Hits	2B	3B	HR	RBI	BA
1951	CLE-A	122	332	51	76	7	0	7	24	.229
1952	CLE	146	545	66	145	21	10	10	65	.266
1953	CLE	82	242	25	55	3	1	7	22	.227
1955	CLE/KC-A	115	397	43	119	16	7	5	52	.300
1956	KC	141	543	76	159	22	11	21	105	.293
1957	KC/NY-A	125	403	51	109	16	9	13	63	.270
1958	NY/KC	102	263	22	67	9	2	7	33	.255
1959	KC/CHI-A/ PIT-N	55	104	9	22	7	1	3	17	.212
Totals										
8 Years		888	2829	343	752	101	41	73	381	.266
World Series										
1957	NY-A	5	12	0	1	0	0	0	1	.083

Arthur Lee "Artie" Wilson

Infield. Batted left. Threw right. 5'11", 168 lbs. Born 10/28/20, Springfield, Alabama.

The New York Giants owed Artie Wilson at least 19 games in the major leagues and then some. As manager of the Negro American League's Birmingham Black Barons and a part-time scout for the Brooklyn Dodgers, Wilson told Oakland Oaks manager Chuck Dressen that a young Barons outfielder who had caught Dressen's interest needed more work hitting a curveball. Had Wilson been a better judge of talent, Willie Mays would have been a Dodger.

A superb shortstop, Wilson led the Negro American League in hitting in 1947 and 1948 with batting averages of .377 and .402, respectively. In 1949, stealing a league-leading 47 bases, he became the first player to win the Pacific Coast League batting title (.348) without hitting a home run. An opposite-field slap hitter, Wilson collected an incredible total of 264 hits in an equally incredible 848 at-bats the following year. Playing for Chuck Dressen's PCL champion Oaks, Wilson scored 168 runs, batted .311, and finished second in the running for the league's Most Valuable Player award. But Wilson's slap hitting was no match for major league pitching. And it was no match for major league managing when the manager happened to be (once again) Chuck Dressen.

In Wilson's only at-bat against Brooklyn, his former skipper countered Wilson's batting style with a shift that positioned Jackie Robinson, Pee Wee Reese, and Billy Cox on the left side of the infield; Don Thompson along the left field line; Duke Snider in straightaway center; Gil Hodges at a normal first base; and right fielder Carl Furillo at second. The shift was a tactic that San Francisco's Lefty O'Doul had used successfully the year before against Wilson. Dressen remembered, and a surprised Wilson grounded weakly to pitcher Don Newcombe.

In any other season Wilson might have stuck. But the Giants were in the throes of their miraculous pennant chase, and Leo Durocher demanded more than slick fielding from a 30-year-old rookie. After just 19 games Wilson was optioned to Minneapolis, which is where the story begins all over again.

Oakland Oaks owner Brick Laws phoned his Giants counterpart, Horace Stoneham, requesting that Wilson be transferred from Minneapolis back to Oakland. Wilson, explained Laws, was one of the most popular players ever to play in the Pacific Coast League, and without Wilson on the roster, Oakland was a bust at the gate. Stoneham approved the transfer.

A floral arrangement, paid for by Oakland fans, awaited Wilson at home plate upon his return from Minneapolis. The Oaks drew better than 23,000 fans for Wilson's first three games back in Oakland. "Agile Artie Wilson," according to the team's public relations hype, "hasn't put the Oaks in first place yet, but he will."

What New York fans never got to enjoy was expressed by San Francisco Seals manager Lefty O'Doul following a doubleheader on June 24 in which Wilson started three double plays and was the pivot on a fourth. "You don't see shortstop played better by anybody than you saw it today," said O'Doul, a .349 lifetime hitter in the major leagues. "I spent a few years in the majors, but I never saw anything like the exhibition Wilson staged."

Wilson was the subject of one of the more bizarre signings in major league history. Needless to say, it involved Bill Veeck. At a league meeting of owners of Negro American League ballclubs in February 1949 in Chicago, Abe Saperstein paid $15,000 of his own money to the Birmingham Black Barons to acquire Wilson's contract on behalf of Veeck and the Cleveland Indians.

Notified of the purchase by Saperstein, Veeck flew unannounced to Puerto Rico to sign Wilson, who was playing winter ball for Mayaguez. Veeck arrived in Mayaguez only to learn that his shortstop of the future had driven to San Juan. Veeck flew his chartered plane over the road between the two cities, all 120 miles of it, but there was no sign of Wilson. Never at a loss for imaginative solutions, Veeck phoned local radio stations and requested that sports commentators announce an all-points bulletin for Wilson over the air waves, the rough translation of the message being "Artie Wilson, go to San Juan; Bill Veeck wants to sign you for the Cleveland Indians organization." The two eventually met, and Wilson signed a Cleveland minor league contract. And that's the beginning of chapter three.

When Yankee owner George Weiss learned that Veeck had signed the shortstop, he accused Veeck of unethical conduct. The Yankees, Weiss argued, had recently announced that they were "close" to signing Wilson. Ultimately, Commissioner "Happy" Chandler ruled against both teams and ordered the Indians to swap Wilson to New York for outfielder Luis Marquez. Neither man ever played for the Yankees or the Indians.

Assigned to Oakland in 1949, Wilson was told he would have to room alone because he was black. His second-base double-play partner offered to room with him. His partner was Billy Martin.

While Wilson never returned to the majors after 1951, he remained a Pacific Coast mainstay. With Seattle from 1952 to 1954, he batted over .300 each season.

Statistics: Artie Wilson

Year	Team	Games	AB	Runs	Hits	2B	3B	HR	RBI	BA
1951	NY-N	19	22	2	4	0	0	0	1	.182

1952

Edmundo "Sandy" Amoros

Outfield. Batted left. Threw left. 5'7½", 170 lbs. Born 1/30/30, Havana, Cuba.

With one swipe of his right hand, Sandy Amoros reached out and saved the soul of Brooklyn.

The date, as any Dodger fan worth his salt will tell you, was October 4, 1955; the place, Yankee Stadium, where Dodger dreams went to die. Five times since 1941 the Dodgers had earned a place in the World Series. Five times they had come up empty, and each time it was the Yankees who celebrated.

After five innings in Game 7, the Dodgers held a shaky 2–0 lead. Starting pitcher Johnny Podres had worked out of jams in the second, third, and fourth. Amoros entered the game in the sixth, taking over for Junior Gilliam, who went in to play second base in place of Don Zimmer, who had been pinch-hit for the previous inning. That innocent move by manager Walt Alston turned into gold a few minutes later.

Billy Martin led off the bottom of the sixth with a walk, and Gil McDougald beat out a bunt to put the tying runs on base for Yogi Berra, the league's Most Valuable Player. Alston waved Amoros into left-center field to defense Berra, a dead pull hitter, but Berra crossed the Dodgers up, stroking an outside change-up high down the left-field line. As the ball headed toward the corner, images of past heartbreaks — Mickey Owen's passed ball in 1941, Billy Martin's miracle catch in 1952, and of course Bobby Thomson's "shot heard round the world" in 1951 — lodged in the throats of Dodger fans everywhere.

But you can be unlucky only so long. Amoros had outstanding speed and with destiny in mind, happened to be left-handed. He raced across the outfield, reached out, and caught the ball. He quickly put on the brakes, wheeled, and threw a strike to shortstop Pee Wee Reese, who easily doubled McDougald at first. The play stunned the Yankees and gave Podres a boost. Three innings later Brooklyn celebrated like never before. "I never seen a town go so wild," said Dodger right fielder Carl Furillo.

71

Amoros, who spoke virtually no English, was an unlikely hero and a tough interview. Asked if he thought he would catch up with Berra's fly, he replied, "I dunno. I just run like hell." Amoros's language barrier probably kept him from having a longer, more successful career in the majors. He had all the tools—speed, power, a good glove—but as Peter Golenbock wrote, "A manager just doesn't trust employing a player when he isn't sure whether the guy understands him or not."

Amoros came to the Dodgers with outstanding credentials. The youngest of six children, his father died when he was three, forcing his mother to work in a local textile mill. Amoros went to work in the mill at 14, also his first season of organized baseball. Four years later he was discovered by Havana Reds owner-manager Mike Gonzalez. He played winters in Cuba and summers in Guatemala until 1950 when he signed to play with the New York Cubans of the Negro American League. Amoros had seen Jackie Robinson train with the Dodgers in Cuba and figured, "If he can do it, I can do it too."

Signed by the Dodgers in January 1952, Amoros celebrated by being named Most Valuable Player in the Caribbean World Series on the strength of a .450 batting average. He was assigned to St. Paul, where he was first called "Sandy" by a teammate who said he was built like boxer Sandy Saddler. He also tore up the league, hitting .337 with 19 home runs, 24 doubles, 10 triples and 78 RBIs. He earned a couple of other nicknames: "Miracle Wrists," and "Second Willie Mays." Amoros finished the season with the Dodgers but then spent the entire 1953 season in Montreal where he had another stellar season, leading the league with a .355 average and adding 23 homers, 40 doubles and 128 runs scored.

Amoros hit .421 in spring training with the Dodgers in 1954, but his emergence as a contender for a starting job brought the team face-to-face with the possibility of putting a lineup on the field that had more black players than white. Bill Roeder wrote that there was "an undercurrent of suspicion" that the Dodgers "were reluctant to add another Negro to the squad." The suspicion was heightened when Amoros was sent back to Montreal in May, but he was recalled two months later, and on July 17 the inevitable happened as Amoros started along with Robinson, Roy Campanella, Junior Gilliam, and Don Newcombe.

Amoros played at least 100 games the next three seasons with Brooklyn. His English barely improved, and he communicated through teammates Roy Campanella and Joe Black, both of whom spoke Spanish. He even lived on Campanella's yacht during the season before sharing a room near Ebbets Field with a fellow Cuban, shortstop Chico Fernandez.

Losing a fly ball in the sun and committing a throwing error in a crucial late September game almost made Amoros the goat of the 1956 season, but he atoned with two home runs and a sparkling catch in the pennant-clinching win on the season's final day. He appeared on television after the game smoking a two-pound cigar. "Lucky, lucky, I'm so lucky," he said, grinning.

Amoros and the Dodgers had a bitter salary dispute before the 1958 season, and he was sold to Montreal after clearing waivers. Sportswriter Bill Nunn, Jr., of the Pittsburgh *Courier* claimed the Dodgers had influenced other teams to "keep their hands off Amoros" to punish him for refusing to sign for the same salary, $10,500, he had made the year before.

It was an unusual position for the happy-go-lucky Amoros to be in. He had spent most of his career smiling. His Brooklyn landlady said, "You can never tell what happened to Sandy at the ballpark by how he looks when he comes home. He's always very happy."

Amoros finished his career back in the minors, moved back to Cuba, then returned to the United States in 1967. He never truly mastered English, but as he once said, "When you hit home runs at the right time, you don't need to speak much English."

Statistics: Sandy Amoros

Year	Team	Games	AB	Runs	Hits	2B	3B	HR	RBI	BA
1952	BKN-N	20	44	10	11	3	1	0	3	.250
1954	BKN	79	263	44	72	18	6	9	34	.274
1955	BKN	119	388	59	96	16	7	10	51	.247
1956	BKN	114	292	53	76	11	8	16	58	.260
1957	BKN	106	238	40	66	7	1	7	26	.277
1959	LA-N	5	5	1	1	0	0	0	1	.200
1960	LA/DET-A	74	81	8	12	0	0	1	7	.148
Totals										
7 Years		517	1311	215	334	55	23	43	180	.255
World Series										
1952	BKN-N	1	0	0	0	0	0	0	0	.000
1955	BKN	5	12	3	4	0	0	1	3	.333
1956	BKN	6	19	1	1	0	0	0	1	.053
Totals										
3 Years		12	31	4	5	0	0	1	4	.161

Joseph "Joe" Black

Pitcher. Batted right. Threw right. 6'2", 220 lbs. Born 2/8/24, Plainfield, New Jersey.

Joe Black was the first African American to win a World Series game. He had an overpowering fastball, a tight-breaking curve, and a tragically short career.

From the time he was a small boy, all Black wanted to do was play baseball. He grew up poor in Plainfield, New Jersey, learning to pitch with a sponge ball and hit with half a bat. He heard that major league players wore spikes, so he jammed his feet into tin cans to get the feel of metal underneath him.

He grew into a tall, powerful young man, 6'2" and 220 pounds. He starred in three sports at Plainfield High, and won a partial scholarship to Morgan State in Baltimore. After a stint in the army during World War II, he signed with the Baltimore Elite Giants of the Negro National League to help pay his tuition. He was the team's best pitcher, but a major league offer was slow in coming. In 1950, at 26 and with a college degree, he signed a minor league contract with Brooklyn and went to play in Montreal. Two years later, he put the Dodgers on his broad back and carried them to a pennant.

Brooklyn won 96 games in 1952. Black won or saved 30 of them. He lost just four, had the league's best ERA, 2.15, and was named Rookie of the Year. Perhaps equally important, he gave the Dodgers something quiet and nasty on the mound. For years, the New York Giants' Sal Maglie had tried to intimidate the Dodgers with a steady diet of beanballs. It worked until Black came along. On September 9, 1952, the Dodgers were slumping, and their lead over the Giants had slipped to five games. Brooklyn trailed New York 2–0 when Black came on in relief in the second inning and began flattening Giant hitters. The Dodgers came back and took the lead, so Giants manager Leo Durocher ordered his pitcher to throw at Black. He did, and missed, and an inning later Black responded with what sportswriter Roger Kahn called "the single most terrifying pitch I have ever seen."

The batter was George Wilson, and when Black fired a fastball at his neck, Wilson went down so hard that his cap came off, and the pitch sailed through the opening between Wilson's cap and his head. The Giants were done, and Black clinched a tie for the pennant in his first start of the season on September 22. Black also fought racism with high tight fastballs. During a game he pitched against Cincinnati, the Reds bench began singing "Old Black Joe." "Black neither responded nor changed expression," Kahn wrote. "He simply threw one fastball each at the heads of Cincinnati's next seven batters." That stopped the music.

Manager Charlie Dressen tabbed Black to start Game 1 of the World Series against the Yankees, even though he had started just two games all season. Black went the distance and gave up just six hits in a 4–2 Dodger win. He also pitched well in starts in Games 4 and 7 but was the losing pitcher both times.

Dressen predicted Black would win 20 games in 1953, but he also tinkered with his ace's success, demanding that Black learn an off-speed pitch to go with his fastball and curve. But Black had been born with stretched tendons on the index and middle fingers of his pitching hand and could not master another pitch. In the meantime, he lost both his control and his confidence. Clem Labine replaced him as the team's top reliever, and Black had a nightmarish season, including a 5.33 ERA. He was traded to Cincinnati in 1955 and was released by the last-place Washington Senators in 1957, ending his major league career.

Black went on to teach at Plainfield Junior High and later became a vice president at the Greyhound Corporation and traveled the country speaking to African American youths. He was an usher at the funeral of Dr. Martin Luther King, Jr.

Statistics: Joe Black

Year	Team	W	L	PCT	G	IP	H	BB	SO	ERA	SV
1952	BKN-N	15	4	.789	56	142.1	102	41	85	2.15	15
1953	BKN	6	3	.667	34	72.2	74	27	42	5.33	5
1954	BKN	0	0	.000	5	7	11	5	3	11.57	0
1955	BKN/										
	CIN-N	6	2	.750	38	117.2	121	30	63	4.05	3
1956	CIN	3	2	.600	32	61.2	61	25	27	4.52	2
1957	WAS-A	0	1	.000	7	12.2	22	1	2	7.11	0
Totals											
6 Years		30	12	.714	172	414	391	129	222	3.91	25
World Series											
1952	BKN-N	1	2	.333	3	21.1	15	8	9	2.53	0
1953	BKN	0	0	.000	1	1	1	0	2	9.00	0
Totals											
2 Years		1	2	.333	4	22.1	16	8	11	2.82	0

James Buster "Buzz" Clarkson

Shortstop. Batted right. Threw right. 5'11", 210 lbs.
Born 3/13/18, Hopkins, South Carolina.

Buzz Clarkson made Satchel Paige do something he almost never did— blink. It was the winter of 1940, and Paige was barnstorming in Puerto Rico. The bases were loaded in the first inning when Clarkson, who was playing for a local team, stepped to the plate. Paige called to his catcher that he wanted to walk Clarkson. "Don't you know the bases are loaded?" the catcher cried. "Don't you know you're going to walk a run home?" As always, Paige had an answer. "Well, I'd rather walk one run home than have him hit three or four home." So Clarkson was walked, and Paige announced his intention of not allowing another run. And he did not.

Clarkson was a burly power-hitting shortstop and outfielder who spent most of his career in the Negro leagues, beginning in 1937 with the peripatetic Crawfords, with whom he moved from Pittsburgh to Toledo to Indianapolis. In 1940 he played in his first East-West All-Star game as a member of the Newark Eagles and was an all-star again in 1949, this time with the Philadelphia Stars, with whom he spent eight seasons.

Clarkson entered organized baseball in 1951 with Milwaukee, the Boston Braves' top farm team, and helped the Brewers win the American Association pennant. He was called up to the majors in early May in hopes of giving the Braves lineup some right-handed punch. "I need his power," said manager Tommy Holmes. "With a fellow like him around, we may not see so many left-handers after." Milwaukee teammate Billy Klaus said, "It's about time they brought that fellow to the major leagues." But the press, as it did with many former Negro league players, assumed Clarkson was older than he actually was. One reporter described him as "a comparatively ancient colored shortstop," whose "indeterminable" age "was the only thing against him."

Clarkson was returned to the minors after just 25 at-bats. He played out the season back in Milwaukee and finished with a .318 average, 12 homers, and 68 RBIs in just 242 at-bats. The next season found him in Dallas of the Texas League, and a year later he was traded to Beaumont, where he ended his career as the team's first black player.

Statistics: Buzz Clarkson

Year	Team	Games	AB	Runs	Hits	2B	3B	HR	RBI	BA
1952	BOS-N	14	25	3	5	0	0	0	1	.200

George Daniel Crowe

First base. Batted left. Threw left. 6'2", 210 lbs. Born 3/22/23, Whiteland, Indiana.

Lots of people played professional baseball with Jackie Robinson. George Crowe played pro basketball with him.

Crowe was a three-time all-state selection in basketball-crazy Indiana in high school, and it was through basketball that he got a shot at a career in major league baseball. In 1946, Crowe had just been released from the army where he had helped truck war materials over the Burma Road into China. He had just gotten married and moved to Los Angeles when he read that a new professional basketball team, the Los Angeles Red Devils, was forming. He got a tryout and made the team as a forward. The other forward was Robinson, and one of the starting guards was Irv Noren, a white guy who went on to play 11 years as a major league outfielder.

The team broke up after a couple of months, and Robinson went off to join the Brooklyn Dodgers. But Crowe hooked on with another team, the New York Renaissance, some of whom also played baseball for the Black Yankees, and got a baseball tryout the next spring. One eye examination and a pair of new glasses later, Crowe was a pro baseball player.

He had played baseball at Indiana Central College where he earned his degree in physical education, played basketball, and put the shot over 50 feet. After two years with the Black Yankees, Crowe was recommended to Harry Jenkins, head of the Boston Braves farm system, by Effa Manley, famed owner of the Newark Eagles of the Negro National League. He became the first black player to sign with the Braves, then played one last season of pro basketball with Dayton of the National Basketball League before reporting to Pawtucket.

Crowe tore up New England League pitching, hitting .354, then moved up to Hartford in 1950 where he was the Eastern League's Most Valuable Player, hitting .353 with 24 homers, 122 RBIs, and 117 runs scored. He capped his year by hitting .375 for Caguas to lead the Puerto Rican League.

Crowe then cleared his last hurdle to the majors, bashing Class AAA pitching with Milwaukee in 1951—.339, 41 doubles, 24 homers, 119 RBIs, and a Rookie of the Year award. Once he got to the majors in 1952, his hurdles included Earl Torgeson, the Braves' starting first baseman, and some questions about his fielding. He played first part-time that year, but the Braves traded for Joe Adcock in 1953, and Crowe became a pinch-hitting specialist, a role he mastered quickly. But apparently a .286 average was not good enough to keep him in the majors, so he spent another year terrorizing Class AAA, hitting .334 with 34 homers and 128 RBIs for Toledo.

Adcock broke his arm midway through the 1955 season, and Crowe got his first chance to play regularly. He played well, but Adcock returned the next spring, and Crowe was traded to Cincinnati just before the start of the season. On April 27 he had the misfortune of starting in place of crowd favorite Ted Kluszewski. Klu got benched, and Crowe got booed mercilessly. "I felt sorry for the poor guy," said Reds manager Birdie Tebbetts. "No matter who played first, they would have booed him." But Crowe was not fazed. "It didn't bother me," he said, despite going one for five in the game. "I hope they all come back tomorrow. I'll show them something." Sure enough, the next day he hit two home runs and added a triple in a 9–1 win over the Cubs. Still, Crowe spent most of the year on the bench.

In 1957 Kluszewski spent most of the year with a bad back. At 34, Crowe played more than 100 games for the first time in his career and came up big. He led the team with 31 home runs, good for sixth in the league, though he was primarily a line-drive hitter. "The best balls I hit," he once said, "don't go out of the park." He was voted to the All-Star team, but obvious ballot stuffing in Cincinnati prompted Commissioner Ford Frick to scrub Crowe and teammates Wally Post and Gus Bell from the game. He was elected again in 1958, and this time it stuck.

Crowe twisted ligaments in his knee late in the 1958 season, and after being traded to the Cardinals, there were reports he would have to retire. "Shucks, I'll never quit," he said. "They'll have to stop playing me first." Stan Musial was playing out his career at first base for the Cardinals, so Crowe went back to pinch-hitting. He led the league with 17 pinch-hits, including four pinch-hit home runs, three in August.

In March 1960, an article in *Sports Illustrated* called him the "Big Daddy" and self-appointed leader of blacks in the major leagues, with an eye to organizing black players. Crowe chafed at the charges. "Maybe some of the other players look up to me, but I haven't encouraged it," he said. "I am older than most, and have a background of some education, and perhaps they have come to me for advice."

When Crowe left the majors after playing just seven games in 1961, he held the major league record for pinch-hit home runs with 14. "Pinch-hitting," he liked to say, "is an art."

Statistics: George Crowe

Year	Team	Games	AB	Runs	Hits	2B	3B	HR	RBI	BA
1952	BOS-N	73	217	25	56	13	1	4	20	.258
1953	MIL-N	47	42	6	12	2	0	2	6	.286
1955	MIL	104	303	41	85	12	4	15	55	.281
1956	CIN-N	77	144	22	36	2	1	10	23	.250
1957	CIN	133	494	71	134	20	1	31	92	.271
1958	CIN	111	345	31	95	12	5	7	61	.275
1959	STL-N	77	103	14	31	6	0	8	29	.301
1960	STL	73	72	5	17	3	0	4	13	.236
1961	STL	7	7	0	1	0	0	0	0	.143
Totals										
9 Years		702	1727	215	467	70	12	81	299	.270

David "Dave" Pope

Outfield. Batted left. Threw right. 5'10", 170 lbs. Born 6/17/25, Talladega, Alabama.

Growing up in the coal-mining town of Library, Pennsylvania, Dave Pope had aspirations of becoming a doctor and the intelligence to make it happen. What he did not have was the money necessary to finance an education. Soon after high school Pope went to work in the mines; nine months later he realized that baseball was his escape route.

Locally renowned for his softball skills, Pope began playing semipro baseball in 1944 before signing with the Homestead Grays of the Negro National League in 1945. A utility player for Homestead during the 1946 season, Pope was scouted and signed by the Cleveland Indians' Hank Greenberg. Making his way through Cleveland's minor league ranks, Pope established his reputation as an excellent hitter with good power. When he was called up to Cleveland to replace Luke Easter, who was sent back down to the minors at the end of June 1952, he was hitting .348 with Indianapolis of the American Association.

A fielder of dubious skills, Pope was knocked unconscious in his major league debut in the third inning of a July 1 game against the St. Louis Browns when he crashed into the right-field wall of Cleveland's Municipal Stadium. Although he batted a respectable .294 in 12 games, his fielding became a liability to Indian pennant hopes. After three Philadelphia Athletics scored when he dropped a fly ball, Pope was sent back to Indianapolis (again in exchange for Easter).

Recalled from Indianapolis in August 1954, Pope filled in for the slumping Dave Philley with consistent and timely hitting. Although he failed to produce at the plate in the 1954 World Series, Pope won a spot on the Cleveland roster going into 1955 spring training. As Cleveland broke camp in Phoenix and headed north to open the 1955 season, a number of ball clubs expressed interest in Pope, who replied, "I'd prefer to stay with the Indians. I like it here."

How much he liked it was apparent early on when in a span of seven games Pope hit four homers. But after 35 games, six home runs, and a .298 batting average, Cleveland traded him and outfielder Wally Westlake to the Baltimore Orioles for outfielder Gene Woodling. Baltimore's spacious Memorial Stadium stymied Pope's power, and he managed just one home run and a .248 average in 86 games with the Orioles.

The next spring, after being struck in the head by a pitch thrown by Cleveland left-hander Dick Tomanek, Pope began to work with Baltimore manager Paul Richards on improving his bunting skills to tighten his strike zone and make use of his speed. Having learned from Richards how to deaden the ball on a bunt, Pope beat out bunts for base hits in three consecutive spring-training games and swore that he could "bunt [his] way over .300" in 1956.

Unfortunately, whatever future lay ahead in Baltimore was cut short by Cleveland general manager Frank "Trader" Lane, who reacquired Pope for the Tribe in May. Sent immediately to the minors, Pope responded by hitting 25 home runs and batting over .300 in less than three months with Indianapolis.

By late August, the Indians were once again battling with the Yankees for first place in the American League. In need of left-handed hitting,

Cleveland recalled Pope from the minors. In his first start after being called up, the 31-year-old prodigy with barely 200 major league at-bats, doubled to right field in Yankee Stadium, a blow that brought Yankee manager Casey Stengel from the dugout to replace his starting pitcher with a left-hander. To counter Stengel's strategy, Cleveland manager Al Lopez replaced Pope with rookie slugger Rocky Colavito in the bottom half of the inning.

Pope finished his career in the minor leagues, primarily in the Pacific Coast League. With San Diego in 1958, he was one of eight black hitters to rank in the top 12 in the league in batting.

Statistics: Dave Pope

Year	Team	Games	AB	Runs	Hits	2B	3B	HR	RBI	BA
1952	CLE-A	12	34	9	10	1	1	1	4	.294
1954	CLE	60	102	21	30	2	1	4	13	.294
1955	CLE/									
	BAL-A	121	326	38	86	13	4	7	52	.264
1956	BAL/									
	CLE	37	89	7	20	3	1	0	4	.225
Totals										
4 Years		230	551	75	146	19	7	12	73	.265
World Series										
1954	CLE-A	3	3	0	0	0	0	0	0	.000

Hector Antonio Rodriguez

Third base. Batted right. Threw right. Born 6/13/20, Villa Alquizar, Cuba.

On April 7, 1952, Hector Rodriguez and Minnie Minoso became the first black ballplayers to play baseball with white men in the city of New Orleans, as the Chicago White Sox played the Pittsburgh Pirates in an exhibition game at Pelican Park. An article by Hap Glaudi in *The Item* the following day, described "a throng of 9,502 [who] paid to see this new era in baseball make a tardy appearance.

"A total of 2,882 Negroes saw the game from their section of the stands in Pelican Park," Glaudi wrote, and he predicted the game would "assist tremendously in erasing the impression which some organizations give our people that there is something wrong with the way God distributes his color."

Rodriguez was nearly 32 years old on that historic day. And while he was a major league rookie, he was hardly a newcomer to baseball. Since 1942, when

Rodriguez broke into the professional ranks in his native Cuba, baseball was the only job he ever knew.

Following nine seasons in the Negro leagues and the Mexican League, Rodriguez was named International League Rookie of the Year in 1951, when he hit .302, drove in 95 runs and stole 26 bases for the Montreal Royals. He was runner-up to Archie Wilson for the league's Most Valuable Player award. Following that season, he was purchased from the Dodgers organization by the White Sox.

At the start of the 1952 season, New York Giants farm director Carl Hubbell told Sox manager Paul Richards, "You won't like him at first. He isn't colorful. He can't speak English at all.... But he can throw strikes to first base, he's an uncanny fielder and he can run faster than players ten years his junior. You'll just get to depend upon him, like an old shoe or an old mule."

Rodriguez returned to the minors in 1953, playing and managing in the International League, the Pacific Coast League and the Mexican League. By the time he retired in 1966, Rodriguez had collected 2,351 hits for a .290 lifetime minor league average.

Statistics: Hector Rodriguez

Year	Team	Games	AB	Runs	Hits	2B	3B	HR	RBI	BA
1952	CHI-A	124	407	55	108	14	0	1	40	.265

Quincy Thomas Trouppe

Catcher. Batted both. Threw right. 6'2", 225 lbs. Born 12/25/12, Dublin, Georgia; died 1983.

Quincy Trouppe was one of the mainstay players of the Negro leagues. From 1930 through 1949, he played for, and often managed, the St. Louis Stars, Detroit Wolves, Homestead Grays, Kansas City Monarchs, Chicago American Giants, Indianapolis ABCs, Cleveland Buckeyes, and New York Cubans. By the time he joined the Indians in 1952 as a 39-year-old "rookie," Trouppe had put 20 years in the Negro leagues in a career that coincided with those of such Negro league greats as Satchel Paige, Josh Gibson, Martin Dihigo, Cool Papa Bell, Ray Dandridge, Willie Wells, Mule Suttles, Buck Leonard, and others.

"Baseball was something like a mother, father and best friend all rolled into one," Trouppe wrote in his autobiography, *Twenty Years Too Soon*, published in 1977.

Recommended to the Cleveland Indians by Dodger catcher Roy Campanella, Trouppe was a smart baseball man and as a catcher, a particularly deft handler of pitchers. Returning from Mexico City in October 1951, Trouppe paid a visit to Abe Saperstein in Chicago with a dim hope of landing a job with a major league team the following season. The owner and coach of the Harlem Globetrotters basketball team advised Trouppe to continue with his plans to play winter ball. A few months later, in the lobby of a Caracas, Venezuela, hotel, Trouppe received the call he had been waiting for all his life. Cleveland's Hank Greenberg was inviting him to join the Indians at the club's Tucson, Arizona, spring-training site.

Greenberg, wanting to make the most of Trouppe's baseball knowledge, particularly with some of Cleveland's minor league pitching prospects, signed the veteran catcher to an Indianapolis contract with the understanding that making the Indians would be based on Trouppe's spring training performance.

Despite catching Early Wynn for 17 consecutive scoreless innings and Bob Feller for a shutout, Trouppe remained with the American Association team. In Indianapolis, Trouppe worked closely with Cleveland's young farmhand pitchers—Ray Narleski, George Zuverink and the phenom left-hander Herb Score. Following six games with Cleveland, Trouppe became a scout for the St. Louis Cardinals in 1953.

The youngest of 10 children born to a sharecropper family in Dublin, Georgia, Trouppe signed his first professional contract with the St. Louis Stars of the Negro National League in 1931. That season, the father of the poet Quincy Trouppe, Jr., had two hits in three at-bats in a game in which the Stars beat a Max Carey all-star team that included Lloyd and Paul Waner and Bill Terry. In 1948, as catcher and manager of Caguas, Trouppe's home run in the top of the ninth inning of the seventh game of the Puerto Rican League championship broke a 6–6 tie against Mayaguez. For bringing the championship to his city, the Caguas mayor declared Trouppe mayor of the city for one week.

Statistics: *Quincy Trouppe*

Year	Team	Games	AB	Runs	Hits	2B	3B	HR	RBI	BA
1952	CLE-A	6	10	1	1	0	0	0	0	100

1953

Eugene Walter "Gene" Baker

**Second base. Batted right. Threw right. 6'1", 170 lbs.
Born 6/15/25, Davenport, Iowa.**

Somehow, Gene Baker managed never to play shortstop for the Chicago Cubs, even though Wid Matthews, Cubs director of player personnel, called him "as good a shortstop as I've ever seen — and that includes Pee Wee Reese," even though he averaged .280 and was dazzling in the field in three seasons with the Chicago's Class AAA farm team in Los Angeles while the lowly Cubs shortstops hovered around .230.

By the time Cub management decided to promote a black player to the major leagues, they had a shortstop they liked better — Ernie Banks. Banks had taken over Baker's shortstop spot with the Kansas City Monarchs after the Cubs bought Baker's contract in 1950. Four years later, they formed the first all-black double-play combination in major league history, but Baker had been moved to second base. Baker had been the first black player to wear a Cubs uniform, but Banks was the first to play.

And while Baker languished in the minors, some speculated that race was his main barrier to the majors. *Jet*'s Doc Young wrote that "the prevailing opinion is that the Cubs just don't want a Negro player at Wrigley Field. After all, they let Junior Gilliam go. They say repeatedly that Baker is 'a year away' and continually harp on their doubts about his hitting." Young quoted an unnamed source as saying, "I feel the same way about the Cubs as Jackie Robinson does about the Yankees. [Starting shortstop Roy] Smalley never was and never will be the shortstop Gene Baker has been for at least two years."

Even Cubs owner P. K. Wrigley blasted the return of Baker to the minors in 1953 as "monkey business." "I don't think the situation has been handled properly," Wrigley said. "I just returned from Los Angeles where I saw Baker play and he was sensational."

Finally in the majors and playing out of position, Baker led National League second basemen in errors in all three of his full seasons with the Cubs. But he also had great range and led the league in assists and putouts in 1955.

He was named to the *Sporting News* all-rookie team in 1954 and the NL All-Star team in 1955. Baker and Banks were a wildly popular pair in Chicago, spawning a fan club whose monthly newspaper was called *Keystone Capers*.

Despite his thin frame, Baker proved to have better than average power and hit almost as well in the majors as he did in the minors. Cub manager Phil Cavarretta called him "one of the best two-strike hitters I've ever seen." He was an outstanding all-around athlete, having been an all-state basketball and track star in high school. He did not start playing baseball until he entered the navy in 1943, then had a successful tryout with the Monarchs in 1947. He was surprisingly durable and singularly tough. He set a Pacific Coast League record by playing in 420 straight games. In August 1956 he was carried off the field after being hit in the left temple by a pitch, and in the clubhouse doctors discovered a gash on his leg he had gotten two innings earlier when a runner spiked him and used four stitiches to close it.

Throughout his career, Baker was praised for his intelligence. Banks called him "Sharp Top." Pirate manager Danny Murtaugh said Baker "knows more baseball than fellows twice his age. He's one of the smartest I've ever met." After tearing up his knee in 1958, Baker finished his major league career as a utility infielder with the Pirates, serving as a scout during his 15-month rehabilitation. The Pirates released him in 1961, then immediately hired him as an instructional assistant in their farm system.

Two years earlier, Baker had spoken about his desire to stay in baseball when his playing days were through. "I'm one of those optimists who like to think the day will come when Negroes are accepted in front-office jobs the same as they are on the playing field," he said. "When that day comes, I would like to be ready to fit into the pattern." That day came for Baker early in the 1961 season when he was named manager of the Pirates Class D club in Batavia, New York, making him the first black manager in U.S. organized baseball.

Statistics: *Gene Baker*

Year	Team	Games	AB	Runs	Hits	2B	3B	HR	RBI	BA
1953	CHI-N	7	22	1	5	1	0	0	0	.227
1954	CHI	135	541	68	149	32	5	13	61	.275
1955	CHI	154	609	82	163	29	7	11	52	.268
1956	CHI	140	546	65	141	23	3	12	57	.258
1957	CHI/PIT-N	123	409	40	108	22	5	3	46	.264
1958	PIT	29	56	3	14	2	1	0	7	.250
1960	PIT	33	37	5	9	0	0	0	4	.243
1961	PIT	9	10	1	1	0	0	0	0	.100
Totals										
8 Years		630	2230	265	590	109	21	39	227	.265
World Series										
1960	PIT-N	3	3	0	0	0	0	0	0	.000

Ernie Banks

Shortstop, first base. Batted right. Threw right. 6'1", 180 lbs. Hall of Fame, 1977. Born 1/31/31, Dallas, Texas.

Ernie Banks just was not the crusading type. He was so grateful to be playing baseball for a living, he did not have time to change the world, and if that meant some people called him an Uncle Tom, well, so be it. Banks was not about changing anyone's mind about the color of his skin; he was about baseball, pure and simple. The greatest power-hitting shortstop in baseball history summed up his feelings on baseball and race this way: "Not everyone will agree with me — and I consider this their privilege — but I've always said the only race we have in baseball is the run to beat the throw."

The way Banks played baseball transcended race. It transcended money and team loyalty. People did not just respect the way Banks played, they almost revered it. Even his opponents did. Giant pitcher Juan Marichal, never one to shy away from dusting off a hitter, refused to knock Banks down after a Cub pitcher had knocked down Willie Mays. "Banks is a nice guy," he explained to Mays in the Giant dugout.

Yet the man who coined the phrase "Let's play two" did not play his first organized game of baseball until he was 17. Banks grew up the son of a ballplayer, a former pitcher and catcher with the Dallas Black Giants who bribed his son with nickels and dimes to get him to play catch. Banks's segregated high school in North Dallas did not have a baseball team, so he played basketball, football, softball, and ran track. At 17, he signed on with the Amarillo Colts, an all-black barnstorming team, for $15 a game. One day the Colts played the Kansas City Monarchs, and Banks had three hits. Banks quickly signed with the Monarchs and joined the team after he graduated from high school.

After two years in the army, he rejoined the Monarchs, but late in the 1953 season owner Tom Baird sold Banks and pitcher Bill Dickey to the Cubs for $35,000. The Yankees and White Sox originally had the inside track on Banks since the Monarchs played games in their stadiums, but Cubs general manager Wid Matthews would not take no for an answer.

So one day in September Banks was handed $10 and a plane ticket, and he was off to Chicago. "I was never so nervous in my life," he said. "There I was, going from the Negro Leagues to the big top in one jump. I was a stranger to Chicago. I knew I would be a stranger to my teammates." Banks was not only entering the majors and soon to become the first black to play in a Cubs uniform but was facing an integrated world for the first time in his life. "During my half-month stay with the Cubs in September 1953, I met more white people than I had known in all my 22 years," he said. "The sudden association with so many white people often left me speechless and wondering why they were so kind."

It was easy to be kind to Banks, especially when people saw him play. Despite his thin frame, Banks demonstrated awesome power, thanks largely to what one scout called "wrists right up to his armpits." Banks's powerful wrists allowed him to wait on pitches longer than most hitters. Matthews called him "the best breaking-ball hitter of any rookie I've ever seen."

Banks opened the 1954 season at shortstop and went on to play every inning that season. His durability was remarkable, and he once played in 717 consecutive games. In 1955 he gave notice that shortstops were no longer singles hitters as he set a major league record for his position with 44 home runs, a record he would break three years later. He also hit five grand slams, a major league record that still stands. From 1955 to 1960, he hit more homers than anyone in baseball — more than Aaron, Mantle, and Mays. He won back-to-back Most Valuable Player awards in 1958 and 1959, even though the Cubs finished below .500 both seasons.

His fielding, erratic at first, soon became stellar. In 1959 he set a record for shortstops with just 12 errors. And amid all the superlatives, Banks maintained his legendary modesty. The Cubs wanted to have a day in his honor late in the 1955 season, but he declined. "I don't want a day until I have proved myself," he said. "I just don't think I deserve one yet."

And with one exception, Banks's graciousness extended to opposing pitchers who tried to move him off the plate. "I thought that was just part of the game," he said. "I felt they were basically paying me a compliment because they thought I was a threat to win the game." But when San Francisco's Jack Sanford hit him three times in 1959, Banks complained publicly. "This is the first time I've ever heard Ernie complain about anything," said Cubs vice president John Holland. Don Drysdale once hit Banks with a pitch at Wrigley Field, which Drysdale said was "worse than hitting the Pope" because Banks was so popular in Chicago. "But Ernie never made a big thing about it," he said.

In 1962 leg injuries forced Banks to move to first base, and all he did was lead NL first basemen in putouts, assists, and double plays. In 1963 Banks ran as an independent candidate for alderman in Chicago's eighth ward. He lost, but learned a lot. "I learned that those professional politicians are a lot tougher than the National League pitchers."

The only great disappointment of Banks's career was that he never played in a World Series or league championship series. His best chance came with the 1969 Cubs when at age 38, he drove in more than 100 runs for the eighth time. And even though the Cubs suffered a historic late-season collapse and lost the NL East flag to the Miracle Mets, Banks said the 1969 season was "the most happiness any of us had ever enjoyed in our lives. Everybody talks about money, the rings, and publicity, but fellowship you develop during that time is worth more than all of that," he said. "We stayed together a long time. That's unique."

But Banks was hardly immune to the racism that marked much of baseball's early days of integration. He was turned away from restaurants, banned from team hotels, and even received a death threat in 1970. "We ran into problems of segregation in the West, East and North as well as in the South," Banks said. "My philosophy about race relations is that I'm the man and I'll set my own patterns in life. I don't rely on anyone else's opinions. I look at a man as a human being; I don't care about his color. If a man doesn't like me because I'm black, that's fine. I'll just go elsewhere, but I'm not going to let him change my life."

"I've never been militant, but that doesn't mean I don't understand."

Statistics: Ernie Banks

Year	Team	Games	AB	Runs	Hits	2B	3B	HR	RBI	BA
1953	CHI-N	10	35	3	11	2	1	2	6	.314
1954	CHI	154	593	70	163	19	7	19	79	.275
1955	CHI	154	596	98	176	29	9	44	117	.295
1956	CHI	139	538	82	160	25	8	28	85	.297
1957	CHI	156	594	113	169	34	6	43	102	.285
1958	CHI	154	617*	119	193	23	11	47*	129*	.313
1959	CHI	155	589	97	179	25	6	45	143*	.304
1960	CHI	156	597	94	162	32	7	41*	117	.271
1961	CHI	138	511	75	142	22	4	29	80	.278
1962	CHI	154	610	87	164	20	6	37	104	.269
1963	CHI	130	432	41	98	20	1	18	64	.227
1964	CHI	157	591	67	156	29	6	23	95	.264
1965	CHI	163	612	79	162	25	3	28	106	.265
1966	CHI	141	511	52	139	23	7	15	75	.272
1967	CHI	151	573	68	158	26	4	23	95	.276
1968	CHI	150	552	71	136	27	0	32	83	.246
1969	CHI	155	565	60	143	19	2	23	106	.253
1970	CHI	72	222	25	56	6	2	12	44	.252
1971	CHI	39	83	4	16	2	0	3	6	.193
Totals										
19 Years		2528	9421	1305	2583	407	90	512	1636	.274

*League leader.

Carlos Bernier

Outfield. Batted right. Threw right. 5'9", 180 lbs. Born 1/28/29, Juana Diaz, Puerto Rico.

Carlos Bernier played only half a season in the major leagues, but in triples he made the most of it. On May 2, 1953, Bernier provided Pirates fans one of their few reasons to cheer during a 104-loss season when he tied a twentieth-century major league record with three triples in a 12–4 win over Cincinnati. Bernier had eight triples that season, eighth in the league, despite playing only 87 games.

Bernier also led the Pirates with 15 stolen bases in 1953, more than twice as many as any other Pirate. Bernier had hit .301 with Hollywood of the Pacific Coast League in 1952, but his .213 mark in 1953 could not earn him a continuing role with the woeful Pirates, who had the lowest team batting average in all of baseball.

Statistics: Carlos Bernier

Year	Team	Games	AB	Runs	Hits	2B	3B	HR	RBI	BA
1953	PIT-N	105	310	48	66	7	8	3	31	.213

William Haron "Billy" Bruton

Outfield. Batted left. Threw right. 6', 169 lbs. Born 12/22/25, Panola, Alabama.

Billy Bruton's journey to integrated America began as a child in a suburb of Birmingham, Alabama, where streets in black neighborhoods were unpaved, baseball fields were homemade, and there was no such thing as Little League. It took him next to Wilmington, Delaware, where the only noticeable new freedom was a seat in the front of a city bus.

Bruton wanted to go to college to study chemistry, but when the time came to choose between science and baseball, he chose baseball. "I took the [baseball] offer because I knew it would be hard for a Negro to get a good job as a chemist," he said. As a member of the semipro San Francisco Cubs, Bruton barnstormed all over the northern plains states in the United States and Canada. He played against white teams in cities big and small, and said he faced little racial harassment from opposing players or fans.

He was discovered by scout John Ogden, who told him that at 24 he was too old to get a good look and suggested he take a few years off his age. So he quickly became 20, and Boston Braves scout Bill Yancey saw him play and got him an invitation to the Braves minor league training camp in 1950. He was assigned to Eau Claire, Wisconsin, in the Northern League, where he and pitcher Roy White were the first blacks in the league. They had trouble finding a place to live, and one of the team's restaurant hangouts would not serve them, but Bruton said, "Ninety-nine percent of the people in Eau Claire welcomed us warmheartedly."

He became even more popular as the season went on as he led the league in runs scored, outfield putouts, and a dazzling 66 stolen bases. Bruton continued up the ladder at Denver the following year, hitting .303 with a league-high 27 triples, then went up another rung to Milwaukee where he hit .325, was the fielding sensation of the Class AAA American Association, and became known as "The Ebony Comet."

In 1953 the majors came to him as the Boston Braves moved to Milwaukee. Bruton was already a local favorite, but he etched his name permanently in Milwaukee baseball history by hitting the first major league home run in County Stadium. The tenth-inning blast in the home opener beat the Cardinals 3–2, and the Braves took off from there, finishing second to the Dodgers and 28 games better than in 1952. Bruton won his first of three straight NL stolen-base titles and finished second in the league with 14 triples.

Bruton worked as hard in the community as he did between the lines, lending his time and concern to local youth agencies and churches. He made Milwaukee his year-round home, and his four children attended integrated local schools. He worked during the off-season in public relations for a local brewery. Bruton got his share of racial abuse, but he was a determined young man and rarely spoke of it. In 1957 he played in baseball's first all-black outfield, flanked in right by Henry Aaron and in left by Wes Covington.

But every spring he got a vivid reminder that real progress came at a snail's pace. When the Braves trained in Florida or traveled through the South, Bruton and his black teammates rediscovered Jim Crow. "When we would arrive in a town," said Aaron, "Duffy Lewis, the traveling secretary, would appoint Bruton to handle the money for cab fares and tips and other things we might need, and Bruton would be in charge of our group until we joined up with the rest of the team again."

Bruton's wife never saw an exhibition game because she refused to sit in the bleachers apart from the wives of white players. "There were beaches everywhere in Florida, but none where she could go with other wives," Bruton said. "I had to eat in the kitchens of roadside restaurants . . . or wait for a Negro cab driver to come along and tell me where I could get a meal. All I could ask myself was—how long would I have to suffer such humiliation?"

Bruton's playing career got a jolt on July 11, 1957, when a collision with teammate Felix Mantilla tore cartilage in his knee, and he had to watch from a hospital bed as his teammates won the pennant and the World Series. He came back 10 months later and helped the Braves win another pennant.

In December 1960 Bruton was traded to Detroit, a very unpopular move with Braves fans. The state legislature passed a resolution urging him to retain his Wisconsin citizenship, and several hundred business and community leaders gathered to honor him. The state's governor called him "a doctor in the science of humanity," and the Wisconsin B'nai B'rith gave him an interfaith award.

But in the end the move worked out for Bruton. He played four solid years for the Tigers, again showing that consistency was the hallmark of his career. In nine of his 12 years in the majors, he hit between .272 and .289, never below .250. He stole bases to help the team, not pad his stats, and in 1954 he led the NL by hitting into only two double plays. In May 1963 he tied a major league record with four doubles in a game.

But Bruton never saw baseball as a lifetime career. "I looked at baseball as a way to open another door for me once my playing days were over, and I thought that way from the very first day I put on a major league uniform." He had gotten a head start in 1961 when he and Aaron opened a real estate investment firm.

Finishing his baseball career in Detroit, Bruton went on to spend the next 23 years working for Chrysler Corporation in customer service, advertising, and promotion.

Statistics: Billy Bruton

Year	Team	Games	AB	Runs	Hits	2B	3B	HR	RBI	BA
1953	MIL-A	151	613	82	153	18	14	1	41	.250
1954	MIL	142	567	89	161	20	7	4	30	.284
1955	MIL	149	636*	106	175	30	12	9	47	.275
1956	MIL	147	525	73	143	23	15*	8	56	.272
1957	MIL	79	306	41	85	16	9	5	30	.278
1958	MIL	100	325	47	91	11	3	3	28	.280
1959	MIL	133	478	72	138	22	6	6	41	.289
1960	MIL	151	629	112*	180	27	13*	12	54	.286
1961	DET-A	160	596	99	153	15	5	17	63	.257
1962	DET	147	561	90	156	27	5	16	74	.278
1963	DET	145	524	84	134	21	8	8	48	.256
1964	DET	106	296	42	82	11	5	5	33	.277
Totals										
12 Years		1610	6056	937	1651	241	102	94	545	.273
World Series										
1958	MIL-N	7	17	2	7	0	0	1	2	.412

*League leader.

James William "Junior" Gilliam

Second base, third base. Batted both. Threw right.
5'10½", 175 lbs. Born 10/17/28, Nashville, Tennessee.
Died 10/8/78, Los Angeles, California.

Junior Gilliam was so talented, he made a utility player out of Jackie Robinson. Robinson had been the Brooklyn Dodger second baseman for five years, but when the 25-year-old Gilliam arrived in the majors in 1953 after a spectacular Negro league and minor league career, manager Chuck Dressen installed him as the team's regular second baseman.

Gilliam returned the favor with a Rookie-of-the-Year season that saw him lead the league with 17 triples, set an NL rookie record with 100 walks, score 125 runs, steal 21 bases, and hit .277. The switch-hitting Gilliam went on to spend 14 versatile, consistently productive years with the Dodgers, splitting his time between second base, third base, and the outfield. He played on seven pennant winners and is the only Dodger ever to play on four world champions. He provided continuity in an era of drastic change for the Dodgers as the team moved from New York to Los Angeles and from heroes like Jackie Robinson, Duke Snider, and Pee Wee Reese, to Sandy Koufax, Maury Wills, and Don Drysdale.

Gilliam got his nickname as the youngest member of the Baltimore Elite Giants of the National Negro League and was a three-time all-star before signing with the Dodgers in 1951. After leading the International League in runs scored in back-to-back seasons, he joined the Dodgers, a wonderfully talented team that had won three pennants in four years but each time were beaten in the World Series by the crosstown Yankees. The Bronx Bombers frustrated the Dodgers again in Gilliam's rookie season, but Junior made some noise by hitting home runs from both sides of the plate.

Two years later, the Dodgers finally beat the Yankees, and Gilliam played a key if inactive role in the Series' most crucial play. Gilliam started Game 7 in left field, but after manager Walter Alston pinch-hit for second baseman Don Zimmer in the top of the sixth, Gilliam took his place, and Sandy Amoros went in to play left. Down 2–0, the Yankees put the tying runs on base with no one out in the bottom of the sixth. Yankee catcher Yogi Berra sliced a fly ball into the left-field corner, but Amoros raced over and made a historic catch that turned into a double play and Brooklyn's first and only world championship.

Gilliam was crucial to the Dodgers' success in their new West Coast home. Gone was the power of the Brooklyn Dodgers. The L.A. Dodgers relied on speed, pitching, and defense, and Gilliam's quick feet, nimble bat, and selflessness made him the perfect man to hit behind baseball's new stolen-base wizard, Maury Wills. In 1958, the Dodgers' first season in their new home, Gilliam led the team in hits, doubles, triples, and steals. The next year, Wills's rookie year, Gilliam drew a league-leading 96 walks, and the Dodgers won the pennant in a two-game playoff sweep of the Milwaukee Braves. Gilliam was robbed of the hero's mantle when in the bottom of the ninth inning of Game 2 Hank Aaron crashed into the wall and speared Gilliam's potential pennant-winning line drive. The Dodgers prevailed and went on to beat the White Sox in the World Series.

The Dodgers ran and pitched their way to another pennant in 1963, and

Gilliam, now the team's oldest player at 34, stole 19 bases, led the team in doubles and walks, and hit .282. In a tight, low-scoring Series sweep against the Yankees, Gilliam got just two hits but scored the only run in Game 3 and the winning run in Game 4. The Series' final run came on a typically heads-up play by Gilliam. With the scored tied 1–1 in the seventh, Gilliam hit a high bouncer to Clete Boyer at third, but first baseman Joe Pepitone lost the throw in a sea of white-shirted fans. As the throw bounced into short right field, Gilliam sped all the way to third, then scored on a sacrifice fly. The Dodgers had swept the two-time defending world champions with a paltry 12 runs and 25 hits in four games.

Gilliam retired after the 1964 season but come spring was talked back onto the field where he became part of baseball's only all-switch-hitting infield. He hit .280 and helped the Dodgers win another world championship. He finally retired for real after the 1966 season and rejoined the team as a coach, a role he filled until his death from a brain hemorrhage just before the start of the 1978 World Series and nine days short of his fiftieth birthday.

Gilliam's uniform number, 19, is one of only eight numbers to be retired by the Dodgers. He was a quiet, disciplined, and consistent ballplayer, even when it came to scouting pitchers. "The guy on the mound could be throwing BBs 200 miles an hour, but Junior always had the same critique," said teammate Don Drysdale. "'Sheeet,' he would say. 'That guy ain't got sheeet.'"

Statistics: Junior Gilliam

Year	Team	Games	AB	Runs	Hits	2B	3B	HR	RBI	BA
1953	BKN-N	151	605	125	168	31	17*	6	63	.278
1954	BKN	146	607	107	171	28	8	13	52	.282
1955	BKN	147	538	110	134	20	8	7	40	.249
1956	BKN	153	594	102	178	23	8	6	43	.300
1957	BKN	149	617	89	154	26	4	2	37	.250
1958	LA-N	147	555	81	145	25	5	2	43	.261
1959	LA	145	553	91	156	18	4	3	34	.282
1960	LA	151	557	96	138	20	2	5	40	.248
1961	LA	144	439	74	107	26	3	4	32	.244
1962	LA	160	588	83	159	24	1	4	43	.270
1963	LA	148	525	77	148	27	4	6	49	.282
1964	LA	116	334	44	76	8	3	2	27	.228
1965	LA	111	372	54	104	19	4	4	39	.280
1966	LA	88	235	30	51	9	0	1	16	.217
Totals										
14 Years		1956	7119	1163	1889	304	71	65	558	.265
World Series										
1953	BKN-N	6	27	4	8	3	0	2	4	.296
1955	BKN	7	24	2	7	1	0	0	3	.292

Year	Team	Games	AB	Runs	Hits	2B	3B	HR	RBI	BA
1956	BKN	7	24	2	2	0	0	0	2	.083
1959	LA-N	6	25	2	6	0	0	0	0	.240
1963	LA	4	13	3	2	0	0	0	0	.154
1965	LA	7	28	2	6	1	0	0	2	.214
1966	LA	2	6	0	0	0	0	0	1	.000
Totals										
7 Years		39	147	15	31	5	0	2	12	.211

League leader.

Ruben Gomez

Pitcher. Batted right. Threw right. 6', 170 lbs. Born 7/13/27, Arroyo, Puerto Rico.

After one year in the New York Yankee farm system, Ruben Gomez reached the conclusion that the greatest franchise in baseball history just was not serious about bringing a black player to the majors. In this he was far from alone. His reaction, however, was unique. He bought his freedom.

Gomez bought his contract from the Yankees for $3,000, promptly signed for a $10,000 bonus with the crosstown Giants, then led the team with 13 wins as a rookie. "How did these saintly gentlemen ever let a good pitcher like [Gomez] get away?" wrote Wendell Smith, a leading critic of Yankee management.

The Yankees, if they were looking to promote a black player at all, were looking for a quiet, even-tempered, gentlemanly one. Gomez was none of those things. In fact, he was in the middle of some of baseball's wildest scenes in the 1950s. Late in 1953, his rookie season, Gomez hit Dodger right fielder Carl Furillo with a pitch. But instead of charging the mound, Furillo went to first, then raced to the Giant dugout to go after manager Leo Durocher, who the Dodgers claimed had ordered beanballs. The fracas cost Furillo a broken finger but probably won him a batting title as he sat out the rest of the season and edged Red Schoendienst by two points.

In 1956 Gomez made the mistake of hitting Braves first baseman Joe Adcock, one of the biggest and strongest men in the game. Adcock took a few steps toward first, then charged the mound. Gomez fired the ball at Adcock, hitting him in the thigh, and as one writer put it, setting a record for "the shortest time interval within which a batter was hit twice by the same pitcher." Gomez took off for the dugout, with Adcock hot on his trail. He dodged a tackle by third-base coach Johnny Riddle and raced into the clubhouse as the Braves team stormed the Giants dugout. Gomez grabbed an ice pick and headed back toward the field but was restrained. Suspended for three days and fined $250, he offered this play-by-play reasoning: "I saw him coming at me so I threw the ball at him. I ran away because I didn't want him to break my ribs."

In July 1957 Gomez and Cardinal pitcher Sam Jones did not throw at the hitters but at each other until the plate umpire threatened to toss both of them out of the game. In January 1959 Gomez's Corvette was pelted with debris and its back window smashed by irate fans after he hit Joe Christopher in the head with a pitch in a Puerto Rican League game. Gomez even got into a fistfight with a teammate — Willie Mays.

But he offered no apologies for moving hitters off the plate. "Baseball can only be played one way — all the time and your best to win," he said. "If my brother is at bat and he crowds the plate when I pitch, then he would have to watch out, just like everybody else. It is the only way to play."

Gomez had great stuff to go along with his intense will to win. "He has a fastball that bursts in on you, a good curveball, and the best screwball of any right-handed pitcher I ever saw," said Giants scout Tom Sheehan. "He hits and runs and slides, and he can field too. The guy's a ballplayer, and he's the most colorful pitcher since Dizzy Dean." He also had a rubber arm, at one point pitching year-round for seven straight years.

Gomez turned pro with Santurce in his native Puerto Rico after college and came to the United States in 1949 to play for an independent minor league team in Bristol, Connecticut. After a year in Canada, the Yankees bought him for their Kansas City farm team. Two years later he helped the Giants win a world championship.

He slumped on the mound in 1955 but hit .300. He went west with the Giants in 1958 and pitched a six-hit shutout in the first major league baseball game ever played in California, beating the hated Dodgers 6–0. He was traded three times in the next few years and left the majors in 1962, only to return five years later at age 40 for a short stint with the Phillies.

Throughout his career, Gomez was a familiar target of angry hitters and those who wanted to crack down on beanballs, but he never flinched. "Let them say what they want," he said. "It doesn't bother me. I get knocked down plenty of times myself, but I don't go crying to the newspapers." And he insisted he never hit anyone on purpose. "I pitch the best way I can. I don't try to hurt anyone. I just try to win."

Statistics: *Ruben Gomez*

Year	Team	W	L	PCT	G	IP	H	BB	SO	ERA	SV
1953	NY-N	13	11	.542	29	204	166	101	113	3.40	0
1954	NY	17	9	.654	37	221.2	202	109*	106	2.88	0
1955	NY	9	10	.474	33	185.1	207	63	79	4.56	1
1956	NY	7	17	.292	40	196.1	191	77	76	4.58	0

Year	Team	W	L	PCT	G	IP	H	BB	SO	ERA	SV
1957	NY	15	13	.536	38	238.1	233	71	92	3.78	0
1958	SF-N	10	12	.455	42	207.2	204	77	112	4.38	1
1959	PHI-N	3	8	.273	20	72.1	90	24	37	6.10	1
1960	PHI	0	3	.000	22	52.1	68	9	24	5.33	1
1962	CLE-A/										
	MIN-A	2	3	.400	21	64.2	67	36	29	4.45	1
1967	PHI-N	0	0	.000	7	11.1	8	7	9	3.97	0
Totals											
10 Years		76	86	.469	289	1454	1436	574	677	4.09	5
World Series											
1954	NY-N	1	0	1.000	1	7.1	4	3	2	2.45	0

*League leader.

David Taylor "Dave" Hoskins

Pitcher. Batted left. Threw right. 6'1", 180 lbs. Born 8/3/25, Greenwood, Mississippi.

On June 9, 1952, Dave Hoskins gave new meaning to pitching under pressure. He was scheduled to start for the Dallas Eagles of the Texas League against Shreveport, but that morning he received three letters, one at a time, all in the same handwriting. The first said he would be shot if he sat in the dugout. The second said he would be shot if he went on the field. And the third said he would be shot if he took the mound.

But Hoskins's biggest fear was that if he revealed the threat, he would not be allowed to pitch. So he said nothing, simply went out and whipped Shreveport 3–2 before its biggest crowd of the season.

Big crowds came out wherever Hoskins pitched in 1952. He was, after all, the first black player in the Class AA Texas League. He soon became known as the league's savior. In a league where attendance averaged between 2,000 and 3,000, Hoskins regularly pitched before crowds of 6,000 or more as black baseball fans poured into stadiums in cities like Beaumont, San Antonio, and Fort Worth. In his Houston debut, Hoskins pitched before a crowd of 11,031, more than half of whom were black. By season's end, Hoskins had drawn sellout crowds to every stadium in the league. He had also gone 22-10 with a 2.12 ERA and hit .328.

From Greenwood, Mississippi, Hoskins's family moved to Flint, Michigan, where he was a four-sport star at Northern High School. He began his professional baseball career in 1942 as an outfielder with the Cincinnati Clowns of the Negro American League. In 1945 he was playing for the legendary

Homestead Grays when sportswriter Wendell Smith managed to get a commitment from Boston's two major league clubs, the Red Sox and Braves, to hold a tryout for a trio of Negro league stars. Smith picked Jackie Robinson, then a rookie with the Kansas City Monarchs; Sam Jethroe of the Cleveland Buckeyes; and Hoskins. But Grays owner Cum Posey refused to give Hoskins the time off to attend the tryout, and Philadelphia Stars second baseman Marvin Williams went instead.

Hoskins began his trek to the majors with Grand Rapids of the Central League in 1948. He was the league's first black player, and despite what he called the harshest treatment of his career, he hit .393 in 46 games as an outfielder.

That season Hoskins faced racial slurs hurled behind his back and fastballs aimed at his head. "The Muskegon club gave me a particularly rough time," he said. "There was one pitcher who seemed to take delight in working me over. The first time he pitched to me, he knocked me down. But I got up and knocked a home run off him. The next time I came up, he threw at me until he finally hit me in the back."

In 1949 Hoskins's friend Satchel Paige, then with the American League's Cleveland Indians, brought Hoskins to Municipal Stadium in Cleveland for a tryout. "You better sign this boy," Paige told Indians general manager Hank Greenberg. "He can hit. I know because I could never get him out easy." Greenberg liked what he saw and signed Hoskins to a minor league contract. He spent 1950 with Dayton of the Central League.

A beanball that nearly ended his life changed his career. After spending three days hospitalized in critical condition, Hoskins decided to become a pitcher. "I was getting tired of having pitchers throw at me," he said. "I made up my mind I would start throwing at other guys." He had pitched a few times while barnstorming with Paige the previous fall, and Paige was impressed with his battery of breaking pitches.

In January 1952, Dallas Eagles owner Dick Burnett announced that he was on the lookout for a black player to add to his roster for the coming season. But a tryout for 200 players yielded just a trio of Class C prospects, far below Burnett's demand for a player "capable of playing Double-A ball." The Eagles signed second baseman Ray Neil of the Negro American League's Indianapolis Clowns, but he was released during spring training.

Burnett contacted Greenberg (the Eagles and Indians had signed a working agreement in 1951), and Greenberg remembered Hoskins, who had spent 1951 with Wilkes-Barre of the Eastern League, finishing with a 5-1 record. Burnett, Greenberg, and Dallas manager Dutch Meyer decided Hoskins could win in the Texas League but realized it could be a rough road and left the decision up to Hoskins. When asked, Hoskins did not hesitate. "I'd like to go down there," he said. Six years after Texas League president J. Alvin Gardner proclaimed, "You will never see any Negro players on teams in Organized Baseball in the South as long as the Jim Crow laws are in effect," Texas League baseball was integrated.

Hoskins was impressive in two exhibition outings, then made his first start April 13 at home against Tulsa. With just 11 career pitching appearances under his belt, Hoskins turned in a gritty veteran performance, stranding 14 runners in a 4–2 complete-game win. By May 4, he had pitched in every ballpark in the league and drawn big crowds at every spot. He won his first four decisions and pitched complete games in his first eight starts. His season included a 2–0 shutout of Beaumont in which Hoskins banged out as many hits (two) as he allowed. His season also included remarkably few problems. "Aside from the scattered jibes thrust at him by a few leather lunged fans, Hoskins's reception has been remarkably mild," wrote Bill Rives in the *Sporting News*. And Hoskins was probably glad to see three of his former teammates at Dayton in Dallas uniforms to start the season. "All I care about is the way my teammates treat me," he said. "And they've been swell."

Hoskins's ability to win games and draw crowds made a distinct impression on other Texas League owners. By August, Hoskins had a black teammate, pitcher Jose Santiago, and had been the losing pitcher in the Texas League's first all-black pitching matchup, a game he lost to Oklahoma City's Bill Greason. Hoskins was a unanimous selection to the league's all-star team and was feted with nights in his honor in both Dallas and Fort Worth. "By the mid–1950s," wrote Jules Tygiel in *Baseball's Great Experiment*, "the Texas League was as thoroughly integrated as any minor league circuit in the nation." "I am proud to state," said Burnett, "that our opinion of Dave was well founded. He has done an excellent job for us. He has shown a great amount of ability and determination. And, the reception accorded Dave by Texas League fans has been tremendous. We are deeply gratified."

But Hoskins moved on, joining the Indians to start the 1953 season. In his second major league appearance, he relieved Bob Feller with Cleveland trailing 3–0. Hoskins pitched three shutout innings, doubled, homered, and drove in four runs for his first major league win. He was a solid reliever and spot starter for the Indians that season, but in 1954 the Indians were stacked with fine pitchers, and although the team won 111 games, Hoskins pitched in just 14 and was not used as the Indians were swept by the Giants in the World Series.

A curveball specialist needs work to stay sharp, and Hoskins was not getting enough. He was cut during spring training in 1955 and was so upset at the news that he became, by his own admission, "sick and nervous and couldn't sleep." Hoskins bounced around the minors for a number of years, playing in Indianapolis and San Diego, then ended his career back in Dallas.

"With bat, glove, and ball," wrote *Jet* magazine, "Dave Hoskins has taken his place alongside Texas pioneers of yesteryear who stood tall in the saddle and manipulated six-guns with the speed of a rattlesnake's fangs."

Statistics: Dave Hoskins

Year	Team	W	L	PCT	G	IP	H	BB	SO	ERA	SV
1953	CLE-A	9	3	.750	26	112.2	102	38	55	3.99	1
1954	CLE	0	1	.000	14	26.2	29	10	9	3.04	0
Totals											
2 Years		9	4	.692	40	139.1	131	48	64	3.81	1

Clifford "Connie" Johnson

Pitcher. Batted right. Threw right. 6'4", 200 lbs. Born 12/27/22, Stone Mountain, Georgia.

In 1957, Baltimore Orioles manager Paul Richards called Connie Johnson "the best right-hander in the American League." Unfortunately, Johnson's breakthrough season did not come until he was 34.

At 6'4" and 200 pounds, Johnson was an imposing sight on the mound. He started his professional career in 1940 with the Indianapolis Crawfords of the Negro American League, then sandwiched seven seasons with the Kansas City Monarchs around three years in the military. Johnson was a staffmate of Satchel Paige's during most of his tenure with the Monarchs and in 1946 went 9-3, allowing just 33 hits in 85 innings as the Monarchs won the Negro American League pennant. He was the winning pitcher in the 1950 East-West all-star game and contributed a triple in the 5–3 win.

Johnson made his debut in organized baseball in 1951 with St. Hyacinthe of the Provincial League and went 15-14. That led to a contract with Colorado Springs, a Western League team with a working agreement with the White Sox. Johnson's fastball overpowered Western League hitters in 1952 as he went 18-9 with 24 complete games and 233 strikeouts in 248 innings and was a unanimous choice for the all-star team.

He opened the 1953 season with the White Sox, but control trouble got him shipped down to Charleston until August. In his first start after being recalled, Johnson got his first major league win, a dazzling seven-hit, 10-strikeout shutout of the Senators. Johnson struck out the side twice, once after loading the bases with no outs. "This guy has ice blood in his veins," said Richards.

But Johnson wound up back in the minors in 1954, helping pitch Toronto to the International League pennant. After winning 12 of his first 14 decisions with Toronto in 1955, Johnson was called up by the White Sox on June 30, and in his first 11 starts went 6-1 with five complete games and two shut-outs.

Richards had taken over the helm in Baltimore and traded for Johnson in May of 1956. Johnson went on to lead Oriole starters in ERA for the next two seasons. His 1957 season included three times as many strikeouts as walks, and he placed third in the league in strikeouts and fourth in shutouts, innings pitched, and complete games. Johnson was gone from the majors after the 1958 season, but in five years in the majors during a hitter's heyday, his ERA never rose above 3.88.

The 1950s were racism's heyday. Whitey Ford recalled a Yankee team meeting at which scout Rudy York, an Alabama native, told hitters that they could read Johnson's pitches by how he held his hands. "You know niggers have white palms, lighter than the backs of their hands," he said, apparently not caring that Elston Howard was in the room.

Statistics: Connie Johnson

Year	Team	W	L	PCT	G	IP	H	BB	SO	ERA	SV
1953	CHI-A	4	4	.500	14	60.2	55	38	44	3.56	0
1955	CHI	7	4	.636	17	99	95	52	72	3.45	0
1956	CHI/										
	BAL-A	9	11	.450	31	196	176	69	136	3.44	0
1957	BAL	14	11	.560	35	242	212	66	177	3.20	0
1958	BAL	6	9	.400	26	118.1	116	32	68	3.88	1
Totals											
5 Years		40	39	.506	123	716	654	257	497	3.44	1

James Edward "Jim" Pendleton

Outfield. Batted right. Threw right. 6', 185 lbs. Born 1/7/24, St. Charles, Missouri.

It was not race that kept Jim Pendleton in the minor leagues from 1949 through 1952 as much as Reese. After playing the 1948 season with the Chicago American Giants of the Negro American League, Pendleton was scouted and signed by the Brooklyn Dodgers out of the Venezuelan winter league. A shortstop with excellent speed and a lively bat, Pendleton led the American Association in runs scored and all shortstops in putouts, assists, and chances. But with future Hall-of-Famer Pee Wee Reese a fixture at shortstop for Brooklyn from 1940 through 1956, Pendleton remained in the minors.

One of the most sought-after players in the Dodgers minor league system, Pendleton became an original member of the Milwaukee Braves when he was finally traded in 1953 in a six-player, four-team deal that brought pitcher Russ Meyer to Brooklyn. Milwaukee moved Pendleton from shortstop to the outfield in hopes of replacing the fading Sam Jethroe. The 29-year-old rookie responded by batting .299, the second-highest batting average among major league rookies in 1953, as the Braves made their "miracle" ascent from seventh place in 1952 to second. In addition to speed, Pendleton showed respectable power and in one game that season hit three home runs as the Braves set a National League one-game record with eight homers.

But by the 1954 season, Pendleton was washed up. Although he played for seven more seasons, he never regained the batting eye he displayed as a rookie. Following trades, abbreviated stints and then two full years in the minors, Pendleton was signed by the Houston Colt .45s in their first season in the National League.

Statistics: Jim Pendleton

Year	Team	Games	AB	Runs	Hits	2B	3B	HR	RBI	BA
1953	MIL-N	120	251	48	75	12	4	7	27	.299
1954	MIL	71	173	20	38	3	1	1	16	.220
1955	MIL	8	10	0	0	0	0	0	0	.000
1956	MIL	14	11	0	0	0	0	0	0	.000
1957	PIT-N	46	59	9	18	1	1	0	9	.305
1958	PIT	3	3	0	1	0	0	0	0	.333
1959	CIN-N	65	113	13	29	2	0	3	9	.257
1962	HOU-N	117	321	30	79	12	2	8	36	.246
Totals										
8 Years		444	941	120	240	30	8	19	97	.255

Alphonse Eugene "Al" Smith

Outfield, third base. Batted right. Threw left. 6', 196 lbs. Born 2/7/28, Kirkwood, Missouri.

In 1955, during his uncontested divorce proceeding, Al Smith called on the Kansas City Athletics' Harry Simpson as a character witness. "How can you be a character witness," the judge asked Simpson, "for a man who took your position away from you?"

That was Al Smith's career in a nutshell: Ballplayers stood up for him; fans and the press underestimated him. With a batting eye that was compared to that of Ted Williams, Smith hit in the clutch and with power despite batting in the leadoff position for much of his career. In a 1956 poll, a majority of American League managers voted that with a game on the line, Al Smith was the one player they would least like to face. An exceptional and versatile fielder—he played every position but catcher, pitcher, and first base in the majors—Smith had speed and a strong, accurate arm.

But it may have been his versatility that made Smith something of an invisible man whose contributions frequently went unacknowledged by everyone *off* the field. Fans did not vote him to the 1955 All-Star team because, they claimed, they did not know where he belonged. Batting leadoff and bunting for base hits and taking more pitches than he would have batting third or fourth, Smith sacrificed power to get on base ahead of the guys who were paid to drive him in. And in the eyes of the public and press, he was always somehow identified with his disappointing rookie season.

In 1953, when he was brought up from Indianapolis, Smith was hitting .332 and leading the International League in home runs. But with Al Rosen at third base, Cleveland manager Al Lopez moved Smith to the outfield. Smith read the switch as a knock on his ability at third, a position he had requested, and excelled at, with Indianapolis. His batting average plunged, and now Cleveland fans had two would-be phenom outfielders to boo. Harry Simpson also managed to hit in the low .240s.

By spring training 1954, Smith's versatility made Simpson expendable (he was sold to Kansas City, where his career turned around), and Smith grew comfortable with his unusual role as a utility man who played every day. Four years later, in December 1957, the syndrome started all over again when Smith and pitcher Early Wynn were traded to the White Sox for Minnie Minoso, the god of Comiskey Park.

Smith was booed in Chicago throughout the 1958 season and well into 1959, even when his repeated clutch hits won the 2–1 and 3–2 games the go-go White Sox, the "hitless wonders," were known for. (Sox fans seemed to ignore the fact that Wynn, a four-time 20-game winner—he made it five when he won 22 games and the Cy Young Award in 1959—was hardly a "throw-in.") The booing finally stopped in late September when Smith hit a sixth-inning home run off Cleveland's Mudcat Grant to clinch Chicago's first pennant since the "Black Sox" scandal of 1919. Earlier in that game, Smith caught up with a line drive to left field off the bat of Rocky Colavito, then fired a strike to catcher John Romano to cut down Minoso trying to score from third. That assist was the eighth time Smith had thrown out a runner at the plate in 1959. Yet ask most fans what they remember about Al Smith and the 1959 season, and they will probably mention the World Series and the cup of beer someone in the Comiskey Park bleachers accidentally knocked onto his head.

Nicknamed "Fuzzy" because of his rough whiskers, Smith started playing semipro ball on the outskirts of St. Louis at 14. An all-around schoolboy athlete who played baseball, was a Golden Gloves boxing champ, and ran track, Smith scored 60 touchdowns at Douglas High School in Webster Grove, Missouri. In one game alone he scored 13 touchdowns, although three were called back.

Smith played the 1947 and 1948 seasons with the Cleveland Buckeyes of the Negro American League, where he was a teammate of Sam Jones and Sam Jethroe. Following a tryout in 1948, he was signed by Cleveland's Hank

Greenberg, along with Satchel Paige, and assigned to Wilkes-Barre, becoming the first black player in Eastern League history and finishing second in the league in hitting with .388.

Al Smith was a ballplayer's ballplayer: He played when he was hurt and did not complain; he always seemed to be playing where someone else was injured or slumping. At any position and with any of four teams, Smith brought out the best in everyone around him. From 1953 through 1959, an Al Smith team won two American League pennants and twice came in second. When he slumped, it was usually because he was injured, yet no one knew about it.

Smith was the first player to homer and set off Bill Veeck's exploding scoreboard in Comiskey Park. In 1960, his .315 batting average was second in the AL to Boston's Pete Runnels. Retiring from baseball in 1964, Smith worked for 18 years supervising youth baseball programs for the city of Chicago.

"I'm a laughing ballplayer," Smith once told Hal Lebovitz of the *Cleveland Plain Dealer*. "I gotta keep it up," he said. "That's me. No sense in being moody."

To Gene Woodling, who played on five consecutive world championship Yankee teams, that translated as "Al Smith was one of the best morale builders I've ever played with."

Statistics: Al Smith

Year	Team	Games	AB	Runs	Hits	2B	3B	HR	RBI	BA
1953	CLE-A	47	150	28	36	9	0	3	14	.240
1954	CLE	131	481	101	135	29	6	11	50	.281
1955	CLE	154	607	123*	186	27	4	22	77	.306
1956	CLE	141	526	87	144	26	5	16	71	.274
1957	CLE	135	507	78	125	23	5	11	49	.247
1958	CHI-A	139	480	61	121	23	5	12	58	.252
1959	CHI	129	472	65	112	16	4	17	55	.237
1960	CHI	142	536	80	169	31	3	12	72	.315
1961	CHI	147	532	88	148	29	4	28	93	.278
1962	CHI	142	511	62	149	23	8	16	82	.292
1963	BAL-A	120	368	45	100	17	1	10	39	.272
1964	CLE-A/									
	BOS-A	90	187	25	33	5	1	6	16	.176
Totals										
12 Years		1517	5357	843	1458	258	46	164	676	.272
World Series										
1954	CLE-A	4	14	2	3	0	0	0	2	.214
1959	CHI-A	6	20	1	5	3	0	0	1	.250
Totals										
2 Years		10	34	3	8	3	0	1	3	.235

*League leader.

Robert Lee "Bob" Trice

**Pitcher. Threw right. Batted right. 6'2", 190 lbs. Born
8/28/28, Newton, Georgia.**

Bob Trice was the first black player on the Philadelphia Athletics and the
first black to play major league ball for a Philadelphia team. It was because of
the presence of Trice and Vic Power on the Athletics roster that Philadelphia
hired former Negro leagues third baseman and future Hall-of-Famer Judy
Johnson in 1954 to assist in their transition to the major leagues.

When the Athletics called him up from their Class AAA affiliate in Ottawa, Trice had a 21-10 won-loss record as well as a .283 batting average as a
part-time outfielder and pinch-hitter. In 1954, Trice earned a spot in the A's
starting rotation and won his first four starts (all complete games), including
a 1–0 shutout of the Yankees on April 24. Trice labored to a 7-7 won-loss record
for the last place A's, and when he lost his eighth game of the season, he asked
to be sent back to the minors.

"I figure that in the long run, this is what's best for me," Trice told the
Sporting News. "And since I cannot seem to win in my present frame of mind,
the team shouldn't miss me. Maybe after a few weeks at Ottawa, I'll be able
to come back and win."

Pitching in the major leagues "just wasn't fun anymore; it was work," he
said. "Maybe I am crazy, as everyone says, but to me the reasons seem logical
enough." Trice did return to the Athletics, in Kansas City, in 1955, but after
just four innings of work and no decisions he was released and never pitched
in the majors again.

Trice starred in football, basketball, and baseball at Weirton (West
Virginia) Dunbar High School, spent two years in the navy, then returned
home to West Virginia to work alongside his father in a steel mill. In 1949 he
signed with the Homestead Grays and roomed with Luke Easter. He joined
organized baseball the following season with Farnham, Ontario, playing the
infield when he was not pitching. When the Farnham franchise folded following the 1951 season, Trice signed with the Athletics organization.

Following a 1952 season in which he won 19 games and hit .297 for St.
Hyacinthe in the Class C Provincial League, Trice made the jump to Class AAA
Ottawa and by the end of the season was in the majors.

In retrospect, Trice's nostalgia for Ottawa was well founded. He "was a
sensation from the start," wrote Art Morrow. "He won such respect in Ottawa
that fans there gave him a day, heaping gifts upon him and bringing his
parents to the Canadian capital for the occasion."

"I can count on a good game any time Trice goes to the mound," said Ottawa manager Frankie Skaff. "He is cool and refuses to get rattled. And he'll

fight to the very end. He refuses to give up." To wit: En route to his eleventh win of the season, a shutout over Montreal, Trice walked the bases loaded in the sixth inning, retired the side by getting Montreal's Dick Williams on a fly out, then singled and scored the only run of the game. Pinch-hitting in games on July 11 and 12, he singled twice and the next day singled, doubled, and homered in beating Toronto 4–3.

As popular as he was in Ottawa, because of his race, Trice was the object of knock-down and brush-back pitches. But according to Skaff, Trice would "get up and practically slam the ball out of the park." "The time to worry," Trice commented, "is when they don't 'get on me.' When they're yelling and trying to rattle me, I know it's because I have them worried."

Statistics: Bob Trice

Year	Team	W	L	PCT	G	IP	H	BB	SO	ERA	SV
1953	PHI-A	2	1	.667	3	23	25	6	4	5.48	0
1954	PHI	7	8	.467	19	119	46	48	22	5.60	0
1955	KC-A	0	0	.000	4	10	14	6	2	9.00	0
Totals											
3 Years		9	9	.500	26	152	185	60	28	5.80	0

1954

Henry Louis "Hank" Aaron

Outfield. Batted right. Threw right. Hall of Fame, 1982. Born 2/5/34, Mobile, Alabama.

Hank Aaron is best known for breaking Babe Ruth's career home-run record in 1974. But 21 years earlier, he quietly broke something that did not attract as much attention but was nearly as unexpected—the color line in the Sally League.

The South Atlantic, or Sally, League, featured teams in Georgia, Alabama, and northern Florida. In 1953, Aaron, Felix Mantilla, and Horace Garner arrived to play for Jacksonville and integrate baseball in the Deep South. Aaron reacted to the situation in characteristic fashion. He let his bat do the talking. "There's only one way to break the color line," he said. "Play so good they can't remember what color you were before the season started."

He hit .362 with 125 RBIs, 208 hits, 36 doubles, and 115 runs scored, and was the league's MVP. As one reporter put it, Aaron "led the league in everything but hotel accommodations." Aaron, who grew up in Mobile, Alabama, was relatively unscathed by the racial barbs and segregated team living. "I'd been raised in the South, and this was the way I was accustomed to seeing blacks treated," he said. He also gave credit to Jacksonville manager Ben Geraghty, a Jersey City native who shielded Aaron as best he could. "I guess he was one reason I didn't realize I was crusading, because he crowded out a lot of stuff and never let it get close to me," Aaron said.

Still, the 18-year-old Aaron experienced the sting of segregation that season. It was especially sharp when the bus arrived at the team hotel. "[We] would sit there watching them unload," he said. "It was a silent kind of thing. The white players might have been joking and laughing when we drove into town, but when the unloading started they would get quiet. They didn't like this any more than we did, but we all knew we couldn't do anything about it."

What Aaron did was play his way out of the Sally League in short order. He had been discovered playing softball on a Mobile playground, and by the time he was 16, was playing shortstop with the Indianapolis Clowns of the

Negro American League. He was hitting .427 when the Boston Braves bought his contract from the Clowns. After his Sally League heroics, Aaron was sent to Puerto Rico for the winter to learn to play the outfield. The next spring he expected to be in the minors at Atlanta or Toledo. But when Braves left fielder Bobby Thomson broke his leg sliding into second, manager Charlie Grimm handed the 21-year-old the job. In 1954, his rookie season, Aaron was named to his first of 23 straight All-Star teams.

Consistency was Aaron's hallmark. He had flashier contemporaries like Willie Mays, Roberto Clemente, and Mickey Mantle, but none was more productive year in and year out than Aaron. For 13 straight seasons, he scored at least 100 runs. He hit at least 24 home runs for 19 straight seasons. He kept himself in outstanding physical condition, especially late in his career. In 1973, at 39, he hit 40 home runs in less than 400 at-bats, giving him the highest home run percentage of his career.

But because he was not flashy, it was not until Aaron threatened Ruth's seemingly unbreakable record that he got the attention he deserved — and some he could have done without. Aaron had a lazy-looking batting style. Hall-of-Fame pitcher Robin Roberts, off whom Aaron hit his first major league home run, said Aaron was the only batter he knew that "could fall asleep between pitches and still wake up in time to hit the next one." But he had tremendously strong wrists and great timing, and while he is best remembered as a power hitter, Aaron won two batting titles and hit over .300 14 times.

He was an outstanding base runner and led the Braves in steals every year from 1961 to 1968. He won four Gold Gloves for his defense, and though he spent most of his career in right field, he moved to center when the need arose. And although he usually went quietly about the business of being a superstar, Aaron backed down from no one. Yankee shortstop Tony Kubek recalled a time he was outside a Tampa hotel with Aaron and some other players when a truckful of rednecks stopped and began harassing Aaron. One challenged him, and Aaron dropped him with three quick punches.

Aaron could rise to the occasion on the field as well. In 1957 he had perhaps his greatest season, winning two-thirds of the Triple Crown and clinching the pennant with a twelfth-inning game-winning homer on September 23. He kept on slugging through the World Series, hitting three homers as the Braves beat the Yankees in seven games.

Steadily, but in unspectacular fashion, he began his assault on Ruth's record. In 1971, at 37, he had a career-best 47 homers. With 34 more in 1972, he passed Willie Mays, and the following year he hit 40 more, the most ever by a player his age. He ended the season with 713 home runs, one behind Ruth. Throughout his pursuit of the record, Aaron received some vicious hate mail. "You can hit all dem home runs over dem short fences, but you can't take that black off yo' face," one correspondent wrote. But Aaron received even more mail supporting his quest.

On his first swing of 1974, he tied Ruth's record. He sat out the next few games so that he could take a shot at breaking the record at home in Atlanta. In the fourth inning of the Braves' home opener against the Dodgers, Aaron sent a 1-0 pitch from Al Downing over the left-center field fence and into the history books. Braves reliever Tom House caught the ball in the bullpen and sprinted across the field to give the ball to baseball's new home-run king.

"In that great crowd around home plate I found him looking over his mother's shoulder, hugging her to him, and suddenly I saw what many people have never been able to see in him — deep emotion," House said. "I looked and he had tears hanging on his lids. I could hardly believe it. 'Hammer, here it is,' I said. I put the ball in his hand. He said, 'Thanks, kid,' and touched me on the shoulder. I kept staring at him. And it was then that it was brought home to me what this home run meant, not only to him, but to all of us."

Statistics: Hank Aaron

Year	Team	Games	AB	Runs	Hits	2B	3B	HR	RBI	BA
1954	MIL-N	122	468	58	131	27	6	13	69	.280
1955	MIL	153	602	105	189	37*	9	27	106	.314
1956	MIL	153	609	106	200*	34*	14	26	92	.328*
1957	MIL	151	615	118*	198	27	6	44*	132*	.322
1958	MIL	153	601	109	196	34	4	30	95	.326
1959	MIL	154	629	116	223*	46	7	39	123	.355*
1960	MIL	153	590	102	172	20	11	40	126*	.292
1961	MIL	155	603	115	197	39*	10	34	120	.327
1962	MIL	156	592	127	191	28	6	45	128	.323
1963	MIL	161	631	121*	201	29	4	44*	130*	.319
1964	MIL	145	570	103	187	30	2	24	95	.328
1965	MIL	150	570	109	181	40*	1	32	89	.318
1966	ATL-N	158	603	117	168	23	1	44*	127*	.279
1967	ATL	155	600	113*	184	37	3	39*	109	.307
1968	ATL	160	606	84	174	33	4	29	86	.287
1969	ATL	147	547	100	164	30	3	44	97	.300
1970	ATL	150	516	103	154	26	1	38	118	.298
1971	ATL	139	495	95	162	22	3	47	118	.327
1972	ATL	129	449	75	119	10	0	34	77	.265
1973	ATL	120	392	84	118	12	1	40	96	.301
1974	ATL	112	348	47	91	16	0	20	69	.268
1975	MIL-A	137	465	45	109	16	2	12	60	.234
1976	MIL	85	271	22	62	8	0	10	35	.229
Totals										
23 Years		3298	12364	2174	3771	624	98	755	2297	.305
League Championship Series										
1969	ATL-N	3	14	3	5	2	0	3	7	.357

Year	Team	Games	AB	Runs	Hits	2B	3B	HR	RBI	BA
World Series										
1957	MIL-N	7	28	5	11	0	1	3	7	.393
1958	MIL	7	27	3	9	2	0	0	2	.333
Totals										
2 Years		14	55	8	20	2	1	3	9	.364

*League leader.

Thomas Edison "Tom" Alston

First base. Batted left. Threw right. 6'5", 210 lbs. Born 1/31/31, Greensboro, North Carolina.

Thomas Edison Alston was a can't-miss prospect who somehow did. Lefty O'Doul, himself a career .349 hitter, called Alston "one of the greatest prospects I have ever seen." He was bright, hardworking, and eager to learn. He was a brilliant defensive first baseman and had good size and power. He just never hit in the majors.

Alston was the first black player on the St. Louis Cardinals roster, and they paid dearly to get him. He earned his degree at North Carolina A&T, then played for an all-black team in Jacksonville, Florida. From there he joined the Saskatchewan Rockets for a tour of western Canada where he played with Chet Brewer. When Brewer became manager of Porterville of the Southwest International League the following year, he told team owner Fido Murphy to find Alston and sign him. Murphy made $93 worth of phone calls tracking Alston down, but it was worth it as the lanky first baseman hit .353 with 69 RBIs in just 54 games.

Porterville had a working agreement with San Diego, of the Pacific Coast League, that allowed the latter to pick one player a year off Porterville's roster for $500. San Diego picked Alston and about 18 months later turned an astronomical profit. Alston hit .297 with 23 home runs and 101 RBIs in 1953, and that winter was sold to the Cardinals for $100,000.

Alston arrived at spring training in 1954 with a sore back and laden with high expectations. "I think we have a real player in this colored boy," said Cardinal manager Eddie Stanky. "He will get every opportunity to show what he has, and to remain with the team." Alston had a fine spring, and after going hitless in his first nine major league at-bats, homered on consecutive days, the latter a game-winning three-run pinch-hit blast. But Alston's hitting spree was brief, and in July he was sent down to Rochester where he hit .295 the rest of the season.

Alston spent most of 1955 struggling with his batting stroke and working to overcome a thyroid condition. "If I can find my hitting stroke, I'll be the happiest man in the world," he said during spring training in 1956. But he did not, and that season Hall-of-Famer Stan Musial had moved in from the outfield to take over first base.

Statistics: Tom Alston

Year	Team	Games	AB	Runs	Hits	2B	3B	HR	RBI	BA
1954	STL-N	66	244	28	60	14	2	4	34	.246
1955	STL	13	8	0	1	0	0	0	0	.125
1956	STL	3	2	0	0	0	0	0	0	.000
1957	STL	9	17	2	5	1	0	0	2	.294
Totals										
4 Years		91	271	30	66	15	2	4	36	.244

Joseph Vann "Joe" Durham

Outfield. Batted right. Threw right. 6'1", 186 lbs. Born 7/31/21, Newport News, Virginia.

Joe "Pop" Durham was the second black player to take the field for the Baltimore Orioles in 1954. Jehosie Heard, the first, pitched in just two games. Durham did not last much longer in Baltimore. He came up at the end of the season to play 10 games in the outfield, then disappeared from the majors for two years. He resurfaced with the Cardinals in 1957 but could not hit enough to stick.

The speedy Durham broke into pro baseball at a St. Louis Browns tryout school in Thomasville, Georgia, in 1952, and was sent to the Chicago Giants of the Negro American League for a season. In 1953 he had a fine season with York of the Eastern League, hitting .308 with a league-leading 28 stolen bases.

With San Antonio in 1954, Durham earned his late-season trial with the Orioles by hitting .318 with 25 doubles, 17 triples, 14 homers, and 108 RBIs.

Statistics: Joe Durham

Year	Team	Games	AB	Runs	Hits	2B	3B	HR	RBI	BA
1954	BAL-A	10	40	4	9	0	0	1	3	.225
1957	BAL	77	157	19	29	2	0	4	17	.185
1959	STL-N	6	5	2	0	0	0	0	0	.000
Totals										
3 Years		93	202	25	38	2	0	5	20	.188

Saturnino "Nino" Escalera

Outfield, infield. Batted left. Threw right. 5'10", 165 lbs. Born 12/1/29, Santurce, Puerto Rico.

Nino Escalera proved time and again that he could hit minor league pitching. Unfortunately, in his one short shot at major league pitching, he did not even hit his weight.

Escalera broke into organized baseball with Bristol, Connecticut, in the Class B Colonial League in 1950. In 1951 he hit a stunning .374 with 16 home runs and 69 RBIs for Muskegon in the Central League. He was signed originally by the Yankees, who then sold his contract to Cincinnati. Neither team had a black player in the majors at the time.

In 1953 he hit .303 for Tulsa in the Texas League but was the victim of a nasty racial incident, along with teammate Chuck Harmon, in Dallas. According to author Jules Tygiel, the pair hopped in one of several cabs hired by the team to transport the team to the train station. Unfortunately, the cab was driven by a white man, and even more unfortunately, the cab was stopped by a police car on the way. The policeman said, "You niggers get out of this cab," then chewed out the cabdriver before handing him a ticket and allowing him to take the black players to the station.

Escalera took a more pleasant trip with Harmon the following season. The pair went to Cincinnati to become the Reds' first black players. But Escalera lasted just a handful of games.

Escalera went back to Puerto Rico where he played for several more seasons. He is currently a scout for the San Francisco Giants.

Statistics: Nino Escalera

Year	Team	Games	AB	Runs	Hits	2B	3B	HR	RBI	BA
1954	CIN-N	73	69	15	11	1	1	0	3	.159

William Henry "Bill" Greason

Pitcher. Batted right. Threw right. 5'10", 170 lbs. Born 9/3/24, Atlanta, Georgia.

Bill Greason's major league career consisted of exactly eight innings on the mound. But in what was arguably the biggest game of his life, he went the distance—and won.

It was August 3, 1952, and Greason was in the first month with the Oklahoma City Indians of the Class AA Texas League. Signed a week earlier, he was the third black ever to play in the league; the other two were Dallas pitchers Dave Hoskins and Jose Santiago. A record crowd of 11,000 jammed the Dallas ballpark to watch the first all-black pitching duel in Texas League history as Greason faced Hoskins, already known as "the savior of the Texas League," who came into the game 16-8. But Greason, who just four days earlier had beaten Shreveport at home before another record crowd, outdueled Hoskins 3–2.

Greason went on to post an 8-1 record with 57 strikeouts in 80 innings. In Game 2 of the league semifinal playoffs against Dallas, Greason pitched before the largest Oklahoma City crowd since 1938 — 10,605.

Greason's Texas League success came immediately on the heels of a two-year hitch in the marines during which he was beaten just once. His wins included a 1–0 duel with Dodger great Don Newcombe.

He got his professional start with the Birmingham Black Barons of the Negro American League in 1948 and tossed three shutout innings in the 1949 East-West all-star game. Greason entered the marines in 1950. After his successful 1952 season, both the Boston Red Sox and New York Yankees, neither of which had yet placed a black player on their major league roster, were said to be pursuing Greason.

But 1953 found him back in Oklahoma City where he turned in another solid season — 16 wins, 13 losses, and 193 strikeouts. In the off-season, Greason was traded, along with Texas League batting champion Joe Frazier, to the St. Louis Cardinals. In 1953, beer magnate August Busch had bought the Cardinals from Fred Saigh, a staunch opponent of integration. Busch changed all that. In October, *Jet* reported, "The St. Louis Cardinals, hastening in their twin-pointed desire to win a National League pennant and break the club's color line, purchased pitcher Bill Greason from the Oklahoma City Indians. While Greason was assigned to the Columbus Redbird farm team, it was reported that he would be given 'every chance' to make the Cardinals next spring."

Busch hired a black scout, and 1954 saw Greason, first baseman Tom Alston, and pitcher Brooks Lawrence integrate the team that probably gave Jackie Robinson more racial grief than any other.

Lawrence had an outstanding rookie season, and while Alston faltered, the Cardinals had spent $100,000 on him and were not about to give up easily. But Greason never got much of a chance. He was already 29 by the time he made the majors and was hit hard and exited early in his two starts with the Cardinals.

But Greason continued to have success in the Texas League and in winter ball for a number of years. He was 7-2 for Santurce in the Puerto Rican League the winter after he was released by St. Louis. Three winters later he was 12-6 with a 2.76 ERA for Santurce, including a 25-inning scoreless streak, which was broken only after Greason, the starting pitcher, had thrown 11 shutout innings.

Statistics: Bill Greason

Year	Team	W	L	PCT	G	IP	H	BB	SO	ERA	SV
1954	STL-N	0	1	.000	3	4	8	4	2	13.50	0

Charles Byron "Chuck" Harmon

Third base, outfield. Batted right. Threw right. 6'2", 175 lbs. Born 4/23/26, Washington, Indiana.

Although he never achieved it as a ballplayer, Chuck Harmon understood star power. The year was 1955, and while the infamous Chase Hotel in St. Louis had buckled to Jackie Robinson's relentless pressure and allowed blacks to room there, they were banned from just about all other hotel facilities. That meant that Harmon and Cincinnati Reds teammate Bob Thurman could not see singer Nat King Cole perform in the hotel's nightclub. The pair went straight to Cole, and he threatened to cancel the concert unless the ban was lifted. The hotel backed down.

Harmon had less success in the majors. He was a fine basketball player in college and led the University of Toledo to the 1943 National Invitational Tournament finals. He was signed by the St. Louis Browns in 1947 and spent the next few years tearing up the minors, including three years with Olean in the Pony League, where he hit .351, .374, and .375. During part of that time Harmon roomed with a white player, Paul Owens, who later became general manager of the Phillies and traded for Harmon in 1957.

Harmon spent four years in the majors as a utility player. He was nicknamed "The Glove" in Cincinnati because he carried around a different glove for each position he played—first base, third base, and outfield.

In an interview with author Jules Tygiel, Harmon talked about being black in the early days of baseball's integration. He said his white teammates often did not even know that black players were staying in different hotels on the road. "They said, 'Boy, you must have some nice stuff in this town, because we never see you around the hotel.'" Harmon said his experience in Cincinnati was largely positive, with the potent exception of a death threat in 1955. Even in the cozy confines of Cincinnati's Crosley Field, Harmon said, "I can't remember anyone saying anything offensive to me."

Harmon, like some other black players in the 1950s, found his southern white teammates friendlier than their northern counterparts, perhaps because they were just more used to having blacks around. "We'd eat together, and go to the movies. They would come looking for me to play cards, and I wasn't a pigeon either."

But Harmon had his share of harsh treatment. Playing at Tulsa, Harmon's blond wife, who was of French, Irish, Indian, and African descent, caused a furor on her first visit to the pass gate. Team officials could not decide whether to seat her in the black or white section, and the situation got so bad the Tulsa general manager actually called the parent club in Cincinnati for advice on what to do. As a result, Harmon's wife came to few games and sat in the black section when she did come. "You know it hurts," he said of the treatment he received. "But you just say, 'Well, one of these days, things are going to get better.' But it puts a little scar on you."

Harmon recalled a white teammate's reaction to what he had to go through. "Hell, you don't know where you're gonna stay the next night; you don't know how you're gonna get to the ballpark; and you don't know where you're gonna eat. . . . This game is hard enough. All I got to worry about is that damn curveball. You guys got to worry about other stuff, and still hit over .300."

Statistics: Chuck Harmon

Year	Team	Games	AB	Runs	Hits	2B	3B	HR	RBI	BA
1954	CIN-N	94	286	39	68	7	3	2	25	.238
1955	CIN	96	198	31	50	6	3	5	28	.253
1956	CIN/ STL-N	33	19	4	0	0	0	0	0	.000
1957	STL/ PHI-N	66	89	16	23	2	2	0	6	.258
Totals										
4 Years		289	592	90	141	15	8	7	59	.238

Jehosie "Jay" Heard

Pitcher. Batted left. Threw left. 5'7", 155 lbs. Born 1/17/20, Atlanta, Georgia.

Before he was drafted for service in World War II, Jehosie Heard had never seen or played in a game of baseball. But one day he saw some soldiers shagging flies and decided to give it a shot. The first ball he tried to catch knocked him out, but he kept trying, and an officer eventually noticed his strong arm. A month later he was the team's star pitcher.

Heard pitched a grand total of 3⅓ innings in the major leagues, but not many 5'7" pitchers make it to the majors. Heard grew up in Birmingham, Alabama, and after the war he returned there to pitch for the Black Barons of the Negro American League. The *Sporting News* said he was nicknamed "Jaybird" for his "bright, cocky attitude." Heard brought a baffling array of breaking pitches to the Barons in 1948 and helped them win the NAL pennant. He pitched with the Memphis Red Sox in 1949 and the Houston Eagles in 1950, and was noticed by Rogers Hornsby and baseball executive Bill Veeck.

Heard made his debut in organized baseball in 1952 with Victoria of the Class A Western International League, going 20-12, with 216 strikeouts and a 2.94 ERA for the league champions. His season featured a no-hitter and a Sunday doubleheader in which Heard pitched both games, losing 1–0 in both.

He was promoted to Portland of the Pacific Coast League in 1953 and won 16 games with a 3.19 ERA. At 34, Heard began the 1954 season as the first black player to play a regular season game for the Baltimore Orioles but was optioned back to Portland in June. The Orioles recalled him in September and sold him back to Portland in October. He finished his career in 1955 with Tulsa.

Statistics: Jay Heard

Year	Team	W	L	PCT	G	IP	H	BB	SO	ERA	SV
1954	BAL-A	0	0	.000	2	3.1	6	3	2	13.50	0

Brooks Ulysses Lawrence

Pitcher. Batted right. Threw right. 6', 205 lbs. Born 1/30/25, Springfield, Ohio.

Brooks Lawrence was sitting in the stands in Tampa watching his teammates play an exhibition game when he became part of a small victory in a massive movement for social change. Lawrence and Reds teammate Ed Bailey had been removed from the lineup and went into the stands to watch the rest of the game. The teammates sat next to each other, a rope separating the white section from the black section. "This is stupid," said Bailey, a native of Strawberry Plains, Tennessee. "I'm gonna change this." Bailey removed the rope, and as Lawrence related the story to author Jules Tygiel, no one ever reattached it.

Lawrence was not your average tobacco-chewing 1950s baseball player. He spent most of his spare time reading; his favorites included Hemingway. He brought a unique perspective to the trials of a racial pioneer. "Being a Negro is an interesting life," he told Ritter Collet, a white sportswriter. "Every morning I wake up with a challenge staring me in the face. You'll never understand that."

He also saw both sides of baseball's effort to integrate. "It was a two-way street," he said. "It was a totally new experience for the white players too." As a veteran, he discouraged black teammates from bunching together in locker rooms. "If we keep huddled up, we're not going to learn anything, and the people around us aren't going to learn anything." Lawrence said black veterans would take black rookies under their wing, advising them where they should and should not go, and black players often hosted visiting black players at local taverns. "You were taking care of me in your town, seeing that I did not jeopardize the situation in baseball," he said. "We didn't necessarily always like each other, but the situation was bigger than our personality conflicts."

Lawrence railed against the discrimination he endured, especially during spring training in Florida. "We can go to the dog races, if we sit in a special section set aside for us," he said. "The only distinction they don't make is the color of our money." He stayed in the home of a black doctor in Tampa and never brought his family to spring training. "The club . . . does what they can. But a man would have to be out of his mind to bring a wife and children down here and expose them to this sort of treatment."

His playing career had its ups and downs. He got into baseball in hopes of making enough money to support his young family. He married at 17 and had two kids by the time he was 23. He worked his way up from the Class D Ohio-Indiana League to the majors in five years and in June 1954 got a shot with the pitching-poor St. Louis Cardinals. Lawrence was a rookie sensation, using a hard sinker and slider to win nine games as a starter and six more in relief. Often he would pitch out of the bull pen the day after starting. "I like to keep busy," he said. "I find I'm more effective when I get plenty of action on the mound."

Lawrence was hospitalized that winter for 10 days because of gastric ulcers, which plagued him throughout the following season. On August 19 he was 3-8 and on his way to Oakland of the Pacific Coast League where he regained his confidence, winning five of six decisions. A winter diet of baby food and a trade away from the strife-ridden Cardinals worked wonders for Lawrence. He won his first 13 decisions in 1956 for Cincinnati, the longest winning streak in the majors since 1949. He finished fourth in the NL in wins, and the Reds won 91 games, their highest total since 1940.

Lawrence was effective again in 1957, but after that the innings began to take their toll. But he had always planned for his postbaseball career. "A guy can't horse around forever," he said.

Statistics: Brooks Lawrence

Year	Team	W	L	PCT	G	IP	H	BB	SO	ERA	SV
1954	STL-N	15	6	.714	35	158.2	141	72	72	3.74	1
1955	STL	3	8	.273	46	96	102	58	52	6.56	1
1956	CIN-N	19	10	.655	49	218.2	210	71	96	3.99	0
1957	CIN	16	13	.552	49	250.1	234	76	121	3.52	4
1958	CIN	8	13	.381	46	181	194	55	74	4.13	5

Year	Team	W	L	PCT	G	IP	H	BB	SO	ERA	SV
1959	CIN	7	12	.368	43	128.1	144	45	64	4.77	10
1960	CIN	1	0	1.000	7	7.2	9	8	2	10.57	1
Totals											
7 Years		69	62	.527	275	1040.2	1034	385	481	4.25	22

Carlos Conill Paula

Outfield. Batted right. Threw right. 6'3", 195 lbs. Born 11/28/27, Havana, Cuba. Died 4/25/83, Miami, Florida.

From the time Branch Rickey signed Jackie Robinson to a Montreal Royals contract in 1945, winter hot-stove league discussion in Washington, D.C., always came back to the same question: When will the Senators sign a black ballplayer? With Senators scout Joe Cambria virtually living in Havana, Cuba, the Senators were familiar with dozens of black American ballplayers who regularly played in the Cuban winter league as well as such native Cubans as Sandy Amoros, Minnie Minoso, and Ray Noble. In addition, with Washington's large black population, a black player on the Senators would have been a natural drawing card. But the Senators remained all-white until late in the 1954 season when Carlos Paula, a 6'3" outfielder, was called up from the minors.

Paula, who was hitting .290 with Charlotte at the time of his promotion, was largely unimpressive in his late-season introduction to the majors. But in 1955 Paula had Griffith Stadium buzzing. His .299 average was highest among all major league rookies; among Senators, only veteran first baseman Mickey Vernon's .301 was higher.

Paula began his campaign for Rookie of the Year honors when he replaced a slumping Roy Sievers in Washington's outfield. When Sievers returned to the lineup, Paula was shifted to right field, where he remained for the rest of the season. Unfortunately, right field was Paula's one liability. Described by *Washington Post* writer Shirley Povich as "something of a crudity in the field," Paula led all American League right fielders in errors in 1955. Perhaps the most surprising aspect of Paula's game, however, was the absence of power from a man his size. Still, Paula delivered what Povich called "destructive singles" that fueled Washingon's few winning streaks.

Paula survived a tendency to swing at bad balls, but in 1956 the bad balls became curveballs, which proved to be the Cuban outfielder's *other* Achilles heel. Despite his request to be optioned to the Pacific Coast League, where he believed he would profit from seeing more curveballs, the Senators sent the

29-year-old Paula to Minneapolis before the start of the 1957 season. Paula eventually got his wish, finishing his career in organized ball in the Pacific Coast League where in 1957 he was one of eight black batters to hit above .300.

A regular in the Cuban winter league, Paula holds the distinction of being the first Cuban to homer under the regime of Fidel Castro. Following a five-day suspension of the season, Castro's army opened the gates to Gran Stadium in Havana on January 6, 1959. Paula and teammate Willie Tasby saluted the former pitcher and new premier with home runs in a doubleheader sweep for the home team.

Statistics: Carlos Paula

Year	Team	Games	AB	Runs	Hits	2B	3B	HR	RBI	BA
1954	WAS-A	9	24	2	4	1	0	0	2	.167
1955	WAS	115	351	34	105	20	7	6	45	.299
1956	WAS	33	82	8	15	2	1	3	13	.183
Totals										
3 Years		157	457	44	124	23	8	9	60	.271

Vic Pellot Power

First base. Batted right. Threw right. 6', 195 lbs. Born 11/1/31, Arecibo, Puerto Rico.

Before Vic Power, first base was the domain of lumberjacks; Vic Power was a figure skater.

Power was to first base what Willie Mays was to center field. His reflexes were incomparable. He attacked the ball one-handed, trailing a foot across the bag as he sailed into the throw or scooped one out of the dirt in a whirlwind motion of his left arm.

Fans liked watching Power play first base the way they liked watching Michael Jordan play basketball. He did things that no one else did, or could do. Yet despite a lifetime fielding average that ranks seventh on the all-time list for first basemen and the highest average number of assists per game, Power was branded a showboat, by the press in particular but also by other players and a few managers. Until he grew tired of people not listening, Power denied this, insisting that he played the game as he felt most comfortable, the most natural to him. And what difference did it make, he argued, whether he caught the ball with one hand as long as he made the out?

That Power spoke up in defense of himself at all was treated as an affront by the press. That he dared insinuate that he would have been better paid if he were white earned him the undeserved reputation for being lazy, that sometimes he did not go "all out." When Yankees catcher Elston Howard agreed with this assessment of Power to the press, Power replied, "That Howard, he's a good boy."

But another Yankee, manager Casey Stengel, called Power the "best I've seen in 20 years at guarding the line against pull hitters. And that includes Lou Gehrig." Stengel would have loved Power at first base in Yankee Stadium. And Power almost was a Yankee.

Growing up in Arecibo, Puerto Rico, Power wanted to be a doctor. Because it would interfere with his studies, Power's father forbade him to play ball. But when Power was 14, his father died. Two years later he was playing as a professional in the Puerto Rican league.

Quincy Trouppe, playing Puerto Rican winter ball, tried to convince Power to come to the United States with him and sign with the Chicago American Giants of the Negro American League. But that was 1948, and Power did not want to quit high school before graduation. Besides, he was making $250 a month playing ball in Puerto Rico.

Both Trouppe and Power played the 1949 season in the Mexican League, and the following season Trouppe signed Power for Drummondville, Ontario, in the Class D Provincial League. It was in Drummondville that Tom Green-wade, the Yankee scout who signed Mickey Mantle, signed Power to a Yankee contract. New York paid Drummondville $7,000 for the rights to Power, who was scheduled for assignment with the Kansas City Blues. Instead, because of a negative racial climate in Kansas City, Power was assigned to Syracuse where he was that city's first professional black ballplayer. In 1951, Power hit .298 but did not draw even a look from the Yankees.

Following a 1952 season in which he hit .331 in Kansas City, Power was again passed over by the Yankees, which led to picketing outside Yankee Stadium. Ignored in New York, Power was all too prominent in Kansas City where he was the first black to play for the Blues. Barred from segregated movie theaters and restaurants, Power was actually booed at home by Kansas City fans despite leading the league in hits, doubles, and triples.

In 1953, Power drove in 97 runs and led the American Association with a .349 batting average and 217 hits. Yankee fans anticipated a spring-training showdown between Power and another Yankee first-base prospect, a former Purdue University football player named Bill Skowron. But the showdown never happened. In December 1953 New York traded Power to the Philadelphia Athletics. When asked why they traded Power, the Yankee front office claimed that Power did not hustle the year before, which prompted one of Power's more famous retorts: "They were just looking for excuses. . . . What did they want me to do? Mow the lawn in the outfield after the game was over?"

Even with the lowly Athletics, Power was happy to have made the majors. "There is only one place to play ball and that is in the majors." When the Athletics moved to Kansas City in 1955, Power returned to Municipal Stadium, hitting the way he had for the Blues—a .319 batting average that was second in the league only to Al Kaline's .340.

Batting from an exaggerated crouch, Power quickly became one of the most respected, and intense, hitters in the American League. A four-time American League All-Star first baseman, Power used his extraordinary reflexes to become one of baseball's best "bad-ball" hitters. "I worry about my hitting," Power told Hal Lebovitz in 1959. "Worry gives me determination."

The year 1958 was a particularly determined one for Power. In addition to hitting .317, Power had the longest batting streak in the American League, 22 games. And on August 14, 1958, he became the first player in American League history to steal home twice in one game. His first steal, in the eighth inning against the Tigers' Bill Fischer, gave the Indians a two-run lead. But it was his second steal that was the masterpiece. With the scored tied in the tenth inning, the bases loaded, and two out, Frank Lary, facing Rocky Colavito, who had already homered twice in the game, was pitching from a full windup. Going on his own, Power faked the steal twice before finally sliding in under the tag of Tiger catcher Charley Lau.

In his book *Baseball Has Done It*, Jackie Robinson described one of the unique problems that black Latin American players experienced in the United States. "Segregation comes as a shock to them," wrote Robinson, "for at home they knew no color barriers. Some stay within their own Spanish-speaking communities. Others react with indignation and refuse to take second-class citizenship in the United States.

"Among the latter is Vic Power."

Statistics: Vic Power

Year	Team	Games	AB	Runs	Hits	2B	3B	HR	RBI	BA
1954	PHI-A	127	462	36	118	17	5	8	38	.255
1955	KC-A	147	596	91	190	34	10	19	76	.319
1956	KC	127	530	77	164	21	5	14	63	.309
1957	KC	129	467	48	121	15	1	14	42	.259
1958	KC/CLE-A	145	590	98	184	37	10*	16	80	.312
1959	CLE	147	595	102	172	31	6	10	60	.289
1960	CLE	147	580	69	167	26	3	10	84	.288
1961	CLE	147	563	64	151	34	4	5	63	.268
1962	MIN-A	144	611	80	177	28	2	16	63	.290
1963	MIN	138	541	65	146	28	2	10	52	.270
1964	MIN/LA-A/									
	PHI-N	105	314	24	75	12	0	3	17	.239
1965	CAL-A	124	197	11	51	7	1	1	20	.259
Totals										
12 Years		1627	6046	765	1716	290	49	126	658	.284

League leader.

Curtis Benjamin "Curt" Roberts

Second base. Batted right. Threw right. 5'8", 165 lbs.
Born 8/16/29, Pineland, Texas. Died 11/14/69,
Oakland, California.

On October 22, 1953, the Pittsburgh Pirates announced the purchase of the first black player in the history of the franchise. His name was Curt Roberts, a 24-year-old Western League all-star second baseman who had hit .291 for the Denver Bears in 1953. Signed by Branch Rickey, Roberts was the Pirates starting second baseman when the team finished spring training and headed north to begin the 1954 season. If anything, Roberts was probably no worse than any of last-place Pittsburgh's starting regulars, and had team expectations not been so high, he might have lasted for more than 171 games.

For the most part, Roberts suffered from the Pirates' absolute need for players. Although anyone who saw him play recognized his incredible fielding ability, his hitting was suspect. But just when Roberts was beginning to learn to hit minor league pitching, the Pirates were desperate for a second baseman. With the color barrier long broken, Rickey lavished none of the attention, care, and advice on Roberts he had on another black second baseman, Jackie Robinson, seven years before. And Roberts, lacking Robinson's hitting skills, would surely have benefited from additional league seasoning in the minor leagues.

Labeled one of the best second baseman in Pirates history, Roberts led the team with 394 assists (nearly twice as many as the nearest Pirate) in 1954. But despite having "the quickest hands in the majors," Roberts also led the team in errors — 24.

Making the jump from Class A baseball to the majors was as difficult in practice as it was in theory, though Roberts proved himself a quick study. After hitting barely .200 for most of the 1954 season, Roberts took the advice of Bears manager Fred Haney and began wearing eyeglasses at bat. In his next 61 trips to the plate, Roberts collected 19 hits for a .311 batting average.

Roberts was recommended to Denver by Andy Cohen, the former Giants infielder, who saw him playing in the Mexican winter league in 1950. Prior to that, Roberts played with the Kansas City Monarchs from 1947 to 1950. The winner of four letters in baseball at Oakland's McClymonds High School — which also produced Frank Robinson, Vada Pinson, Willie Tasby, Curt Flood, and basketball player Bill Russell — Roberts returned to the minors for good in 1956, replaced at second for the next 17 years by a new Pirates rookie, Bill Mazeroski.

Statistics: Curt Roberts

Year	Team	Games	AB	Runs	Hits	2B	3B	HR	RBI	BA
1954	PIT-N	134	496	47	115	18	7	1	36	.232
1955	PIT	6	17	1	2	1	0	0	0	.118
1956	PIT	31	62	6	11	5	2	0	4	.177
Totals										
3 Years		171	575	54	128	24	9	1	40	.223

Jose Guillermo Santiago

Pitcher. Threw right. Batted right. 5'10", 175 lbs. Born 9/4/28, Coamo, Puerto Rico.

When Hank Greenberg signed Jose Santiago to a $6,000 Cleveland Indians contract, the Tribe general manager said, "We're glad to have him with us. Every minor league team he ever played with won the pennant."

Santiago's minor league pennant winners included Dayton in 1949, Wilkes-Barre in 1950 and 1951, and Dallas in 1952 and 1953. Commenting on Cleveland's chance in 1954, Santiago said, "This is a very good team. Yankees not so good. We win pennant by ten games if I stay here." Which proves that Santiago was not only a winner but a sage. Cleveland finished eight games ahead of the second-place Yankees. For Santiago, six pennants in six years.

With a slow, easy windup and a delivery that belied his intensity, Santiago was a workhorse pitcher in the minor leagues and the New York Cubans of the Negro American League where he pitched in 1947 and 1948. Signed to an Indians minor league contract by Bill Killefer following the 1948 season, Santiago won 21 games with Wilkes-Barre in 1951. In a 13-game stretch in 1953, including the playoffs of the Dixie League championships, Santiago appeared in 11 games.

Midway through 1954, Santiago went on the voluntary retired list rather than accept demotion from Cleveland to Indianapolis. And during spring training in 1955, Santiago threatened to repeat his retirement if he did not make the big club. His rationale: "I do not like to pitch in [Indianapolis] and will not. I still say every team I have ever played with won a pennant, and I can throw the 'get-them-out' ball."

Santiago saw his pennant-winning streak end in 1955. Finally consenting to return to the minors, Santiago was signed by Kansas City in 1956. After 21⅔ innings with the Athletics, Santiago (not to be confused with Jose Rafael Santiago of the 1967 pennant-winning Red Sox), Jose Guillermo Santiago returned to the minors for good.

Statistics: Jose Santiago

Year	Team	W	L	PCT	G	IP	H	BB	SO	ERA	SV
1954	CLE-A	0	0	.000	1	1.2	0	2	1	0.00	0
1955	CLE	2	0	1.000	17	32.2	31	14	19	2.48	0
1956	KC-A	1	2	.333	9	21.2	36	17	9	8.31	0
Totals											
3 Years		3	2	.600	27	56	67	33	29	4.66	0

William Michael "Joe" Taylor

Outfield. Batted left. Threw left. 6'1", 185 lbs. Born 12/30/29, Alhambra, California.

Joe Taylor's baseball career was launched by a sportswriter. Writing for the Pittsburgh *Courier*, Earl Johnson covered Taylor's exploits as a sandlot catcher in the Pittsburgh area. Johnson's articles and personal encouragement helped Taylor gain the confidence to pursue a career in baseball.

Taylor entered the professional ranks in 1949 with the Chicago American Giants of the Negro National League. After a season of semipro ball in Canada, Taylor signed his first organized baseball contract in 1951 with Farnham, Quebec, a Class C Provincial League club. As a teammate of pitcher Bob Trice's, the power-hitting Taylor batted .360 with Farnham and was promoted, along with Trice, to St. Hyacinthe in 1952. Following two seasons with Class AAA Ottawa of the International League, Taylor was called up to Philadelphia late in 1954, becoming the third black ballplayer to play for the Athletics. Taylor divided the 1955 season between Portland, where he hit three home runs in his first game, and Toronto, where he batted .324 for manager Luke Sewell's International League club. In 1956, Sewell brought Taylor with him to Seattle where he hit 24 home runs for the Rainiers.

Always a streak hitter, Taylor divided the remainder of his professional career between Class AAA minor league teams and brief stints in the majors. In the 1957 Rainier home opener at Sicks Stadium, he hit three home runs and drove in nine runs. "When Taylor is right," said Seattle manager Lefty O'Doul, "he is definitely a major league hitter."

Taylor holds the dubious distinction of being one of the least risky investments in the history of organized baseball. The contracts of Taylor and Hector Lopez were purchased from their minor league teams for $750 each.

Statistics: Joe Taylor

Year	Team	Games	AB	Runs	Hits	2B	3B	HR	RBI	BA
1954	PHI-A	18	58	5	13	1	1	1	8	.224
1957	CIN-N	33	107	14	28	7	0	4	9	.262

Year	Team	Games	AB	Runs	Hits	2B	3B	HR	RBI	BA
1958	STL-N/									
	BAL-A	54	100	13	28	7	0	3	12	.280
1959	BAL	14	32	2	5	1	0	1	2	.156
Totals										
4 Years		119	297	34	74	16	1	9	31	.249

Charles "Charlie" White

**Catcher. Batted left. Threw right. 5'11", 192 lbs. Born
9/12/28, Kinston, North Carolina.**

After playing the 1950 season with the Philadelphia Stars of the Negro
American League, Charlie White rose through the minors in the St. Louis
Browns and Baltimore Orioles organizations. In exchange for veteran pitcher
Vern Bickford, he was acquired by the Braves on February 10, 1954, as a backup
for catcher Del Crandall.

From 1955 through 1961, White played Class AAA ball in the American
Association and the International and Pacific Coast leagues. In 1958 he was
voted to the Pacific Coast League managers' all-star team.

Statistics: Charlie White

Year	Team	Games	AB	Runs	Hits	2B	3B	HR	RBI	BA
1954	MIL-N	50	93	14	22	4	0	1	8	.237
1955	MIL	12	30	3	7	1	0	0	4	.233
Totals										
2 Years		62	123	17	29	5	0	1	12	.236

1955

Earl Jesse Battey

Catcher. Batted right. Threw right. 6'1", 205 lbs. Born 1/5/35, Los Angeles, California.

Earl Battey learned the tricks of the catching trade from an unlikely source—his mother. The oldest of 11 children, Battey grew up in a suburb of Los Angeles where his father was a pitcher and his mother a catcher for their church softball teams. With catching in his blood, Battey developed into one of the finest defensive backstops of his era, his skills reminiscent of the great Roy Campanella.

Like Campanella, Battey was a fine all-around athlete. He was such a good basketball player that Abe Saperstein tried to sign him to play for the Harlem Globetrotters. Instead, Battey signed out of high school with the Chicago White Sox and wound up playing in the minors in Louisville, Kentucky, a far cry from his Los Angeles neighborhood and its mix of black, Mexican, and Chinese residents. Battey recalled his fellow Californians on the Louisville team asking him to go out with them after games, "never thinking there were places I couldn't go."

Later, when he was an established star, Battey protested the paucity of endorsement opportunities available to black athletes. "National advertisers of such things as cigarettes, shaving creams, and foods do not use Negroes enough," he said.

Battey spent his first few years in the majors backing up Chicago's Sherm Lollar, then was traded to Washington where he earned the starting job and began showing off his rifle arm. He led American League catchers in assists and putouts in each of his first four years with the franchise, which moved to Minnesota in 1961. He threw out three speedy former teammates—Chicago's Luis Aparicio, Jim Landis, and Jim Rivera—in one game in 1960 and made White Sox manager Al Lopez put the brakes on his team. "Notice what a difference he has made in that club? You can't run on them anymore. Last year we ran them dizzy."

Battey helped turn the Minnesota Twins into a pennant contender, handling the pitching staff and contributing to a power-packed lineup. In 1962 Battey hit a career-high 26 homers to help the Twins to a total of 225, the second-highest total ever. He also threw out 24 runners trying to steal and picked off 13 more. Battey won three Gold Gloves and made four All-Star teams, including 1965, when he was the league's top vote getter. He ranks in the top 20 all-time in fielding percentage, putouts per game, and chances per game.

Like Campanella, Battey played much of his career despite nagging injuries. He had knee trouble, several dislocated fingers, and a goiter problem. Twice he suffered broken cheekbones from pitched balls, and he wore a special helmet after 1962. In Game 3 of the 1965 World Series against the Dodgers, he was chasing a foul pop when he ran neck-first into a pole. He played the rest of the Series with almost no voice and a stiff neck. Still, Battey played in 805 of the Twins' first 970 games.

Statistics: Earl Battey

Year	Team	Games	AB	Runs	Hits	2B	3B	HR	RBI	BA
1955	CHI-A	5	7	1	2	0	0	0	0	.286
1956	CHI	4	4	1	1	0	0	0	0	.250
1957	CHI	48	115	12	20	2	3	3	6	.174
1958	CHI	68	168	24	38	8	0	8	26	.226
1959	CHI	26	64	9	14	1	2	2	7	.219
1960	WAS-A	137	466	49	126	24	2	15	60	.270
1961	MIN-A	133	460	70	139	24	1	17	55	.302
1962	MIN	148	522	58	146	20	3	11	57	.280
1963	MIN	147	508	64	145	7	1	26	84	.285
1964	MIN	131	405	33	110	17	1	12	52	.272
1965	MIN	131	394	36	117	22	2	6	60	.297
1966	MIN	115	364	30	93	12	1	4	34	.255
1967	MIN	48	109	6	18	3	1	0	8	.165
Totals										
13 Years		1141	3586	393	969	150	17	104	449	.270
World Series										
1965	MIN	7	25	1	3	0	1	0	2	.120

Julio Becquer

**First base. Batted left. Threw left. 5'11½", 178 lbs.
Born 11/20/31, Havana, Cuba.**

Julio Becquer was good in a pinch. Twice he led the American League in pinch-hits.

And in a real pinch he could pitch. Twice in his seven-year major league career Becquer was asked to pitch, and twice it became clear why he was better off at the plate instead of the mound. His lifetime ERA was 15.43.

For most of his career Becquer was a part-time first baseman for the Washington Senators, one of a host of Cuban black players recruited by Senators scout Joe Cambria. The oldest of eight children, he played baseball in his spare time while attending Havana University and working as a bookkeeper.

He began his professional career in 1952 with Drummondville of the Canadian Provincial League, hitting .299. He got to go home to Havana for the 1953 season and hit .296 with 11 triples. In 1954 the Senators invited seven black Cubans, Becquer among them, to the team's minor league spring training in Winter Garden, Florida. But an unnamed city official allegedly called minor league director Ossie Bluege and told him to get the players out of town. The players were moved to nearby Orlando, and Winter Garden officials quickly denied that they were unwelcome, but the players refused to return.

Carlos Paula became the first to break the color line with the Senators that year, but Becquer continued to hit near .300 in the minors and had his first taste of major league life at the end of the 1955 season. In 1957 he had 18 pinch-hits, the eighth-highest total ever. He had 23 more over the next two years. And on July 4, 1961, Becquer got the ultimate pinch-hit, a grand slam.

Becquer, a left-handed pull hitter with a fine glove and a .993 lifetime fielding percentage, believed he could have been a much better hitter had he played regularly. But he was just happy to play, and in a 1958 interview he offered thoughts that are almost inconceivable today. "Money is a secondary thing with me," he said. "I love the game, and I believe this is true of most major league players. In fact, many would play for nothing because they love the game so much."

Statistics: Julio Becquer

Year	Team	Games	AB	Runs	Hits	2B	3B	HR	RBI	BA
1955	WAS-A	10	14	1	3	0	0	0	1	.214
1957	WAS	105	186	14	42	6	2	2	22	.226
1958	WAS	86	164	10	39	3	0	0	12	.238
1959	WAS	108	220	20	59	12	5	1	26	.268
1960	WAS	110	298	41	75	15	7	4	35	.252
1961	LA-A/									
	MIN-A	68	92	13	20	1	2	5	18	.217
1962	MIN	1	0	1	0	0	0	0	0	—
Totals										
7 Years			488	974	100	238	37	16	12	114	.244

Roberto Walker Clemente

Outfield. Batted right. Threw right. 5'11", 175 lbs.
Born 8/18/34, Carolina, Puerto Rico. Died 12/31/72,
San Juan, Puerto Rico.

Going into the 1971 World Series, Roberto Clemente was 37. He had battled injuries and illness throughout his brilliant career, but a rocky relationship with the press earned him a reputation as a hot dog hypochondriac and kept his brilliance hidden from many baseball fans.

Clemente knew this was perhaps his last chance to showcase his talent to the baseball world, so he made the Series his personal showcase. He hit .414 with two homers and played spectacular defense, including a 300-foot throw that shocked the Orioles. "It had to be the greatest throw I've ever seen," said Orioles second baseman Davey Johnson. "One moment he's got his back to the plate at the 309-foot mark and the next instant here comes the throw, right on the chalk line."

Sportswriter Roger Angell described Clemente's play as "something close to the level of absolute perfection, playing to win but also playing the game almost as if it were a form of punishment for everyone else on the field."

Clemente battled baseball every step of the way. When he was healthy, his game was bigger than life. Dodger scout Al Campanis called him "the most complete ballplayer I ever saw." But when he hurt, he said so, and he hurt often. Clemente was plagued with back pain throughout his career. He hurt his arm in 1959, got malaria in 1965, and in 1960 spent five days in the hospital after crashing into a concrete wall to make a catch. Yet from 1960 through 1967 he played at least 140 games each season. Still, he was seen by managers, writers, and even some fans as a loafer. "I don't understand it," Clemente said. "They say I am not a team player, that I do not give my best. But I have won four batting titles. I kill myself in the outfield. I try to catch any ball hit in the park. I throw my arm out for the Pirates and I play when I am hurt. Mickey Mantle is like a god. But if a black or a Latin American is hurting, they say he is imagining things."

Even with the injuries and the bitterness, there were not many players in baseball who could beat you as many ways as Clemente. His arm was legendary, made strong by throwing the javelin as a youth in his native Puerto Rico. He roamed Forbes Field's spacious outfield with fluid strides and once ran from right into short-left center to field a bunt that slipped past the shortstop, then threw out a runner trying to go from first to third. He never stole more than 12 bases in a season but was one of the best and most aggressive baserunners of his era. And as a hitter he had no weakness, slashing line drives to all fields and hitting at least 10 home runs in 13 straight seasons.

Clemente fell in love with baseball early and as a child was rarely without a baseball in his hand. "I became convinced that God wanted me [to play baseball]," he said. "I was sure I came to this world for a reason." Campanis must have agreed when he happened upon Clemente among 72 young ballplayers at a tryout camp in Puerto Rico. First the players threw to the plate from center field. "I couldn't believe my eyes," Campanis said. "This one kid throws a bullet, on the fly." Then they ran a 60-yard dash. Clemente was clocked in 6.4 seconds. "Hell, the world record was only 6.1," Campanis said. "I'm behind the cage and I'm saying to myself, we gotta sign this guy if he can even hold a bat in his hands." Then for 20 minutes Clemente ripped line drives off a Dodger minor league pitcher.

Campanis wanted to sign him on the spot, but he could not. Clemente was still in high school and as such was off-limits to major league teams. So he signed with a Puerto Rican team instead, but at the end of the season he signed with the Dodgers for a $10,000 bonus and a $5,000 salary. Under the bonus rules at the time, the Dodgers would have to keep him in the majors for his entire rookie season or risk losing him after a year for just $4,000 in a player draft. As it turns out, the Dodgers knew they would not be able to keep Clemente; they just did not want the hated Giants to get their hands on him. It worked. The Pirates, dead last in the standings, picked first in the draft and took Clemente. At the time, he did not even know where Pittsburgh was.

Clemente had trouble adjusting to life as a black Hispanic in the majors. Pittsburgh had few Hispanics and only a small black community in one neighborhood. He was lonely and confused by the constant prejudice he faced. He could not believe his teammates would hurl racial slurs at opponents as if he were not there. "Sometimes I acted like I didn't hear [the word 'nigger']," he said. "But I heard it."

He also felt unappreciated. In 1960 he had his best season, and the Pirates won the World Series, but he finished eighth in the MVP voting. His pride was deeply hurt. "He changed after that," said manager Danny Murtaugh. But if Clemente was bitter, it just made him play harder. In 1966 he finally won an MVP award. For his career, he won 12 Gold Gloves, tying Willie Mays for most by an outfielder, and led NL outfielders five times in assists. He played in 14 All-Star games. And on September 30, 1972, Clemente smacked a Jon Matlack curve off the wall for his 3,000th career hit. It turned out to be his last.

In December 1972, a severe earthquake rocked Nicaragua. Clemente, a hero throughout Latin America, immediately volunteered to head the Puerto Rican relief effort. Enough supplies were gathered to overfill a DC-7, and Clemente, who had heard soldiers were stealing relief aid, decided to go along for the New Year's Eve trip. "If I go, the stealing will stop," he said. "They would not dare steal from Roberto Clemente." Pirate teammate Manny

Sanguillen was with Clemente at the airport and urged him not to go because the plane was overloaded.

Shortly after takeoff, the plane's engines sputtered. When the pilot tried to turn the plane around, the load shifted, and the plane crashed into heavy seas. Clemente's death was a national tragedy. On New Year's Day, thousands of Puerto Ricans went down to the beach near where the plane crashed. The inauguration of Puerto Rico's new governor was postponed.

The following spring Clemente finally got the recognition he deserved as the nation's baseball writers voted unanimously to waive the mandatory five-year waiting period and elected Clemente to the Hall of Fame. The Pirates retired his number, and fans poured into the streets of Pittsburgh to pay tribute. While Clemente feuded with umpires, management, and the press, he had a special relationship with Pirate fans. After the Pirates won the 1960 World Series, he quickly left the clubhouse to join the public celebration.

"I came out of the clubhouse, Clemente said later, "and saw all those thousands of fans in the streets. It was something you cannot describe. I did not feel like a player at the time. I felt like one of those persons, and I walked the streets among them."

Teammate Steve Blass called Clemente "the most decent man I ever met. . . . And yet, no one seemed to understand him."

Statistics: Roberto Clemente

Year	Team	Games	AB	Runs	Hits	2B	3B	HR	RBI	BA
1955	PIT-N	124	474	48	121	23	11	5	47	.255
1956	PIT	147	543	66	169	30	7	7	60	.311
1957	PIT	111	451	42	114	17	7	4	30	.253
1958	PIT	140	519	69	150	24	10	6	50	.289
1959	PIT	105	432	60	128	17	7	4	50	.296
1960	PIT	144	570	89	179	22	6	16	94	.314
1961	PIT	146	572	100	201	30	10	23	89	.351*
1962	PIT	144	538	95	168	28	9	10	74	.312
1963	PIT	152	600	77	192	23	8	17	76	.320
1964	PIT	155	622	95	211*	40	7	12	87	.339*
1965	PIT	152	589	91	194	21	14	10	65	.329*
1966	PIT	154	638	105	202	31	11	29	119	.317
1967	PIT	147	585	103	209*	26	10	23	110	.357*
1968	PIT	132	502	74	146	18	12	18	57	.291
1969	PIT	138	507	87	175	20	12*	19	91	.345
1970	PIT	108	412	65	145	22	10	14	60	.352
1971	PIT	132	522	82	178	29	8	13	86	.341
1972	PIT	102	378	68	118	19	7	10	60	.312
Totals										
18 Years		2433	9454	1416	3000	440	166	240	1305	.317

Year	Team	Games	AB	Runs	Hits	2B	3B	HR	RBI	BA
League Championship Series										
1970	PIT	3	14	1	3	0	0	0	1	.214
1971	PIT	4	18	2	6	0	0	0	4	.333
1972	PIT	5	17	1	4	1	0	1	2	.235
Totals										
3 Years		12	49	4	13	1	0	1	7	.265
World Series										
1960	PIT	7	29	1	9	0	0	0	3	.310
1971	PIT	7	29	3	12	2	1	2	4	.414
Totals										
2 Years		14	58	4	21	2	1	2	7	.362

*League leader.

Lino Donoso

Pitcher. Batted left. Threw left. 5'11", 160 lbs. Born 9/23/22, Havana, Cuba.

In 1954, Lino Donoso was the Pacific Coast League's Rookie of the Year. He was also 32 years old.

Lino Donoso picked up most of his career wins south of the border, far from the glitter of the major leagues. By the time he made the majors, some of the zip had gone off his fastball, which made his array of other pitches, including a screwball and knuckleball, less formidable.

A 9.00 ERA in spring training with the 1955 Pirates got him a ticket back to Hollywood. But he was soon recalled and completed three of his nine starts, his only major league starts, that season.

Donoso also spent three seasons with the New York Cubans of the Negro National League, where his teammates included other future major-leaguers Minnie Minoso and Ray Noble. In 1955 he became the thirteenth player from the NNL to make the majors.

And he made the majors largely on the strength of his 1954 season with Hollywood. He was 15-3 and on his way to a 20-win season when he had to undergo an emergency appendectomy. Still, he wound up 19-8 with a 2.37 ERA and 141 strikeouts with only 55 walks.

By 1956, he was back in Mexico and came within one out of a no-hitter pitching for Mazatlan in the Mexican Pacific Coast League. He continued to pitch for teams in Veracruz, Puebla, and Mexico City, and in August 1960 became the tenth pitcher ever to win 100 games in Mexican baseball.

Statistics: Lino Donoso

Year	Team	W	L	PCT	G	IP	H	BB	SO	ERA	SV
1955	PIT-N	4	6	.400	25	95	106	35	38	5.31	1
1956	PIT	0	0	.000	3	1.2	2	1	1	0.00	0
Totals											
2 Years		4	6	.400	28	96.2	108	36	39	5.21	1

William "Billy" Harrell

Infield. Batted right. Threw right. 6'1½", 180 lbs. Born 7/18/28, Norristown, Pennsylvania.

Billy Harrell never played in a World Series. He never hit a major league grand slam and never even held a solid starting job in the bigs. But he was versatile, and in 1960 he did something that perhaps no other player in baseball history has done. He played in three countries in two days.

Harrell began his odyssey in Cuba, where a doubleheader began on June 25 and ended in the wee hours of June 26. After the games, Harrell caught a plane to Toronto where he played that night in an International League all-star game. The following night, June 27, he played a regular-season game in Rochester, where by that point in the season he had played every position but pitcher and catcher for the Red Wings.

A former basketball star at Siena College, Harrell got his start in organized baseball with Cedar Rapids in 1952 and hit .325. In 1953 he was the Eastern League's Most Valuable Player, hitting .330 and playing such spectacular shortstop that manager Kerby Farrell said, "Billy has such tremendous hands, he could play the infield without a glove." Farrell and Harrell moved up to Indianapolis of the American Association in 1954, and the latter made the former look good again, hitting .307, playing third base, shortstop, and left field.

The following spring, Cleveland manager Al Lopez said Harrell was "a cinch to become a big league shortstop." Harrell had another solid season at Indianapolis, and responded well when called up to the Indians near the end of the season, hitting .412 in 13 games. Harrell looked to ward earning a shot at the starting job, but in late October the Indians traded for veteran shortstop Chico Carrasquel. With Al Rosen at third base and Bobby Avila at second base, the Indians infield was solid, consigning Harrell to another year in the minors. In May 1956, the *Sporting News* said, "Harrell's speed, a strong throwing arm . . . his all-around versatility and knack for hitting should qualify him for any major league club if for no other purposes than a utility player and pinch-hitter."

Harrell showed off his defensive versatility for two more years with the Indians, playing three infield positions and the outfield, but never hit well enough to win a starting job. He did lead the Puerto Rican League with a .316 average in the winter of 1957-58, but in February 1959 he was sold to the Cardinals, who shipped him to Rochester. Harrell had two solid years with the Red Wings and became something of a power hitter for the first time in his career, hitting 30 homers in two years. He was drafted by the Red Sox in 1961 but hit under .200 in his last season in the majors.

Statistics: Billy Harrell

Year	Team	Games	AB	Runs	Hits	2B	3B	HR	RBI	BA
1955	CLE-N	13	19	2	8	0	0	0	1	.421
1957	CLE	2	57	6	15	1	1	1	5	.263
1958	CLE	101	229	36	50	4	0	7	19	.218
1961	BOS-A	37	37	10	6	2	0	0	1	.162
Totals										
4 Years		173	342	54	79	7	1	8	26	.231

Elston Gene "Ellie" Howard

Catcher. Batted right. Threw right. 6'2", 200 lbs. Born 2/23/29, St. Louis, Missouri. Died 12/14/80.

Elston Howard grew up in the shadow of major league baseball, but until the day Jackie Robinson was signed by the Dodgers, he never dreamed he would play it.

Howard grew up across the street from Sportsman's Park in St. Louis and remembered the day vividly. "I was 16 and already dreaming of a baseball career, but not in organized baseball. A friend of mine came into the store and said, 'Ellie, have you heard the news? Branch Rickey just signed one of our boys. His name is Jackie Robinson.' I felt like dancing all over that floor. The path was opening up. Maybe I could become a major league player."

Howard not only became a major-leaguer; he became the first black to play with baseball's most storied franchise, the New York Yankees. The Yankees were among the most reluctant to integrate, and it is likely that that reluctance prevented other, less "suitable" players from beating Howard into pinstripes.

A four-sport star at Vashon High School in St. Louis, Howard won the Missouri state shot-put title and had a dozen college scholarship offers in various sports. But he decided to stay home and play baseball with the St. Louis Braves, an all-black semipro team. William Desmuth, a scout for the Kansas

City Monarchs, spotted Howard and signed him for a $600 bonus and $400 a month. An outfielder with the Monarchs, Howard hit .270 in 1949 and .318 in 1950. Yankee scout Tom Greenwade, who in 1945 had been one of several Dodger scouts Branch Rickey sent out looking for black players, sold the Yankees on Howard, and they signed him and Monarch pitcher Frank Barnes to minor league contracts.

But the army intercepted Howard. He was assigned to Special Services, where he got to play baseball, and spent some time in a noncombat unit in Japan. Two years and one divorce later, he returned to play for the Yankee farm team in Muskegon of the Central League. A solid season got Howard promoted to Class AAA Kansas City in 1953, where he became a teammate of the player many thought would be the first black Yankee, first baseman Vic Power. Power was coming off a season in which he hit .331 and drove in 109 runs. In 1953, Power had an even better year, while Howard hit a solid but modest .286.

But Power was not the kind of person the Yankees wanted to be their first black player, if one is willing to concede they wanted one at all. Powers was flamboyant and exciting, possessed a sharp tongue, and rumor had it he dated white women. The Yankees solved the Power problem by trading him to the Philadelphia Athletics in December 1953. "The first requisite of a Yankee is that he be a gentleman, something that has nothing to do with race, color, or creed," wrote New York *Daily Mirror* sports editor Dan Parker, apparently ignoring the rowdy exploits of Yankee stars Whitey Ford, Mickey Mantle, and Billy Martin.

Meanwhile, the team went about the task of turning the quiet, easygoing Howard into a catcher. Yankee critics saw this as an attempt to keep him in the minors, since at the time the Yanks' starting catcher was one Yogi Berra, he of the three Most Valuable Player awards. Sam Lacy of the Baltimore *Afro-American* called Howard "a lad . . . so young, so trusting, so naive as to still have faith in human nature, Yankee version." But Howard was not bothered. "If they decide to send me back to Kansas City, I won't lose heart," he said during spring training in 1954. "I'll just try my best again to make it."

Howard was sent back to the minors, prompting one correspondent to write, "For years I defended the Yankees. After watching developments this spring, however, I am convinced they don't want a Negro player; they want a Negro superman." Howard was very nearly a superman that season with Toronto, hitting .331 with a league-high 15 triples — not bad for a player about whom Casey Stengel once said, "When I finally get a nigger, I get the only one that can't run." Howard added 22 homers and 108 RBIs, and was named the International League's MVP.

So in 1955, at 26, Howard became a Yankee. Berra was coming off one of those pesky MVP seasons, which left Howard a half-time outfielder on the American League champions. He would play on nine pennant winners in his first 10 years in the majors. By 1958, he was splitting the catching duties with

Berra and finally got a chance to demonstrate the skills he had learned from Yankee great Bill Dickey. "I worked hard," Howard said of his minor league training. "Dickey worked harder."

Howard proved to be an outstanding defensive catcher. He ranks second all-time in fielding percentage among catchers and was regarded as a fine handler of pitchers. "When Ellie caught me, I always felt like I would win, even if I didn't have anything working," said Bill Stafford. "There were games I had absolutely nothing, and Ellie kept me pumped up."

In 1961 former catcher Ralph Houk took over from Casey Stengel as Yankee manager, and that was the first season Howard caught more than 100 games. He also hit .348, although he was overshadowed by teammates Roger Maris and Mickey Mantle. Two years later, with Maris and Mantle hampered by injuries, Howard put together an MVP season and carried the Yanks to another pennant. His modest demeanor belied "an inner toughness and a burning desire" to win, according to teammate Tony Kubek.

Howard never griped when he had to board with a black family in Sarasota while his teammates spent spring training in a hotel. "Elston wasn't the kind of guy to get up on a soapbox," said his wife, Arlene. "He never personalized racism. He realized that when he started playing, segregation was a law, and a lot of people just didn't know better." Still, while Howard was no rebel, he shied away from no one. According to Kubek, Howard was given a particularly rough time by Yankee pitcher Jim Coates, a beanball specialist with a distinctly southern approach to race relations. Once, after an exhibition game at West Point, the Yankees went to play some basketball at a nearby gym. Whitey Ford, who apparently was tired of Coates's attitude, coaxed him into the boxing ring to square off with Howard. Howard promptly flattened Coates, putting an end to the abuse.

And Howard's career was not free of resentment. Although he became the American League's first black coach with Yankees in 1969, a job he held for 11 years, he never got a shot at being a big-league manager. "His dream was to manage the Yankees," Arlene said. "We always thought that since they acted like great white liberals, they might give Elston a chance." But it never happened. "Elston wondered why he had to be better than everyone else, why he had to be superman to manage a baseball team. They wanted you to have a Ph.D. to manage if you were black, and about any white guy could manage. To Elston, it was like a slap in the face."

Howard was named to the All-Star team every year from 1957 through 1965. He played in 54 World Series games; only Berra and Mantle played in more. And like Jackie Robinson, Howard was picked perhaps as much for his character as for his ability. "The Yankees were very anxious that the first black player that they brought up would be somebody with the right type of character," said American League president Lee MacPhail, who was the Yankees' minor league director in the 1950s. "Elston was ideal."

Statistics: Elston Howard

Year	Team	Games	AB	Runs	Hits	2B	3B	HR	RBI	BA
1955	NY-A	97	279	33	81	8	7	10	43	.290
1956	NY	98	298	35	76	8	3	5	34	.262
1957	NY	110	356	33	90	13	4	8	44	.253
1958	NY	103	376	45	118	19	5	11	66	.314
1959	NY	125	443	59	121	24	6	18	73	.273
1960	NY	107	323	29	79	11	3	6	39	.245
1961	NY	129	446	64	155	17	5	21	77	.348
1962	NY	136	494	63	138	23	5	21	91	.279
1963	NY	135	487	75	140	21	6	28	85	.287
1964	NY	150	550	63	172	27	3	15	84	.313
1965	NY	110	391	38	91	15	1	9	45	.233
1966	NY	126	410	38	105	19	2	6	35	.256
1967	NY/									
	BOS-A	108	315	22	56	9	0	4	28	.178
1968	BOS	71	203	22	49	4	0	5	18	.241
Totals										
14 Years		1605	5363	619	1471	218	50	167	762	.274

World Series

Year	Team	Games	AB	Runs	Hits	2B	3B	HR	RBI	BA
1955	NY-A	7	26	3	5	0	0	1	3	.192
1956	NY	1	5	1	2	1	0	1	1	.400
1957	NY	6	11	2	3	0	0	1	3	.273
1958	NY	6	18	4	4	0	0	0	2	.222
1960	NY	5	13	4	6	1	1	1	4	.462
1961	NY	5	20	5	5	3	0	1	1	.250
1962	NY	6	21	1	3	1	0	0	1	.143
1963	NY	4	15	0	5	0	0	0	1	.333
1964	NY	7	24	5	7	1	0	0	2	.292
1967	BOS-A	7	18	0	2	0	0	0	1	.111
Totals										
10 Years		54	171	25	42	7	1	5	19	.246

Hector Headley Lopez

**Outfield, third base. Batted right. Threw right. 5'11",
180 lbs. Born 4/8/32, Colon, Panama.**

Hector Lopez grew up among American GIs and civil servants in the
Panama Canal Zone, where he worked part-time in a bowling alley on an

American military base. A high school track star and the son of a pitcher for the Panama national team, Lopez began playing semipro baseball for $100 a month while still in high school in his hometown, Colon. After graduation, he signed with St. Hyacinthe of the Canadian Provincial League where he teamed with pitcher Connie Johnson.

One of four black players (Vic Power, Jose Santiago, and Harry Simpson the others) with the 1955 Athletics, Lopez enjoyed an outstanding rookie season in Kansas City. A consistent and frequently powerful hitter, Lopez batted .290, second only to Washington's Carlos Paula among all major league rookies. If not for Herb Score's 16 wins, 2.85 ERA, and a league-leading 245 strikeouts, Lopez would probably have won the league's Rookie of the Year award in 1955. Despite leading all American League third basemen in errors, Lopez solidified a Kansas City infield desperate for a third baseman.

According to his Kansas City manager, Lou Boudreau, Lopez had "great instincts" at bat and in the field. And he always hustled, a quality that Lopez attributed to the presence of his KC teammate Enos Slaughter. Slaughter "makes you hustle just by watching him," he once said.

Throughout his major league career, Lopez spent his winters playing in the Panama winter league, winning three batting titles and regularly leading the league in home runs. But critics argued that winter baseball only drained his strength and detracted from his play during the major league season. In 1957, Lopez, having learned to pace himself over the course of the winter league, hit safely in 22 consecutive games, batting .439 from June 15 to July 16. That summer, batting over .300 for most of the season and displaying equal power to all fields, Lopez earned the respect of American League pitchers, many of whom called him the toughest batter to fool in the league.

While his reputation as a third baseman continued to improve—Dan Daniel compared him with Pepper Martin, "a great player despite his tendency to take a few on the chest"—Lopez's strong suit in the field was his adaptability. Other than pitcher and catcher, the only position he did not play in Kansas City was first base, a position he later tried with the Yankees under manager Ralph Houk.

The combination of hitting and fielding versatility made Lopez a prime candidate for Casey Stengel's platoon system in New York. Midway through the 1959 season, Lopez was traded to the Yankees along with pitcher Ralph Terry for infielder Jerry Lumpe and pitchers Johnny Kucks and Tom Sturdivant. In his first game with New York, Lopez doubled off Sturdivant to drive in the winning run in an extra-inning game.

A member of five consecutive pennant winning Yankee teams, Lopez homered and drove in five runs in New York's World Series–clinching Game 5 win over the Cincinnati Reds in 1961.

Statistics: Hector Lopez

Year	Team	Games	AB	Runs	Hits	2B	3B	HR	RBI	BA
1955	KC-A	128	483	50	140	15	2	15	68	.290
1956	KC	151	561	91	153	27	3	18	69	.273
1957	KC	121	391	51	115	19	4	11	35	.294
1958	KC	151	564	84	147	28	4	17	73	.261
1959	KC/NY-A	148	541	82	153	26	5	22	93	.283
1960	NY	131	408	66	116	14	6	9	42	.284
1961	NY	93	243	27	54	7	2	3	22	.222
1962	NY	106	335	45	92	19	1	6	48	.275
1963	NY	130	433	54	108	13	4	14	52	.249
1964	NY	127	285	34	74	9	3	10	34	.260
1965	NY	111	283	25	74	12	2	7	39	.261
1966	NY	54	117	14	25	4	1	4	16	.214
Totals										
12 Years		1451	4644	623	1251	193	37	136	591	.269
World Series										
1960	NY-A	3	7	0	3	0	0	0	0	.429
1961	NY	4	9	3	3	0	1	1	7	.333
1962	NY	2	2	0	0	0	0	0	0	.000
1963	NY	3	8	1	2	2	0	0	0	.250
1964	NY	3	2	0	0	0	0	0	0	.000
Totals										
5 Years		15	28	4	8	2	1	1	7	.286

Roman Mejias

Outfield. Batted right. Threw right. 6', 175 lbs. Born 8/9/30, Abreus, Cuba.

Roman Mejias provided baseball with one of its first true cold-war success stories. When Mejias was traded to Boston for AL batting Pete Runnels in November 1962, he had not seen his family in almost a year. His wife, two children, and two sisters were in his native Cuba, now controlled by Fidel Castro, and unable to join him in the United States.

Without Mejias's knowledge, Red Sox executives contacted the U.S. State Department and the Red Cross to secure his family's release. In classic cold-war parlance, sportswriter Hy Hurwitz reported that the Red Sox "had been working to 'ransom' the outfielder's brood from the clutches of Castroism." On the afternoon of March 15, Red Sox vice president Dick O'Connell handed Mejias a phone. On the line was his wife, and she and the rest of his family were in Florida. The next day the Mejiases were reunited. Overjoyed and obviously not a student of Red Sox history, he said, "I hope very soon I'll be helping [Boston] win the pennant."

In fact, Mejias was a big disappointment in Boston. The Red Sox were counting on his right-handed power to be a big hit in Fenway Park with its short left-field wall. But like many right-handed hitters, Mejias could not take his eyes off the Green Monster and tried to pull everything, even though he saw mostly right-handers who pitched him outside. By August 1963, he was hitting .223 and trying to go to the opposite field. By 1965, he was back in the minors.

But it was not a bad run for Mejias, who was working in a sugarcane field in Cuba when he signed with Hall-of-Fame first baseman George Sisler for the Pirates in 1953. He went to the Pirates' minor league training camp in Georgia, but the language barrier kept his stomach growling. "I thought I would have to go back to Cuba for food," he said. After a while someone taught him to say "ham and eggs" and "fried chicken," and he "ate that for a long while."

But hitting is a universal language, and Mejias spoke volumes in his first professional season, hitting .354 for Waco in the Big State League, including a 54-game hitting streak. He was up with the Pirates in 1955, but quickly lost his right-field job to Roberto Clemente and spent the next seven years trying unsuccessfully to crack the Pirates' starting outfield. He and Clemente also spent time fighting for respect, often from their own teammates. He showed occasional power, hitting three home runs in one game in 1958, and he had good speed. He made basket catches in the outfield, Willie Mays–style, but dropped a few too many. He finally got a break in 1962 when the expansion Houston Colt .45s drafted him for $75,000 and gave him the right-field job.

Mejias responded with his finest season, leading Houston in homers, hits, batting average, runs scored, runs batted in, and stolen bases. But it was his last good season in the majors.

Statistics: Roman Mejias

Year	Team	Games	AB	Runs	Hits	2B	3B	HR	RBI	BA
1955	PIT-N	71	167	14	36	8	1	3	21	.216
1957	PIT	58	142	12	39	7	4	2	15	.275
1958	PIT	76	157	17	42	3	2	5	19	.268
1959	PIT	96	276	28	65	6	1	7	28	.236
1960	PIT	3	1	1	0	0	0	0	0	.000
1961	PIT	4	1	1	0	0	0	0	0	.000
1962	HOU-N	146	556	82	162	12	3	24	76	.286
1963	BOS-A	111	357	43	81	18	0	11	39	.227
1964	BOS	62	101	14	24	3	1	2	4	.238
Totals										
9 Years		627	1728	212	429	57	12	54	202	.254

Humberto Valentino Robinson

Pitcher. Threw right. Batted right. 6'1", 155 lbs. Born 6/25/30, Colon, Panama.

Humberto Robinson pitched well enough in the major leagues to deserve a longer career. And had he pitched in the 1980s or 1990s, the age of pitching "specialists," he may well have had one.

The first black to pitch for Jacksonville, Florida, of the South Atlantic League, Robinson set a Sally League record with 23 wins in 1954. That season made the lanky Robinson one of four young pitchers on whom the Milwaukee Braves were banking their future. In 1958, Robinson, Joey Jay, Juan Pizarro, and Carleton Willey combined for 22 wins as the Braves won their second consecutive National League pennant. While his 3.02 ERA was highest among the four, Robinson emerged as manager Fred Haney's most reliable relief pitcher by the end of the season.

The Braves traded Robinson to Cleveland for Mickey Vernon at the start of the 1959 season. One month later, Cleveland traded him to Philadelphia for Granny Hamner, ending Hamner's 16 consecutive years with the Phillies.

Robinson's single moment of fame in the major leagues was in 1959 when he reported a bribery offer to throw a game he was pitching for the Phillies. Robinson turned down the $1,500 offer from a Philadelphia cafe owner and won the game 3–2.

Statistics: Humberto Robinson

Year	Team	W	L	PCT	G	IP	H	BB	SO	ERA	SV
1955	MIL-N	3	1	.750	13	38	31	25	19	3.08	2
1956	MIL	0	0	—	1	2	1	2	0	0.00	0
1958	MIL	2	4	.333	19	41.2	30	13	26	3.02	1
1959	CLE-A/										
	PHI-N	3	4	.429	36	81.2	79	28	38	3.42	1
1960	PHI	0	4	.000	33	49.2	48	22	31	3.44	0
Totals											
5 Years		8	13	.381	102	213	189	90	114	3.25	4

Milton "Milt" Smith

Infield. Batted right. Threw right. 5'10", 165 lbs. Born 3/27/29, Columbus, Georgia.

Milt Smith played for the Philadelphia Stars in the Negro American League in 1950. In 1955, Smith was hitting .338 with San Diego in the Pacific

Coast League when he was called up to the Cincinnati Reds at the end of the season. Traded to the St. Louis Cardinals in exchange for Paul LaPalme on May 1, 1956, Smith spent the remainder of his professional career in the minors, primarily with Class AAA clubs.

Statistics: Milt Smith

Year	Team	Games	AB	Runs	Hits	2B	3B	HR	RBI	BA
1955	CIN-N	36	102	15	20	3	1	3	8	.196

Robert Burns "Bob" Thurman

Outfield. Batted left. Threw left. 6'1", 205 lbs. Born 5/14/21, Wichita, Kansas.

After a Negro league pitching career with the Homestead Grays and the Kansas City Monarchs, Bob Thurman saw a future for himself as an outfielder in organized baseball.

Originally signed by the Yankees and assigned to the Newark Bears, Thurman immediately showed why he had given up pitching, hitting three tape-measure home runs in his first week at Newark. Thurman spent five seasons in the minors before making the majors as a 34-year-old rookie in 1955. A part-time player, Thurman was one of the most popular players of the slugging Cincinnati Reds teams of Frank Robinson, Ted Kluszewski, George Crowe, Wally Post, and Gus Bell that dominated the National League home-run parade in the 1950s.

Off the field, Thurman, the lone black player on four Class AAA teams, served as an informal traveling secretary, arranging road-trip accommodations for black players on the Reds. "The white players would usually be all checked into their hotels," Thurman told Hank Aaron in his autobiography, *Aaron.* "But they didn't know that we would be having some problems trying to find a decent place."

Known as "Big Swish" because he would always get his cuts at the plate and "The Owl," Thurman fit right into the Cincinnati power mold. After being recalled from Seattle in 1957, he hit four home runs in his first four games, driving in 12 runs in his first five games. When the Reds sent him back to Omaha later that season, the irrepressible Thurman told Reds manager Birdie Tebbetts, "I know I'll be back and when I am I'll make you play me."

Statistics: Bob Thurman

Year	Team	Games	AB	Runs	Hits	2B	3B	HR	RBI	BA
1955	CIN-N	82	152	19	33	2	3	7	22	.217
1956	CIN	80	139	25	41	5	2	8	22	.295

Year	Team	Games	AB	Runs	Hits	2B	3B	HR	RBI	BA
1957	CIN	74	190	38	47	4	2	16	40	.247
1958	CIN	94	178	23	41	7	4	4	20	.230
1959	CIN	4	4	1	1	0	0	0	2	.250
Totals										
5 Years		334	663	106	163	18	11	35	106	.246

Roberto Enrique Vargas

Pitcher. Threw left. Batted left. 5'11", 170 lbs. Born 5/29/29, Santurce, Puerto Rico.

Roberto Vargas was a junkballing left-hander with a reputation for excellent control. Unfortunately, when he made the Milwaukee Braves in 1955, all he brought with him was the reputation.

Sent back to the minors midway through the season, Vargas, who had pitched for the Chicago American Giants of the Negro National League in 1948, eventually had a long career coaching and managing in the Puerto Rican League. There, he advised young pitching prospects of the difference between control and reputation.

Statistics: Roberto Vargas

Year	Team	W	L	PCT	G	IP	H	BB	SO	ERA	SV
1955	MIL-N	0	0	.000	25	24.2	39	14	13	8.76	2

1956

Charles Alfonzo "Charlie" Beamon, Sr.

Pitcher. Batted right. Threw right. 5'11", 195 lbs. Born 12/25/34, Oakland, California.

Charlie Beamon won a total of three games in the major leagues, but for one golden season in the minors, he could do no wrong. The year was 1955, and Beamon was a 20-year-old starting pitcher for the Stockton Ports in the Class C California League.

Using his fastball to set up an array of breaking pitches, Beamon mowed down the league. He went 16-0, completing all 15 of his starts and winning one game in relief. He beat every team in the league at least once and posted a 1.36 ERA with 112 strikeouts in 139 innings. He broke league records for most consecutive wins and most wins in a season without a loss. He even hit .281.

When he was promoted to Oakland near the end of the season, he ran his winning streak to 19, counting two wins at the end of 1954, with a four-hit shutout. Beamon impressed Oakland manager Lefty O'Doul. "If ever there was a prospect, this kid is one," O'Doul said. "He has all the poise in the world. They give bonuses to untried kids, and here's a kid who has won nineteen in a row in organized baseball."

Zeroes followed Beamon throughout his career. He grew up in Oakland and was 12-0 as a high school senior, a schoolmate of basketball great Bill Russell's. He caught the eye of scout Roosevelt Tyson and was married and signed to a pro contract by the time he graduated from high school.

Described by the *Sporting News* as "owner of a wide, friendly grin, a gleaming gold tooth and a blazing fastball," Beamon ran into trouble with Oakland in the second half of the 1955 season, winning just two of 10 decisions. But he bounced back in 1956, going 13-6 for Vancouver, who finished last in the Pacific Coast League. Late in the season his contract was purchased by the Baltimore Orioles, and in his major league debut on September 26, he blanked the six-time defending world-champion New York Yankees 1–0 on four hits.

Beamon was the most talked-about player in the Orioles' spring camp in

1957, but arm trouble cut short his career. Baltimore tried to convert him into an outfielder, but the effort did not work. Beamon did get another major league thrill in 1978 when his son, Charlie Beamon, Jr., made his debut with the Seattle Mariners.

Statistics: Charlie Beamon

Year	Team	W	L	PCT	G	IP	H	BB	SO	ERA	SV
1956	BAL-A	2	0	1.000	2	13	9	8	14	1.38	0
1957	BAL	0	0	—	4	8.2	9	7	5	5.19	0
1958	BAL	1	3	.250	21	49.2	47	21	26	4.35	0
Totals											
3 Years		3	3	.500	27	71.1	64	36	45	3.91	0

Joseph Clifford "Joe" Caffie

Outfield. Batted left. Threw right. 5'10½", 180 lbs.
Born 2/14/31, Ramer, Alabama.

Had Joe Caffie reached the major leagues about 10 years later, he probably could have made a career on his speed alone. But baseball in the mid–1950s was more about power than speed, and Caffie's major league career lasted just 44 games over two seasons.

Luke Easter said Caffie was the fastest player he ever saw. "We clocked him at three seconds flat from home to first," he said. "I have seen a lot of fast ones, but Caffie is the fastest, and that includes guys like Sam Jethroe." Caffie was a four-sport star in high school, lettering in baseball, football, track, and boxing in Warren, Ohio. He signed a pro contract with the Indians in 1950, and two years later exploded across the Northern League, named Most Valuable Player and leading the league with a .342 average, 105 runs scored, 171 hits, and 18 triples.

Caffie worked his way up through the minors, leading the International League with 24 steals in 1955. That winter he hit .360 in the Venezuelan League. After hitting .311 with Buffalo, he was called up to the majors very late in the season and hit .342 in 12 games with three steals.

Despite hitting well the next spring, he was sent back to Buffalo. "What does a fellow have to do to make it up here?" he asked. He answered his own question by hitting .331 with 30 doubles and a 21-game hitting streak in 1957. And despite Easter's advice to quit swinging for the fences — "Just poke and go, Joe" was the slugger's advice — on June 30 Caffie won $1,000 from a local Pepsi-Cola distributor for hitting the bottle cap atop the Pepsi sign above the scoreboard at Buffalo's Offerman Stadium.

Caffie was back in the majors on July 30 and again performed well. On August 24 he hit his first major league homer, and he hit two more before the season ended. But the following spring he found himself back in the minors, this time for good. He led the International League with 39 doubles in 1958 and finished his career with Charlotte in 1961.

Statistics: Joe Caffie

Year	Team	Games	AB	Runs	Hits	2B	3B	HR	RBI	BA
1956	CLE	12	38	7	13	0	0	0	1	.342
1957	CLE	32	89	14	24	2	1	3	10	.270
Totals										
2 Years		44	127	21	37	2	1	3	11	.291

John Wesley "Wes" Covington

Outfield. Batted left. Threw right. 6'1", 205 lbs. Born 3/27/32, Laurinburg, North Carolina.

Throughout his career, the rap on Wes Covington fell squarely on his glove. So naturally he is remembered most for the World Series he saved with it.

It was 1957, and Covington was in his first season as the starting left fielder for the Milwaukee Braves. He added a potent bat to a lineup that included Hank Aaron and Eddie Mathews, and that established a franchise record with 199 home runs. The Braves lost Game 1 of the Series to the Yankees and Whitey Ford. With two on and two out in the second inning of a 1–1 tie in Game 2, Yankee pitcher Bobby Shantz drove a Lew Burdette pitch deep into the left-field corner of Yankee Stadium. But Covington ran the ball down and made a backhanded catch, saving two runs, then drove in the go-ahead run an inning later in a 4–2 Braves win. Before the series, Covington had consulted Jackie Robinson for tips on fielding in Yankee Stadium. "He told me to forget about the shadows. That helped a lot. The shadows are there all right, but I just made up my mind not to pay attention to them."

Back home in Milwaukee, Covington saved Burdette again in Game 5. In the fourth inning of a scoreless tie, Covington leaped above the left-field fence to rob Gil McDougald of a home run. The Braves went on to win 1–0, and Burdette came back in Game 7 to shut the Yankees out again.

But for most of his career it was Covington's bat that got him noticed. Football was his first love, and he was an all-state fullback in high school. He was also a track star, and ran a 9.9 hundred. But his wife convinced him to concentrate on baseball, and at age 20 he signed with the Braves and was assigned to their Eau Claire, Wisconsin, farm team. With Aaron as a teammate, Covington hit .330 with 24 homers and 99 RBIs. But while Aaron fast-tracked it to the majors, Covington got called into the army, where he played baseball for the next two years.

In 1955 he led the Sally League with a .326 average, then dealt calmly with reports that he was "the next Aaron." "You can't afford to take press clippings seriously," he said. "You have to make the club on the field, not in the newspapers, and you have to do it on your own. I'm not going to try to be another Aaron or another anybody else."

Covington finally made the majors in 1956 and was a sensation as a pinch-hitter with 10 pinch-hits in 31 trips. In May 1957 he was sent down to Wichita when the Braves cut their roster, and the team tried to make a trade for a left fielder but could not, so Covington was back in June and helped the Braves win a pennant. A spring-training knee injury limited Covington to about half a season's worth of play in 1958, but what a half season it was. Although he did not have enough at-bats to qualify, Covington's .622 slugging average and 8.2 home run percentage were the best in the National League.

The injury bug bit Covington again in August 1959, this time on his right ankle. He played on sore legs for seven more seasons and in 1961 was traded three times in seven weeks. And despite 11 years in the majors, Covington never batted more than 373 times in a season. Still, he could flat-out hit and drove in a run every six at-bats in his career. As for the rap on his fielding, "What someone else says about me being a bad outfielder doesn't bother me. I've heard it all before. They don't pay outfielders for what they do with the glove."

Statistics: Wes Covington

Year	Team	Games	AB	Runs	Hits	2B	3B	HR	RBI	BA
1956	MIL-N	75	138	17	39	4	0	2	16	.283
1957	MIL	96	328	51	93	4	8	21	65	.284
1958	MIL	90	294	43	97	12	1	24	74	.330
1959	MIL	103	373	38	104	17	3	7	45	.279
1960	MIL	95	281	25	70	16	1	10	35	.249
1961	MIL/CHI-A/									
	KC-A/PHI-N	105	289	34	78	11	0	12	47	.270
1962	PHI	116	304	36	86	12	1	9	44	.283
1963	PHI	119	353	46	107	24	1	17	64	.303
1964	PHI	129	339	37	95	18	0	13	58	.280
1965	PHI	101	235	27	58	10	1	15	45	.247
1966	CHI-N/									
	LA-N	46	44	1	5	0	1	1	6	.114
Totals										
11 Years		1075	2978	355	832	128	17	131	499	.279

Year	Team	Games	AB	Runs	Hits	2B	3B	HR	RBI	BA
World Series										
1957	MIL-N	7	24	1	5	1	0	0	1	.208
1958	MIL	7	26	2	7	0	0	0	4	.269
1966	LA-N	1	1	0	0	0	0	0	0	.000
Totals										
3 Years		15	51	3	12	1	0	0	5	.235

Solomon Louis "Solly" Drake

Outfield. Batted both. Threw right. 6', 170 lbs. Born 9/23/30, Little Rock, Arkansas.

Center fielder Solly Drake was the sensation of the Chicago Cubs spring-training camp in 1955. He was hitting .478, and had been timed in a blurry 3.3 seconds going from home to first. The Cubs had been through three center fielders in three years. But on the last day of camp one bad slide ended what may have been his best shot at a starting job in the majors. Drake slid late into second and suffered a severely dislocated ankle. He did not play again until August, and then it was in the Pacific Coast League.

Drake earned his way back to the majors in 1956, hit reasonably well, and despite playing in only 65 games, tied for the team lead with nine stolen bases. But the following year he was back in the minors. Curt Roberts, who played with Drake in the Cuban winter league, could not figure it out. "Every time I hear the Cubs are seeking a center fielder I laugh, because all they have to do is let [Drake] play and there is no doubt he'll produce," Roberts said. "[In Cuba] his fielding was hotter than the weather. The only thing hotter was the uprising."

Drake was a switch-hitting speedster who once ran a 10-flat hundred. He graduated from Philander Smith College, then hit .324 with Topeka in his first pro season, his first of three .300-plus seasons in the minors. In 1958 he led the International League with 183 hits for Montreal, earning another shot in the majors in 1959. But this time his hitting was abysmal, including 0 for 22 as a pinch-hitter.

His brother Sammy also played in the majors.

Statistics: Solly Drake

Year	Team	Games	AB	Runs	Hits	2B	3B	HR	RBI	BA
1956	CHI-N	65	215	29	55	9	1	2	15	.256
1959	LA-N/									
	PHI-N	76	70	1	11	1	0	0	3	.157
Totals										
2 Years		141	285	41	66	10	1	2	18	.232

Humberto "Chico" Fernandez

Shortstop. Batted right. Threw right. 6', 170 lbs. Born 3/3/32, Havana, Cuba.

Chico Fernandez was one of the few players to make peace with the often brutal fans of the Philadelphia Phillies. After three years of playing solid defensive shortstop, the light-hitting Fernandez said the constant booing no longer bothered him. "I used to think they booed me when I didn't hit," he said. "I've found out that they boo me whether I play good or bad."

Even with the boos, Philadelphia was a welcome change of scenery for Fernandez, who spent too many years trying to win the shortstop job from Dodger Hall-of-Famer Pee Wee Reese. The Dodgers always considered him a bright prospect, but by the time Reese was ready to give up his job, a brighter prospect came along—Charley Neal. So in 1957 the Phillies gave up five players to get him, and Fernandez finally got a chance to play every day.

After breaking into organized baseball in 1951 with Billings, Montana, Fernandez made his reputation with his glove with AAA Montreal. In 1955 he had his finest year at the plate, hitting .301, and International League president Frank Shaughnessy called him "the greatest fielding shortstop in league history." Fernandez was a fine winter-league hitter as well, going over .300 for three straight seasons in Cuba.

After the trade to the Phillies, Fernandez went to spring training where he and John Kennedy were the first black players to train with the Phillies. "This is the chance I've been waiting for," he said. With the Dodgers, "I got to play a few days, do all right, then I go back to the bench. If I play every day, I think I'll do all right." Manager Mayo Smith said Fernandez would be given the shortstop job "until he shows he can't do the job."

Although Kennedy was the first black Phillie to play in a regular season game, he was gone after two at-bats. Fernandez stayed for three years. Fernandez hit a surprising .262 in his first season with the Phillies and led the team with 18 stolen bases. After the 1959 season he was traded to the Detroit Tigers, where he continued his steady play. He was the starting shortstop for the Tigers again in 1961 when Detroit won 101 games yet finished eight games behind the champion Yankees. In 1962 Fernandez put on a shocking display of power, hitting 20 home runs; his previous career high was six.

On May 8, 1963, Fernandez had the unique distinction of being traded twice in one day. The Tigers dealt him to the Braves, who immediately swapped him to the woeful New York Mets. Fernandez went with the program and hit a whopping .200 in his final season in the majors.

Statistics: Chico Fernandez

Year	Team	Games	AB	Runs	Hits	2B	3B	HR	RBI	BA
1956	BKN-N	34	66	11	15	2	0	1	9	.227
1957	PHI-N	149	500	42	131	14	4	4	51	.262
1958	PHI	148	522	38	120	18	5	6	51	.230
1959	PHI	45	123	15	26	5	1	0	3	.211
1960	DET-A	133	435	44	105	13	3	4	35	.241
1961	DET	133	435	41	108	15	5	3	40	.248
1962	DET	141	503	64	125	17	2	20	59	.249
1963	DET/									
	NY-N	73	194	15	36	7	0	1	11	.186
Totals										
8 Years		856	2778	270	666	91	19	40	259	.240

Curtis Charles "Curt" Flood

Outfield. Batted right. Threw right. 5'9", 165 lbs. Born 1/18/38, Houston, Texas.

Babe Ruth changed the way baseball was played. Jackie Robinson changed who played it. Curt Flood changed its balance of power.

Flood's lawsuit challenging baseball's "reserve clause" — a contractual agreement binding players to a single team unless traded, sold, or released — led to free agency and the huge salaries enjoyed by today's major-leaguers. Flood never reaped any benefits from the suit. It effectively ended his playing career and made him the target of abuse, derision, even death threats. But he was a man of immense pride who developed a keen sense of injustice playing baseball under Jim Crow laws in the Deep South.

The youngest of six children, Flood grew up in a two-bedroom apartment in West Oakland. He was a teammate of Frank Robinson's at McClymonds High, which also produced major-leaguers Vada Pinson and Charlie Beamon as well as basketball great Bill Russell and star running back Ollie Matson. Flood and the others played for George Powles, a white coach who had a great influence on him. "If I now see whites as human beings of variable worth rather than as stereotypes, it is because of a process that began with George Powles," Flood said.

He was signed by the same Cincinnati scout who signed Robinson, and the first plane ride of his life landed him in Tampa, home of the Reds' spring-training camp. Flood got his introduction to Jim Crow at the airport when he saw drinking fountains labeled *White* and *Colored*. "For a wild instant I wondered whether the signs meant club soda and Coke," he wrote in his autobiography. "Then the truth struck, like a door slammed in my face." The brochure the Reds sent him said the team stayed at the Floridian Hotel, but when Flood got there he was turned away, put in a cab, and sent to Mrs. Felder's boardinghouse, where he found other black players, including Robinson, Joe Black, and Brooks Lawrence.

Just 18, Flood was impressive enough that spring to be assigned to High Point–Thomasville in the Class B Carolina League. As Flood put it, "I was ready for High Point–Thomasville, but the two peckerwood communities were not ready for me. . . . Wherever we played in that league, at home or away, the stadiums resounded with 'nigger,' 'eight-ball,' 'jigaboo' and other pleasantries." Most of his teammates would not talk to him off the field. Flood played on pride alone and "solved my problem by playing my guts out." He led the league with a .340 batting average, 128 runs scored, 190 hits, and 29 home runs, a remarkable total considering he weighed just 135 pounds by season's end.

The Reds tried to convert him to a third baseman in 1957 at Savannah, probably because if he was promoted to the majors, the team would have to deal with the possibility of having an all-black outfield. So they traded him to the Cardinals after the 1957 season, and he quickly became one of the National League's best center fielders.

Over the next dozen years, Flood hit above .300 six times, and was matched as a defensive center fielder only by Willie Mays. Flood led National League outfielders in putouts four times, and in 1966 he was perfect, setting a major league record for busiest errorless season, handling 396 chances. He played on three NL champions and two world champions but is best remembered for the fly ball he let get over his head in Game 7 of the 1968 World Series against Detroit. The drive, hit by Jim Northrup, broke a scoreless tie in the seventh, and the Tigers went on to a 4–1 win.

Things got worse after the season. Flood had a contract dispute with Cardinal owner August Busch, Jr., with whom he had enjoyed a good relationship. Flood, an accomplished artist, had even painted a portrait of Busch two years earlier but now wanted a raise from $70,000 to $100,000. "I don't mean $99,999.99 either," Flood said, irritating Busch, who felt betrayed after helping Flood with personal and financial problems over the years.

Flood settled for $90,000, but after the 1969 season he was traded to Philadelphia. Or at least that is what the Cardinals intended. "There's no way I'm going to pack up and move twelve years of my life away from here," Flood said. "No way at all." Flood talked to Marvin Miller, executive director of the Players Association, and gained the union's support. On Christmas Eve he sent a now-famous letter to Commissioner Bowie Kuhn. "After twelve years in the major leagues, I do not feel that I am a piece of property to be bought and sold irrespective of my wishes," he wrote, and announced his availability to all other major league teams.

Represented by former Supreme Court Justice Arthur J. Goldberg, Flood filed a $1.4 million lawsuit against Kuhn, the league presidents, and all 24 team owners. He was vilified by the game's powers and many in the press. He was seen as ungrateful and willing to bring the game to its knees to serve his own ends. Sportswriter Dick Young called his case "superficial rhetoric, a sickness of the times." Flood pointed out that "a $90,000 slave is nonetheless a slave."

The case began in May 1970, and as it dragged on, Flood's financial situation worsened. He moved to Denmark, then was offered a contract by Washington owner Bob Short for the 1971 season. His case had been rejected by a federal district judge and was awaiting a Supreme Court hearing. Flood was nearly bankrupt and signed with the Senators for $110,000. But after just 13 games and several death threats, he quit the game for good and moved his family to Majorca.

On June 6, 1972, the Supreme Court ruled against him, despite admitting that the reserve clause was an "aberration" and an "anomaly." Flood made his way back to baseball in the 1980s as commissioner of youth sandlot leagues in Oakland and later played in old-timers' games. In 1989 he was named commissioner of the newly formed Senior League.

Flood's determination to challenge the reserve clause paved the way for a more lucrative, equitable future for the men who play the game and whom fans come out to watch. But all it really got him was a lot of grief. "I am pleased that God made my skin black," he said, "but I wish He had made it thicker."

Statistics: Curt Flood

Year	Team	Games	AB	Runs	Hits	2B	3B	HR	RBI	BA
1956	CIN-N	5	1	0	0	0	0	0	0	.000
1957	CIN	3	3	2	1	0	0	1	1	.333
1958	STL-N	121	422	50	110	17	2	10	41	.261
1959	STL	121	208	24	53	7	3	7	26	.255
1960	STL	140	396	37	94	20	1	8	38	.237
1961	STL	132	335	53	108	15	5	2	21	.322
1962	STL	151	635	99	188	30	5	12	70	.296
1963	STL	158	662*	112	200	34	9	5	63	.302
1964	STL	162	679*	97	211*	25	3	5	46	.311
1965	STL	156	617	90	191	30	3	11	83	.310
1966	STL	160	626	64	167	21	5	10	78	.267
1967	STL	134	514	68	172	24	1	5	50	.335
1968	STL	150	618	71	186	17	4	5	60	.301
1969	STL	153	606	80	173	31	3	4	57	.285
1971	WAS-A	13	35	4	7	0	0	0	2	.200
Totals										
15 Years		1759	6357	851	1861	271	44	85	636	.293

Year	Team	Games	AB	Runs	Hits	2B	3B	HR	RBI	BA
World Series										
1964	STL-N	7	30	5	6	0	1	0	3	.200
1967	STL	7	28	2	5	1	0	0	3	.179
1968	STL	7	28	4	8	1	0	0	2	.286
Totals										
3 Years		21	86	11	19	2	1	0	8	.221

League leader.

Felix Lamela Mantilla

Infield. Batted right. Threw right. 6', 170 lbs. Born 7/29/34, Isabela, Puerto Rico.

There is an axiom in baseball that a team cannot compete for a pennant without a strong bench. In the late 1950s, the Milwaukee Braves called their strong bench Mantilla.

From 1956 through 1961, Felix Mantilla did everything the Milwaukee Braves asked him to do. Most of the time that meant riding the bench. But when a Braves starter was injured, Mantilla was always the irreplaceable replacement. During the 1957 and 1958 seasons, he filled in for the injured Red Schoendienst at second base, Johnny Logan at shortstop, Wes Covington in left field, and Billy Bruton in center. When slugging third baseman Eddie Mathews needed a breather, Mantilla was ready. While Mantilla hit just .228 over those two seasons, it is a safe bet that the Braves would not have been in the World Series those two years if manager Fred Haney had not had Felix Mantilla to call on.

Originally a shortstop and third baseman, Mantilla broke into the professional ranks as a teenager in Puerto Rico. When he returned to winter ball in Puerto Rico after the 1956 season, the Braves asked him to try his hand at second base. Mantilla took to the new position quite easily and going into spring training, appeared to be the odds-on favorite to beat out veteran Danny O'Connell and rookie Ed Charles for the starting job. That he did not led to another fortuitous turn of events for Milwaukee. When O'Connell did not hit, the Braves traded for veteran second baseman Red Schoendienst, a lifetime .289 hitter who hit .310 for the Braves during the remainder of the season. The trade allowed manager Haney to make the most of Mantilla's versatility.

But Felix Mantilla was more than just a fill-in. The Braves typically received an offensive boost from Mantilla whenever he replaced an injured starter in the lineup. After taking over for an injured Schoendienst midway through the 1957 season, the Braves won six straight games, during which Mantilla hit

.364, including his first two home runs in the majors, one of which was a ninth-inning, game-tying shot against the Pirates, a game the Braves won in the thirteenth. That kind of inspired play was typical of Mantilla.

While Milwaukee always seemed to be grooming Mantilla to take over the starting second base position, they could rarely afford *not* to have him on the bench. Nicknamed "The Cat," Mantilla finally got his chance as a starter when he was drafted by the expansion New York Mets following the 1961 season. As the Mets' regular third baseman, Mantilla batted .275, second highest of Casey Stengel's now-infamous "regulars."

Traded to the Red Sox in December 1962 for Pumpsie Green, Tracy Stallard, and Al Moran, Mantilla's .315 batting average was second highest on the Boston team in 1963. In 1964, Mantilla's surprising 30-home-run season was second only to Dick Stuart's team-high 33 homers.

Statistics: *Felix Mantilla*

Year	Team	Games	AB	Runs	Hits	2B	3B	HR	RBI	BA
1956	MIL-N	35	53	9	15	1	1	0	3	.283
1957	MIL	71	182	28	43	9	1	4	21	.236
1958	MIL	85	226	37	50	5	1	7	19	.221
1959	MIL	103	251	26	54	5	0	3	19	.215
1960	MIL	63	148	21	38	7	0	3	11	.257
1961	MIL	45	93	13	20	3	0	1	5	.215
1962	NY-N	141	466	54	128	17	4	11	59	.275
1963	BOS-A	66	178	27	56	8	0	6	15	.315
1964	BOS	133	425	69	123	20	1	30	64	.289
1965	BOS	150	534	60	147	17	2	18	92	.275
1966	HOU-N	77	151	16	33	5	0	6	22	.219
Totals										
11 Years		969	2707	360	707	97	10	89	330	.261
World Series										
1957	MIL-N	4	10	1	0	0	0	0	0	.000

Charles Lenard "Charlie" Neal

Second base. Batted right. Threw right. 5'10", 165 lbs.
Born 1/30/31, Longview, Texas.

In 1957, after 14 consecutive seasons as the Dodger regular shortstop, Pee Wee Reese was moved to third base. Charlie Neal was the man who unseated him.

One of eight black players in the Dodgers 1955 spring-training camp,

Neal was rated by many as the best second-base prospect in baseball, including Brooklyn's Junior Gilliam, the 1953 National League Rookie of the Year. Tabbed as a Rookie-of-the-Year candidate for the upcoming season, Neal was pursued by the Red Sox in 1954 when owner Tom Yawkey offered Brooklyn $125,000 for their young infielder. But Neal was destined to spend the 1955 season with the Montreal Royals. According to New York sportswriter Dick Young, baseball was not yet ready for a team with seven or eight black ballplayers.

Neal finally made the Brooklyn club in 1956 and was named as the second baseman on the *Sporting News* all-rookie team. Following 100 games at shortstop in 1957, Neal was moved back to second during the Dodgers' first season in Los Angeles in 1958. Neal's 22 home runs that season tied Gil Hodges for the team lead, broke Jackie Robinson's team record for a second baseman (19), and made Neal only the third National League second baseman in history to hit 20 or more home runs in a season. (Granny Hamner hit 21 in 1953; Rogers Hornsby did it seven times, with a high of 42 in 1922.) Neal's home-run outburst was surely aided by a screen erected 250 feet down the left-field line of the Dodgers' temporary home, the Los Angeles Coliseum. But Neal's power surge was not limited to left field; that season he was the only right-handed hitter to clear the right-field wall in the Coliseum, a feat he accomplished twice. In addition, he led the Dodgers in runs scored (87) and total bases (207).

Despite his ability with a bat, hitting did not come naturally to Neal. As a child playing softball in Longview, Texas, Neal was afraid of getting hit by the ball when batting. His father and brother helped him overcome his fear by pitching batting practice to him and actually aiming at the young Neal. In time he learned to stand his ground at the plate.

Neal enjoyed his finest all-around season in 1959. He fielded a league-leading .989, tied Junior Gilliam for a team-high 14 stolen bases, and led the team in hits and runs scored. In one game against the Cardinals, he tied a major league record for putouts by a second baseman with 11.

But his crowning moment of 1959 came in the World Series. After committing two errors in Game 1, his two home runs in the second game helped gain the Dodgers gain a split in the series. And one of those home runs made his name the answer to a frequently asked World Series trivia question: Who hit the home run that resulted in a fan knocking a cup of beer on Al Smith's head?

Statistics: *Charlie Neal*

Year	Team	Games	AB	Runs	Hits	2B	3B	HR	RBI	BA
1956	BKN-N	62	136	22	39	5	1	2	14	.287
1957	BKN	128	448	62	121	13	7	12	62	.270
1958	LA-N	140	473	87	120	9	6	22	65	.254

Year	Team	Games	AB	Runs	Hits	2B	3B	HR	RBI	BA
1959	LA	151	616	103	177	30	11*	19	83	.287
1960	LA	139	477	60	122	23	2	8	40	.256
1961	LA	108	341	40	80	6	1	10	48	.235
1962	NY-N	136	508	59	132	14	9	11	58	.260
1963	NY/CIN-N	106	317	28	67	13	1	3	21	.211
Totals										
8 Years		970	3316	461	858	113	38	87	391	.259
World Series										
1956	BKN-N	1	4	0	0	0	0	0	0	.000
1959	LA-N	6	27	4	10	2	0	2	6	.370
Totals										
2 Years		7	31	4	10	2	0	2	6	.323

League leader.

Charles "Charley" Peete

Outfield. Batted left. Threw right. 5'10", 190 lbs. Born 2/22/31, Franklin, Virginia. Died 11/27/56, Caracas, Venezuela.

Charley Peete, a bright prospect in the St. Louis Cardinals organization, was killed in an airplane crash outside of Caracas, Venezuela, in November 1956. En route to Valencia, where he was scheduled to play winter ball, Peete and his wife and three children were among the 25 passengers killed when a commercial plane struck the side of a mountain.

In 1953, following a tour of duty in the army during the Korean War, Peete signed his first minor league contract with Portsmouth of the Piedmont League. In his first at-bat, he hit a 3-2 pitch for a pinch-hit grand slam home run. Peete hit .275 in his first year at Portsmouth, followed by a .311 season in 1954 that included 17 home runs and 79 runs batted in. Blessed with great speed and a strong arm, Peete had 19 outfield assists in 1954.

Signed by the Cardinals organization, Peete hit .317 for Omaha in 1955. In 1956, a split thumb curtailed his stay in St. Louis and made him ineffective against major league pitching. He was sent back to Omaha where he batted .350 and won the American Association batting title.

Statistics: *Charley Peete*

Year	Team	Games	AB	Runs	Hits	2B	3B	HR	RBI	BA
1956	STL-N	23	52	3	10	2	2	0	6	.192

Frank Robinson

Outfield, designated hitter, first base. Batted right.
Threw right. 6'1", 190 lbs. Born 8/31/35, Beaumont,
Texas. Hall of Fame, 1982.

"When I was about 11 years old," Frank Robinson told Cynthia Wilber in her book *For the Love of the Game*, "a wonderful man named George Powles came into my life. . . . He was the *biggest* influence. He felt I had a career in baseball and a life in baseball."

That life began in 1953 and is still going strong. During those 41 years, Robinson has been a National League Rookie of the Year, the first player ever to win the Most Valuable Player award in both the National and American leagues, a Triple Crown winner, the first black manager in major league history, a first-ballot inductee to the Hall of Fame, and an assistant general manager of the Baltimore Orioles.

According to Robinson, Powles, the baseball coach at McClymonds High School in Oakland, California, would "take on kids" for instruction and guidance before they reached high school. Powles became the father Robinson never knew. By the time he was 14 and the youngest player on a championship American Legion team, Robinson was regarded by scouts as having major league potential. Following his graduation from McClymonds High (where he also played basketball with Boston Celtics legend Bill Russell) Robinson was signed by the Cincinnati Reds' Bobby Mattick.

In his first at-bat in the Class C Pioneer League that summer, Robinson tripled, then went on to hit .348 for the Ogden, Utah, ball club. In 1954 he hit .336 with 25 home runs and 110 RBIs for Class A Columbia, South Carolina, of the South Atlantic League. Robinson had all but made the Cincinnati starting lineup when he injured his arm during 1955 spring training.

In pain and unable to throw, Robinson was sent to a dozen doctors, but the injury seemed to defy diagnosis. The arm swelled to twice its normal size. Finally, after months of self-imposed rest, Robinson was able to resume play with Columbia, where he led his team to the league championship by hitting 10 home runs in the final month of play. By the end of the 1956 season, Robinson was the National League Rookie of the Year. He had won a starting berth on the NL All-Star team, led the league in runs scored and game-winning hits, and tied Wally Berger's all-time record for home runs by a rookie, 38. In the off-season, he attended Xavier University.

From 1956 through 1965, Robinson was one of the most potent all-around players in baseball. He averaged more than 32 home runs, 100 RBIs, and 14 stolen bases a season; he batted .303 and led the National League in slugging from 1960 to 1962. In 1961 Robinson was named National League MVP (the first Red to win the award since Frank McCormick in 1940) as he led Cincinnati to its first pennant in 21 years. He was Cincinnati's answer to Willie Mays or Mickey Mantle, a folk hero even to his manager, Birdie Tebbetts, who frequently accused opposing pitchers of throwing at Robinson because he was black. Among the accused, however, were Sam Jones and Ruben Gomez, who, Tebbetts conveniently forgot, were black. Such was Robinson's status until an off-season incident changed the minds of Reds management.

On the evening of February 9, 1961, Robinson was arrested for carrying a concealed weapon during an incident provoked by a chef in a Cincinnati restaurant. The chef, armed with a butcher's knife, had made a threatening gesture toward Robinson, who, responding in defense of himself, brandished a pistol. Robinson was fined $250, but the arrest aroused bad blood between Reds general manager Bill DeWitt and Robinson. DeWitt refused to negotiate contracts with Robinson, who felt that the general manager should have come to his assistance after the arrest.

Management won out. On December 9, 1965 (the day Branch Rickey died at age 83), DeWitt traded Robinson to the Baltimore Orioles for Milt Pappas, Jack Baldschun, and Dick Simpson. When asked to explain the trade, DeWitt said, "Robinson is an old thirty years of age; he has an old body."

The next year, in an even older body and a brand-new uniform, Robinson became the first player since Mickey Mantle in 1956 to win the Triple Crown, was named American League MVP, and hit the World Series–clinching home run in Baltimore's four-game sweep of the Los Angeles Dodgers. Not surprisingly, Robinson continued to age. From 1969 to 1971, he led the Orioles to three consecutive pennants and another world championship.

Robinson concluded his full-time playing career in 1974, hitting 22 home runs at age 39. That fall, Cleveland made him the first black manager in major league history and the first playing manager since Lou Boudreau. While he later managed the San Francisco Giants and the Orioles, Robinson's managerial debut in Cleveland is one of the most memorable in history.

On April 8, 1975, before an opening-day crowd of more than 55,000 in Cleveland's Municipal Stadium, player-manager Robinson homered off Yankee Doc Medich in his first time at bat. "It gave me goose bumps," said Indians first baseman Boog Powell.

Rounding the bases to a standing ovation, Robinson tipped his cap to the crowd as he crossed the plate. "That was for my wife," he said.

Statistics: Frank Robinson

Year	Team	Games	AB	Runs	Hits	2B	3B	HR	RBI	BA
1956	CIN-N	152	572	122*	166	27	6	38	83	.290
1957	CIN	150	611	97	197	29	5	29	75	.322
1958	CIN	148	554	90	149	25	6	31	83	.269
1959	CIN	146	540	106	168	31	4	36	125	.311

Year	Team	Games	AB	Runs	Hits	2B	3B	HR	RBI	BA
1960	CIN	139	464	86	138	33	6	31	83	.297
1961	CIN	153	545	117	176	32	7	37	124	.323
1962	CIN	162	609	134*	208	51*	2	39	136	.342
1963	CIN	140	482	79	125	19	3	21	91	.259
1964	CIN	156	568	103	174	38	6	29	96	.306
1965	CIN	156	582	109	172	33	5	33	113	.296
1966	BAL-A	155	576	122*	182	34	2	49*	122*	.316*
1967	BAL	129	479	83	149	23	7	30	94	.311
1968	BAL	130	421	69	113	27	1	15	52	.268
1969	BAL	148	539	111	166	19	5	32	100	.308
1970	BAL	132	471	88	144	24	1	25	78	.306
1971	BAL	133	455	82	128	16	2	28	99	.281
1972	LA-N	103	342	41	86	6	1	19	59	.251
1973	CAL-A	147	534	85	142	29	0	30	97	.266
1974	CAL/CLE-A	144	477	81	117	27	3	22	68	.245
1975	CLE	49	118	19	28	5	0	9	24	.237
1976	CLE	36	67	5	15	0	0	3	10	.224
Totals										
21 Years		2808	10006	1829	2943	528	72	586	1812	.294

League Championship Series

Year	Team	Games	AB	Runs	Hits	2B	3B	HR	RBI	BA
1969	BAL-A	3	12	1	4	2	0	1	2	.333
1970	BAL	3	10	3	2	0	0	1	2	.200
1971	BAL	3	12	2	1	1	0	0	1	.083
Totals										
3 Years		9	34	6	7	3	0	2	5	.206

World Series

Year	Team	Games	AB	Runs	Hits	2B	3B	HR	RBI	BA
1961	CIN-N	5	15	3	3	2	0	1	4	.200
1966	BAL-A	4	14	4	4	0	1	2	3	.286
1969	BAL	5	16	2	3	0	0	1	1	.188
1970	BAL	5	22	5	6	0	0	2	4	.273
1971	BAL	7	25	5	7	0	0	2	2	.280
Totals										
5 Years		26	92	19	23	2	1	8	14	.250

League leader.

Patricio Athelstan "Pat" Scantlebury

Pitcher. Threw left. Batted left. 6'1", 180 lbs. Born 11/11/25, Gatun, Panama.

Pat Scantlebury was a journeyman pitcher who divided his career between the minor leagues, the Negro leagues, and six games with the Cincinnati Reds in 1956. He was also the last player to go directly from a Negro league team to the majors, though he made that jump in a rather roundabout fashion.

From 1944 through 1950, Scantlebury pitched for the New York Cubans of the Negro National League. Joining organized ball in 1951, Scantlebury won 24 games for Texarkana in 1953. Used frequently as a pinch-hitter and pinch-runner, Scantlebury also managed to hit .300 that season.

Virtually ignored by major league teams, Scantlebury returned to the New York Cubans, where he pitched in 1955. Invited to spring training by Cincinnati, Scantlebury was tabbed by the *Sporting News* as one of the most promising rookie pitchers of 1956. But at 30 Scantlebury hardly seemed like a rookie. As short on patience as they were on pitching, the Reds cut Scantlebury after just 19 innings of work.

Four years later, the Negro American League folded, ending Negro league baseball forever.

Statistics: Pat Scantlebury

Year	Team	W	L	PCT	G	IP	H	BB	SO	ERA	SV
1956	CIN-N	0	1	.000	6	19	24	5	10	6.63	0

Osvaldo Jose "Ozzie" Virgil

Infield. Batted right. Threw right. 6'1", 174 lbs. Born 5/17/33, Montecristi, Dominican Republic.

The first black player to wear the uniform of the Detroit Tigers, Ozzie Virgil made his debut before Tiger fans a game to remember. Acquired by Detroit in January 1958, Virgil had never played a game in Briggs Stadium when manager Bill Norman penciled his name into the lineup of a June 17 night game against the Washington Senators.

Having vowed to "stay loose," Virgil doubled in his first at-bat before 29,794 appreciative fans. He followed that hit with four consecutive singles, finishing the night a perfect five-for-five. "I'd made up my mind that this would be just another ball game," said Virgil afterward. "I'd like one like that every day."

Virgil made his way to the majors in leaps and bounds, jumping from winter ball in the Dominican Republic to Class B, followed by a stop with Class AA Dallas of the Texas League before being called up to the Giants late in the 1956 season. Named to the *Sporting News* all-rookie team as a utility player in 1957, Virgil played every position but pitcher in his nine-year major league career.

One of the first black major leaguers to have a son play in the major leagues, Virgil holds the curious distinction of having played with the last New York Giants team and being traded by the San Francisco Giants before that team played a game.

Statistics: Ozzie Virgil

Year	Team	Games	AB	Runs	Hits	2B	3B	HR	RBI	BA
1956	NY-N	3	12	2	5	1	1	0	2	.417
1957	NY	96	226	26	53	0	2	4	24	.235
1958	DET-A	49	193	19	47	10	2	3	19	.244
1960	DET	62	132	16	30	4	2	3	13	.227
1961	DET/									
	KC-A	31	51	2	7	0	0	1	1	.137
1962	BAL-A	1	0	0	0	0	0	0	0	.000
1965	PIT-N	39	49	3	13	2	0	1	5	.265
1966	SF-N	42	89	7	19	2	0	2	9	.213
1969	SF	1	1	0	0	0	0	0	0	.000
Totals										
9 Years		324	753	75	174	19	7	14	73	.231

William DeKova "Bill" White

First base. Batted left. Threw left. 6', 195 lbs. Born 1/28/34, Lakewood, Florida.

Bill White attributes his success as a major league hitter to an umpire seeking shelter in a sandstorm. In other words, pure serendipity.

Thirty-five years after the fact, White told the story of a chance meeting with umpire Jocko Conlon in 1956. "We played in a little place called Chandler [Arizona] and we had a sandstorm. I had sand in my bathroom.... Somehow it got through, and I happened to walk out and ran into Jocko Conlon. We started talking.

"Jocko came to my room, and he says, 'Kid, you might be a good player one day; let me give you some advice. If a pitcher misses the first pitch when you're hitting, look for a fastball on the second pitch. I've been around here twenty years and I've noticed that if the first pitch is a ball, the next pitch is going to be a fastball.'

"And that's the way I hit for fourteen years. So when I say I couldn't hit the curveball I'm telling the truth. When I say I had an awful lot of trouble — probably couldn't hit a change-up either — I'm telling the truth.

"That's why I only hit .286. Of course, today .286 would be worth $6 million."

Surely the Giants thought White was worth the 1957 equivalent of $6 million when they traded for Jackie Robinson in December 1956. White, playing for Santurce in the Puerto Rican winter league, had just received his Selective Service draft notice, leaving the Giants with a major hole to fill at first base.

Of course, Robinson refused the trade, and the Giants made do with veteran first baseman Whitey Lockman, who hit 15 fewer homers and drove in half as many runs as White had in his rookie season. By the time of his discharge in 1958, White found the Giants in San Francisco and a rookie named Orlando Cepeda with a toehold on first base.

In St. Louis, White ran into another first-base roadblock — namely, Stan Musial — when he was traded to the Cardinals at the end of spring training 1959. But he won a spot in the St. Louis outfield that season, shifted back to first base full time in 1960, and for the next seven years was one of the most productive hitters in the National League.

The only child of a sharecropper family, White was born three miles from the Alabama-Florida state line and grew up in Warren, Ohio, where his father worked in the steel mill and his mother clerked for the air force. Wanting to be a doctor, White attended Hiram College, the second black student in the school's history, and majored in science. An excellent student, he played halfback on the Hiram football team and first base in baseball. White was scouted at Hiram by the Giants' Tony Ravich. "I figured I could make some money in the sport," White recalled 40 years later. "I figured I could make some money in the sport and I could play in the big time, sit down half of the time, and not get beaten up."

White began his professional career with Danville, Virginia, the only black player in the Carolina League in 1952. Repeatedly baited by fans and forced to live and eat alone, White asked to be transferred to St. Cloud, Minnesota. But he was hitting .324, and his manager would not hear of it.

"Perhaps the Giants weren't sensitive to the problems I faced in the Carolina League," White explained in Jackie Robinson's *Baseball Has Done It*. But "the more the fans gave it to me, the harder I hit the ball. . . . They eventually decided to leave me alone, which was a victory over bigotry.

"Taking it out on the ball was, you might say, but one of the psychological effects of segregation on me. The other was — I rebelled. I yelled back at the name callers. I was only 18 and immature."

Immature, perhaps, but as always, White was principled. Five years later, while stationed at Fort Knox, Kentucky, White quit the post baseball team when, after he and another black ballplayer were refused service in an off-post restaurant, his teammates abandoned the two players for the convenience of a whites-only NCO club.

White hit .298 with 20 home runs for Danville in 1952 and followed that with 30 homers the next year with Sioux City in the Western League. After a season with Dallas in 1955, White was promoted to Minneapolis, where he was hitting .293 when he was called up to New York on May 6, 1956. In his first game with the Giants, White became the twenty-sixth player in history to homer in his first major league at-bat. He added a single and a double to his hit total that day as New York lost to White's future employer, the Cardinals.

White's single drove in the tying run in the second 1961 All-Star game, the only midseason classic to end in a tie. After retiring from baseball, White remained in St. Louis, where he broadcast a weekly sports show on KMOX radio. After broadcasting Cardinals games with Harry Carey, White went on to announce for the Yankees and CBS television. On April 1, 1989, he replaced A. Bartlett Giamatti as president of the National League.

Statistics: Bill White

Year	Team	Games	AB	Runs	Hits	2B	3B	HR	RBI	BA
1956	NY-N	138	508	63	130	23	7	22	59	.256
1958	SF-N	26	29	5	7	1	0	1	4	.241
1959	STL-N	138	517	77	156	33	9	12	72	.302
1960	STL	144	554	81	157	27	10	16	79	.283
1961	STL	153	591	89	169	28	11	20	90	.286
1962	STL	159	614	93	199	31	3	20	102	.324
1963	STL	162	658	106	200	26	8	27	109	.304
1964	STL	160	631	92	191	37	4	21	102	.303
1965	STL	148	543	82	157	26	3	24	73	.289
1966	PHI-A	159	577	85	159	23	6	22	103	.276
1967	PHI	110	308	29	77	6	2	8	33	.250
1968	PHI	127	385	34	92	16	2	9	40	.239
1969	STL-N	49	57	7	12	1	0	0	4	.211
Totals										
13 Years		1673	5972	843	1706	278	65	202	870	.286
World Series										
1964	STL	7	27	2	3	1	0	0	2	.111

1957

Frank Barnes

Pitcher. Batted right. Threw right. 6', 170 lbs. Born 8/26/28, Longwood, Mississippi.

Frank Barnes was a professional pitcher for 16 years. He started his career in the Negro American League and finished it in the Mexican League. In between he played on both coasts, in Canada, and all over America's heartland. And more often than not, he won.

Barnes got an early start, making his professional debut at age 18 with the 1947 Indianapolis Clowns of the Negro American League. He also played for the Kansas City Monarchs before being sold to the New York Yankees along with Elston Howard, who later became the first black player to wear Yankee pinstripes.

Barnes had a lot of success in the minor leagues. He went 15-6 with 152 strikeouts in as many innings with Muskegon in 1951 and in 1952 posted a 2.00 ERA with Scranton of the Eastern League. In 1955 he pitched a no-hitter for Oklahoma City in the Texas League. But it was not until 1957 — when he led the American Association with a 2.41 ERA and six shutouts, and broke a 42-year-old record with 41⅓ straight scoreless innings — that he got his first cup of coffee in the major leagues. Back in the minors at Omaha in 1958, Barnes pitched another no-hitter, recording 11 strikeouts in a 3–0 win over Louisville.

While with Omaha, Barnes showed that he was not afraid to dust a hitter off now and again. In a game against Denver, Barnes' brush-back pitches so incensed third-base coach Tommy Lasorda that when Lasorda fielded a foul grounder, he fired it at Barnes' head. Barnes ducked, and the ball sailed into the Omaha dugout where infielder Ed Jok picked it up and fired it into the Denver dugout, setting off a mild melee.

By the time Barnes pitched his first major league game, he was 29. But even after his short major league career was over, he kept on pitching. In fact, he did not stop pitching until he was 45.

Statistics: Frank Barnes

Year	Team	W	L	PCT	G	IP	H	BB	SO	ERA	SV
1957	STL-N	0	1	.000	3	10	13	9	5	4.50	0
1958	STL	1	1	.500	8	19	19	16	17	7.58	0
1960	STL	0	1	.000	4	7.2	8	9	8	3.52	1
Totals											
3 Years		1	3	.250	15	36.2	40	34	30	5.89	1

Bennie Daniels

Pitcher. Batted left. Threw right. 6'1½", 193 lbs. Born 6/17/32, Tuscaloosa, Alabama.

When Dick Rand was asked in 1958 to describe the movement on Bennie Daniels's fastball, he simply wagged his broken left index finger back and forth. "That's the best example I know," said the Columbus Jets catcher. "He broke the finger on my mitt hand, and how often does that happen?"

"I can't be sure myself what it's going to do," Daniels said. Unfortunately, his career was as difficult to control as his fastball. Daniels was brilliant at times, awful at others. He went 12-11 with a team that lost 100 games, but that was the only winning record he posted in nine years in the majors. He was an outstanding hitter and fielder, but he walked almost as many batters as he struck out.

Daniels, a four-sport star at Compton High School in southern California, worked his way through the minors. In 1955 he was one of three black players sent by the Pirates to Huntsville, Texas, to train with the New Orleans Pelicans, an all-white team in the Southern Association. He landed in Class AAA with Hollywood in 1957 and was the Pacific Coast League Rookie of the Year on the strength of a 17-8 record, a .292 batting average, and five home runs. He got called up to start the Pirates' last game of the season and lost a 2–0 decision despite allowing just five hits and one earned run. Pirate management had concerns about Daniels's control, but after a 14-6 season and a 2.31 ERA with Columbus in 1958, he got his first shot at a full major league season. His pitching was erratic, but he hit .310.

After seeing limited duty with the NL champion Pirates in 1960, he was traded to the Washington Senators. He led the team in wins in 1961 and was fourth in the league in complete games. The following year he was the winning pitcher in the first game played at D.C. Stadium, now known as RFK Stadium, then lost 10 straight decisions. In 1964 he shut out the White Sox twice in September, and they wound up second to the Yankees by one game.

Bob Addie of the *Washington Post* wrote that Daniels "baffled his bosses with his often brilliant and then mediocre performances," and by the end of the 1965 season, Senators general manager George Selkirk was frustrated enough with Daniels's inconsistency that he sold the 33-year-old pitcher to the team's Hawaii minor league affiliate. He never made it back to the majors.

Daniels was an affable and popular player, but he could be tough on hitters. In 1959, Cardinal player-manager Solly Hemus, a man not known for his racial tolerance, tabbed himself to pinch-hit against Daniels. According to Cardinal outfielder Curt Flood, Daniels knocked Hemus down with his first pitch. Hemus swung at the second pitch and let his bat fly out to the mound. Daniels's third pitch hit Hemus in the back.

Statistics: Bennie Daniels

Year	Team	W	L	PCT	G	IP	H	BB	SO	ERA	SV
1957	PIT-N	0	1	.000	1	7	5	3	2	1.29	0
1958	PIT	0	3	.000	8	27.2	31	15	7	5.53	0
1959	PIT	7	9	.438	34	100.2	115	39	67	5.45	1
1960	PIT	1	3	.250	10	40.1	52	17	16	7.81	0
1961	WAS-A	12	11	.522	32	212	184	80	110	3.44	0
1962	WAS	7	16	.304	44	161.1	172	68	66	4.85	2
1963	WAS	5	10	.333	35	168.2	163	58	88	4.38	1
1964	WAS	8	10	.444	33	163	147	64	73	3.70	0
1965	WAS	5	13	.278	33	116.1	135	39	42	4.72	1
Totals											
9 Years		45	76	.372	230	997	1004	383	471	4.44	5

Leonard Charles "Lenny" Green

Outfield. Batted left. Threw left. 5'11", 170 lbs. Born 1/6/33, Detroit, Michigan.

Lenny Green made a great first impression.

Four times in his 12-year major league career, Green homered on opening day. He did it three years in a row, 1961–1963, with the Minnesota Twins, then bashed two homers in his first game with the Red Sox in 1964 with President Lyndon Johnson and Vice President Hubert Humphrey looking on. In 1961 he opened the season with a 24-game hitting streak, a Twins record that stood for 19 years, and in 1963 he started the season with a 12-game hitting streak.

Green was quick out of the batter's box too. He ran a 10-flat hundred in high school and led the Washington Senators–Minnesota Twins in stolen bases four years running. Green's speed helped him become an outstanding outfielder, and in 1962 he committed just two errors in 156 games in center field for the Twins.

Green had a journeyman's career in the American League, playing for five teams in 12 years, including two stints with the Baltimore Orioles. He was signed out of a Detroit high school by the St. Louis Browns (who later moved to Baltimore) in 1953 but had to spend two years in the military before beginning his career in Wichita. In 1956 he became one of three black players to break the color line with Columbus, Georgia, of the Sally League. He went on to lead the league with a .318 batting average, and after cracking .300 for most of 1957 with Vancouver, he was called up to Baltimore near the end of the season.

Green was traded to Washington in 1959, and in 1960 he led the team in batting, coming just two hits shy of a .300 season. The team then moved to Minnesota where Green led the Twins in doubles and scored at least 90 runs for the next two seasons. After that, his playing time diminished, and he was traded twice more. The Orioles were set to send him to the minors, but Green got the Red Sox to take a chance on him. He hit almost .400 in spring training and took the center-field job away from Gary Geiger.

On June 13, 1966, the Red Sox acquired two black players, John Wyatt and Jose Tartabull, to increase the number of blacks on their roster to seven. Green was rooming with pitcher Earl Wilson, and that night they figured seven was too many for the Red Sox, the last major league team to integrate. To no one's surprise, the phone rang the next morning, and Wilson and Joe Christopher were traded. Green was released at the end of the season.

Statistics: Lenny Green

Year	Team	Games	AB	Runs	Hits	2B	3B	HR	RBI	BA
1957	BAL-A	19	33	2	6	1	1	1	5	.182
1958	BAL	69	91	10	21	4	0	0	4	.231
1959	BAL/WAS-A	115	214	32	53	6	1	3	17	.248
1960	WAS	127	330	62	97	16	7	5	33	.294
1961	MIN-A	156	600	92	171	28	7	9	50	.285
1962	MIN	158	619	97	168	33	3	14	63	.271
1963	MIN	145	280	41	67	10	1	4	27	.239
1964	MIN/LA-A/									
	BAL-A	79	128	16	27	2	0	2	5	.211
1965	BOS-A	119	373	69	103	24	6	7	24	.276
1966	BOS	85	133	18	32	6	0	1	12	.241
1967	DET-A	58	151	22	42	8	1	1	13	.278
1968	DET	6	4	0	1	0	0	0	0	.250
Totals										
12 Years		1136	2956	461	788	138	27	47	253	.267

John Irvin Kennedy

Infield. Batted right. Threw right. 5'10", 175 lbs. Born 11/23/34, Sumter, South Carolina.

John Kennedy arrived in Philadelphia to a hero's reception. He left almost unnoticed.

In January 1957, Jackie Robinson retired and took a parting shot at those teams—the Phillies, Tigers, and Red Sox—that had yet to promote a black player to the majors. "If thirteen major league teams can come up with colored players, why can't the other three?" he said. The local chapter of the NAACP and other civic organizations had been after the Phillies for several years to integrate.

Kennedy had been a football star at Edward Waters College, once running a kickoff back 102 yards for a touchdown. He had begun his professional baseball career in the Giants organization but was released at the end of the 1953 season after hitting .262 with 30 doubles and 33 stolen bases for St. Cloud in the Northern League. He spent two seasons with the Birmingham Black Barons of the Negro American League, then in 1956 was an NAL all-star shortstop, hitting .385 with 17 home runs for the Kansas City Monarchs.

Late in the season he had a tryout with the Phillies at Connie Mack Stadium, and they invited him to their rookie school the following spring in Clearwater, Florida. Kennedy was impressive enough to make the major league roster and became the last player to make the jump from the Negro leagues to the majors. In early April the Phillies went out and got another black shortstop, Chico Fernandez, from the Dodgers.

Philadelphia's black leaders and others turned out in force to greet Kennedy and Fernandez upon their arrival, and on April 22 Kennedy became the first black to play in a Phillies uniform. His major league career lasted exactly two at-bats and featured a strikeout and an error. He injured his shoulder and was sent down to a Class B team in Thomasville, North Carolina. Fernandez wound up as the Phillies' starting shortstop that season.

Kennedy bounced around the minors for a few years, playing in Des Moines, Jacksonville, Miami, and Tulsa. But he never made it back to the majors. And his departure, according to sportswriter Bob Queen, featured "no great crowd of well-wishers at the station such as the cordon of leaders who met him when he arrived."

Statistics: *John Kennedy*

Year	Team	Games	AB	Runs	Hits	2B	3B	HR	RBI	BA
1957	PHI-N	5	2	1	0	0	0	0	0	.000

Juan Cordova Pizarro

Pitcher. Threw left. Batted left. 5'11", 185 lbs. Born 2/7/38, Santurce, Puerto Rico.

From the time he was 13, when he was a batboy for Santurce in the Puerto Rico League, Juan Pizarro practically lived on the ball field. And for Pizarro, living meant pitching. By the age of 17, he was pitching year round: fall and winter in the Puerto Rican winter league, spring and summers in the minor leagues, and then the majors. One of the most durable pitchers of his era, Pizarro pitched in three decades. Yet for as long and hard as he worked at his trade, many people wondered if Pizarro ever pitched up to his potential.

Pizarro joined the pitching-rich Milwaukee Braves as a 19-year-old rookie in spring training 1957. He was coming off a phenomenal season with Class A Jacksonville, where he went 23-6, struck out 318 batters in 274 innings, and posted a 1.77 ERA. In his first seven starts at Jacksonville, he won five games, lost one, and struck out 95 batters in 63 innings. In a 12-inning 1–0 win against Charlotte, he struck out 21 batters. A few weeks later he beat Columbus 1–0, striking out 17. Pizarro easily won the South Atlantic League's MVP award in 1956. He was 18 and had just completed his first year in organized ball.

Pizarro arrived at the Braves' Bradenton, Florida, spring-training site to considerable fanfare. Milwaukee manager Fred Haney called him "another Warren Spahn"; others said he was the fastest pitcher since Bob Feller. On the morning of March 13, outside Mrs. K. W. Gibson's boardinghouse, where the team's black players lived, Bob Wolf of the *Sporting News* asked Pizarro what he had to improve on in 1957. "Nothing," Pizarro replied. And based on what everyone had seen of the rookie, it was hard to disagree.

Pizarro lived up to expectations that spring and made the Braves roster. Although Haney planned to use him primarily in relief, Pizarro was given an occasional starting assignment. On May 4 he scattered seven hits in a 1–0 loss to Vern Law and the Pirates. By the end of the season, Pizarro showed poise and potential that belied his record and his ERA. The Braves went on to beat the Yankees in seven games in the World Series. And with a pitching staff of Warren Spahn, Lew Burdette, Bob Buhl, Don McMahon, and the rookie Pizarro, they seemed like a dynasty in the making.

Pizarro spent the 1957-58 winter league developing a curveball to complement his screwball (a pitch he learned from the Giants' Ruben Gomez) and his blazing fastball (which he perfected as a teenager by throwing rocks at bottles). Throwing curveballs 50 percent of the time, Pizarro set a Puerto Rico League record, striking out 19 batters in one game. (Satchel Paige and Bob Turley each struck out 18 in 1937 and 1954, respectively.) In his next three starts, Pizarro pitched a no-hitter (striking out 11), a two-hitter, and a one-hitter.

Pizarro took a 14-5 record and a 1.32 ERA to the Braves camp that spring. But the 178 innings he had pitched during winter ball seemed to have taken their toll. Pizarro started the season with Class AAA Wichita and was called up to the Braves after coming within one strike of pitching a no-hitter.

From 1958 through 1960, Pizarro showed flashes of brilliance. On July 3, 1959, he pitched a two-hit shutout against the Pirates, striking out 11. Disappointed with his inconsistency, however, Milwaukee traded him to Chicago.

Over the next four seasons, Pizarro's career flourished in the American League. His 19 wins in 1964 were second in the AL to teammate Gary Peters's 20. But while he seemed to thrive on work, over the next 10 seasons he never pitched more than 118 innings as he bounced among seven major league teams.

Along with Dennis Lamp, Pizarro shares the distinction of being the only pitcher to throw one-hitters against both the Chicago Cubs and the White Sox.

Statistics: Juan Pizarro

Year	Team	W	L	PCT	G	IP	H	BB	SO	ERA	SV
1957	MIL-N	5	6	.455	24	99.1	99	51	68	4.62	0
1958	MIL	6	4	.600	16	96.2	75	47	84	2.70	1
1959	MIL	6	2	.750	29	133.2	117	70	126	3.77	0
1960	MIL	6	7	.462	21	114.2	105	72	88	4.55	0
1961	CHI-A	14	7	.667	39	194.2	164	89	188	3.05	2
1962	CHI	12	14	.462	36	203.1	182	97	173	3.81	1
1963	CHI	16	8	.667	32	214.2	177	66	163	2.39	1
1964	CHI	19	9	.679	33	239	193	55	162	2.56	0
1965	CHI	6	3	.667	18	97	96	37	65	3.43	0
1966	CHI	8	6	.571	34	88.2	91	39	42	3.76	3
1967	PIT-N	8	10	.444	50	107	99	52	96	3.95	9
1968	PIT/BOS-A	7	9	.438	31	118.2	111	54	90	3.56	2
1969	BOS/CLE-A/										
	OAK-A	4	5	.444	57	99.1	84	58	52	3.35	7
1970	CHI-N	0	0	.000	12	16	16	9	14	4.50	1
1971	CHI	7	6	.538	16	101	78	40	67	3.48	0
1972	CHI	4	5	.444	16	59	66	32	24	3.97	1
1973	CHI/HOU-N	2	3	.400	17	27.1	34	12	13	7.24	0
1974	PIT-N	1	1	.500	7	24	20	11	7	1.88	0
Totals											
18 Years		131	105	.555	488	2034	1807	888	1522	3.43	28
League Championship Series											
1974	PIT-N	0	0	.000	1	.2	0	1	1	0.00	0
World Series											
1957	MIL-N	0	0	.000	1	1.2	3	2	1	10.80	0
1958	MIL-N	0	0	.000	1	1.2	2	1	3	5.40	0
Totals											
2 Years		0	0	.000	2	3.1	5	3	4	8.10	0

Lawrence Glenn Hope "Larry" Raines

Infield. Batted right. Threw right. 5'10", 165 lbs. Born
3/9/30, St. Albans, West Virginia. Died 1/28/78,
Lansing, Michigan.

A cynical Cleveland Indians fan might say that Larry Raines made two
significant contributions to baseball. He gave third base back to Al Smith, and
he gave number 9 back to Minnie Minoso.

Raines was the *Sporting News* all-rookie third baseman in 1957, despite
the fact that he played only 27 games at that position. But he made the
team on the strength of his bat, not his glove, as Cleveland manager Kirby Farrell knew all too well. By June, Raines was the sixth player Farrell had tried
at third. The job was his to lose, which he did, because of his fielding, to
Smith.

The next year, when the Indians reacquired Minnie Minoso from the
White Sox, Raines was wearing number 9, the number that Minoso had worn
in Chicago. Minoso asked Raines to switch numbers with him, and Raines
obliged. Wearing his number 9, Minoso hit .302 in 1958. Raines wore number
16, went to bat nine times with no hits, and disappeared from the major
leagues forever.

An Abe Saperstein discovery, Raines began his professional baseball
career in Japan, where he batted .328 and .345 in 1953 and 1954, respectively.
Playing primarily shortstop with Class AAA Indianapolis in 1956, Raines hit
.309 with 22 stolen bases. When the Indians opened camp in the spring of
1957, the rookie headliners were Raines and an outfielder from that same Indianapolis club, Roger Maris, whose 61 home runs in 1961 broke Babe Ruth's
single-season record for round-trippers.

Curiously, Raines' fielding improved dramatically once the Indians sent
him back to the minors in 1958. He overcame his habit of flipping the ball
across the infield and learned to "fire" it. By the end of the season, he was hitting over .300 with San Diego, where he was playing the best shortstop in the
Pacific Coast League.

Statistics: Larry Raines

Year	Team	Games	AB	Runs	Hits	2B	3B	HR	RBI	BA
1957	CLE-A	96	244	39	64	14	0	2	16	.262
1958	CLE	7	9	0	0	0	0	0	0	.000
Totals										
2 Years		103	253	39	64	14	0	2	16	.253

Kenneth Andre Ian Rodgers

Shortstop. Batted right. Threw right. 6'3", 195 lbs.
Born 12/2/34, Nassau, Bahamas.

Cubs fans know Andre Rodgers as the man who replaced Ernie Banks at shortstop. To San Francisco Giants fans, he was the player sent to the minors to make room for a 21-year-old rookie named Willie McCovey. But to Bahamanians, Andre Rodgers was the cricket player who never gave himself the chance to be as good as his father.

Rodgers, the son of a famous Bahamian cricket player, captained the St. John's College cricket team in Nassau. Although he had participated in softball, Rodgers had never actually played baseball when he was recommended to the Giants by a Nassau businessman who did not know the difference between the two games. In the spring of 1954, when Rodgers arrived in Melbourne, Florida, to try out for the Giants, New York's minor league director, Hall-of-Fame pitcher Carl Hubbell, thought someone was pulling his leg. A cricket player? A cricket player who had never played baseball? But Hubbell gave Rodgers a chance, and the cricket player stuck.

Rodgers's transition to baseball was remarkable. In his first year in organized ball, with Olean in the Pony League, he hit .286. The next year, with St. Cloud, he won the Northern League batting title with a .387 average, driving in 111 runs and hitting 28 home runs, one shy of the league leader, teammate Leon Wagner.

Promoted to Dallas in 1956, Rodgers was rudely introduced to the phenomenon known as the curveball. But he still managed to finish the season with a .267 batting average, 21 home runs, and the reputation as the best-fielding shortstop in the league.

In 1957, Rodgers was invited to the Giants' spring-training camp because Bill White, Jackie Brandt and the team's top minor league prospect, Willie Kirkland, had been drafted into military service. When he arrived in Arizona, Rodgers was asked if he thought he could hit major league pitching. "I cannot say," he answered. "I have never seen it." And while Rodgers's true love remained cricket, he knew his baseball history. "The team is a very old organization," he said of the Giants, "and it was a distinction to be asked to play for it."

But the feeling was mutual. Rodgers proved himself to be a solid all-around player. Veteran second baseman Red Schoendienst was just one of many players who were impressed with the rookie's skills. Batting fourth, behind Willie Mays, Rodgers hit two home runs—the second a tape-measure shot—in one game against Baltimore Orioles veteran Connie Johnson. The Giants, considered mediocre at best the previous winter when Jackie Robinson retired rather than accept a trade from Brooklyn to New York, were the talk of the Cactus League. At the start of the 1957 season, Rodgers and Juan Pizarro were the top two rookies in the National League.

But Rodgers's promise was short-lived. Inconsistent play and a leg injury consigned him to the bench, and after just 32 games he was optioned to the American Association. By mid–June, however, he had hit in 20 consecutive games and raised his batting average to .400. That earned Rodgers a promotion to Spokane of the Pacific Coast League where in his first 28 at-bats he collected 19 hits, including six home runs in seven games, for a .672 average.

After hitting .354 with 31 homers and a league-leading 295 total bases, Rodgers was recalled to the Giants, now relocated in San Francisco, at the end of the 1958 season. Rodgers remained with the Giants until July 31, 1959, when he was sent down to Phoenix to make room for Willie McCovey.

Despite hitting .438 as a pinch-hitter (seven for sixteen) with the Giants in 1960, Rodgers was traded to the Braves on October 31 for Alvin Dark, whom the Giants immediately hired as their manager. By the end of spring training in 1961, however, he was traded again, this time to the Cubs for Moe Drabowsky and Seth Morehead. Rodgers made an opportunity for himself with Chicago, and in 1962 replaced "Mr. Cub," future Hall-of-Famer Ernie Banks, as the team's regular shortstop.

Statistics: Andre Rodgers

Year	Team	Games	AB	Runs	Hits	2B	3B	HR	RBI	BA
1957	NY-N	32	86	8	21	2	1	3	9	.244
1958	SF-N	22	63	7	13	3	1	2	11	.206
1959	SF	71	228	32	57	12	1	6	24	.250
1960	SF	81	217	22	53	8	5	2	22	.244
1961	CHI-N	73	214	27	57	17	0	6	23	.266
1962	CHI	138	461	40	128	20	8	5	44	.278
1963	CHI	150	516	51	118	17	4	5	33	.229
1964	CHI	129	448	50	107	17	3	12	46	.239
1965	PIT-N	75	178	17	51	12	0	2	25	.287
1966	PIT	36	49	6	9	1	0	0	4	.184
1967	PIT	47	61	8	14	3	0	2	4	.230
Totals										
11 Years		854	2521	268	628	112	23	45	245	.249

John Junior Roseboro

Catcher. Batted left. Threw right. 5'11", 195 lbs. Born 5/13/33, Ashland, Ohio.

Johnny Roseboro followed the same carefully charted route to the Brooklyn Dodgers that virtually every black player before him had taken. From

1952 through 1955, Roseboro played in America's heartland with teams in Illinois, Wisconsin, and Colorado. He was often the only black person in the community, suffering the consequences of de facto segregation.

But as early as 1956 Roseboro was being touted as the likely successor to Brooklyn's future Hall-of-Famer catcher Roy Campanella. Following a season in Montreal, he was one of five young catchers in the 1957 Dodgertown spring-training camp where, as he states in his *Glory Days with the Dodgers and Other Days with Others*, players "were segregated by ability, not by color." And with his ability Roseboro was clearly the man to beat. But by opening day he was back in Montreal in need of some finishing touches.

By the latter part of the 1957 season, Brooklyn's plans for the 24-year-old catcher were right on schedule. He was called up to the Dodgers with enough games left in the season for him to benefit from Campanella's wisdom and advice. The Dodgers finished a respectable third to the Braves in 1957, with prospects for 1958 looking even brighter.

As the organization prepared to move to Los Angeles, there was no reason to believe that Campy would not continue to tutor his successor in much the same way that the Yankees' Bill Dickey and Yogi Berra worked with Elston Howard in the years 1955–1957. But when Campanella was paralyzed in an auto accident in late 1957, Roseboro was thrust into a starting role, ready or not.

Despite their new image and their sunny new climate, the Los Angeles Dodgers looked, more than ever, like the "Bums" of Flatbush. Playing their home games in the Los Angeles Coliseum, a cavernous football arena originally built for the 1932 Olympics, the Dodgers finished in seventh place, 21 games behind league-leading Milwaukee. But Roseboro quietly did the job required of him, hitting .271 and leading all catchers in total fielding chances per game, a category in which he led the league in five of his 10 years with Los Angeles.

The following season the Dodgers won it all, and despite a very mediocre year at the plate, Roseboro pulled together a pitching staff that carried L.A. to a tie for the pennant, a two-game playoff sweep of the Braves, and a World Series championship in six games over the Chicago White Sox.

From 1958 to 1967, Roseboro worked one of the best pitching staffs of all time. Sandy Koufax, Don Drysdale, Johnny Podres, Ron Perranoski, Larry Sherry, Claude Osteen, Don Sutton, Phil Regan — all had the luxury of pitching to Roseboro, the most skilled backstop of the 1960s. Roseboro caught each of Koufax's four no-hitters, every inning of the Dodgers' four-game sweep of the Yankees in the 1963 World Series and their seven-game Series win over the Minnesota Twins two years later. In 1962, he hit the last National League home run in the major leagues' ill-fated twice-a-year All-Star competition.

Along with relief ace Perranoski, Roseboro was traded to the Twins in the fall of 1967 in exchange for Zoilo Versalles and Mudcat Grant. Two years later, with Roseboro leading AL catchers in double plays, Dave Boswell and Jim Perry each won 20 games, Jim Kaat won 14, and Perranoski saved a league-leading

31 as the Twins, under first-year manager Billy Martin, won the first-ever American League West Division title.

　　Whatever Roseboro accomplished behind the plate and in the way he "handled" pitchers, one pitcher whom he never caught will always be linked with Roseboro's name. On August 22, 1965, in one of the ugliest donnybrooks in baseball history, the Dodgers came close to losing Roseboro for the rest of the season, possibly forever. The game featured a wild exchange of brush-back pitches by two future Hall-of-Famers, Juan Marichal of the Giants and Roseboro's batterymate Sandy Koufax. Believing that Roseboro was partly to blame for Koufax's contribution to the fray—or at the very least in retaliation against Koufax—Marichal came up to bat, settled into the batter's box, then turned and clobbered Roseboro over the head with his bat. Roseboro threw off his catching mask and came up swinging. Marichal, bat still in hand, tried to thwart Roseboro's punches as both benches emptied. Marichal was suspended for nine games and fined $1,750, then the largest fine in league history.

Statistics: John Roseboro

Year	Team	Games	AB	Runs	Hits	2B	3B	HR	RBI	BA
1957	BKN-N	35	69	6	10	2	0	2	6	.145
1958	LA-N	114	384	52	104	11	9	14	43	.271
1959	LA	118	397	39	92	14	7	10	38	.232
1960	LA	103	287	22	61	15	3	8	42	.213
1961	LA	128	394	59	99	16	6	18	59	.251
1962	LA	128	389	45	97	16	7	7	55	.249
1963	LA	135	470	50	111	13	7	9	49	.236
1964	LA	134	414	42	119	24	1	3	45	.287
1965	LA	136	437	42	102	10	0	8	57	.233
1966	LA	142	445	47	123	23	2	9	53	.276
1967	LA	116	334	37	91	18	2	4	24	.272
1968	MIN-A	135	380	31	82	12	0	8	39	.216
1969	MIN	115	361	33	95	12	0	3	32	.263
1970	WAS-A	46	86	7	20	4	0	1	6	.233
Totals										
14 Years		1585	4847	512	1206	190	44	104	548	.249
League Championship Series										
1969	MIN-A	2	5	0	1	0	0	0	0	.200
World Series										
1959	LA-A	6	21	0	2	0	0	0	1	.095
1963	LA	4	14	1	2	0	0	1	3	.143
1965	LA	7	21	1	6	1	0	0	3	.286
1966	LA	4	14	0	1	0	0	0	0	.071
Totals										
4 Years		21	70	2	11	1	0	1	7	.157

Valmy Thomas

Catcher. Batted right. Threw right. 5'9", 160 lbs. Born 10/21/39, St. Thomas, Virgin Islands.

Valmy Thomas holds the distinction of being the last starting catcher for the New York Giants and the first backup catcher for the San Francisco Giants.

Thomas was the Giants' surprise player of 1957. "I didn't know a thing about Thomas when I first saw him in camp this spring," New York manager Bill Rigney told the Pittsburgh *Courier*. "I'd never seen him. All I knew was that Eddie Stanky at Minneapolis didn't keep him."

Thomas learned baseball by playing a Virgin Islands version of stickball with a shaved tennis ball and a broomstick handle when he was 13. He started playing professionally in Puerto Rico, where he was signed to a Class D league contract in the Pittsburgh Pirates farm system. When Thomas and the Pirates could not agree on a contract after the 1954 season, the catcher remained in Puerto Rico and played for Herman Franks, who recommended him to Horace Stoneham of the Giants. When Thomas told Stoneham that he wanted to return to the United States to play ball, he was drafted by New York in 1955.

But do not mention Valmy Thomas to Philadelphia Phillies fans. On December 3, 1958, Philadelphia traded Jack Sanford, a 19-game winner in 1957, to San Francisco in exchange for the Giants battery of Thomas and an aging Ruben Gomez. Thomas lasted only one season with the Phils, Gomez two. Thomas hit .200; Gomez won three games and lost 11. Sanford, meanwhile, won 89 games in 6½ years with the Giants, including 24 wins in San Francisco's pennant-winning 1962 season.

On the surface, Philadelphia had every reason to make the trade. Thomas looked like a catcher of major league caliber. As Philadelphia general manager Roy Hamey put it, "I'm particularly fond of Thomas because he's aggressive, has a good arm and he livens up a ball club."

And Thomas half concurred. "Baseball is a funny game," he once said. "You get lucky and the next thing you know things are going your way."

Statistics: *Valmy Thomas*

Year	Team	Games	AB	Runs	Hits	2B	3B	HR	RBI	BA
1957	NY-N	88	241	30	60	10	3	6	31	.249
1958	SF-N	63	143	14	37	5	0	3	16	.259
1959	PHI-N	66	140	5	28	2	0	1	7	.200
1960	BAL-A	8	16	0	1	0	0	0	0	.063
1961	CLE-A	27	86	7	18	3	0	2	6	.209
Totals										
5 Years		252	626	56	144	20	3	12	60	.230

Rene Gutierrez Valdes

Pitcher. Threw right. Batted right. 6'3", 175 lbs. Born 6/2/29, Guanabocco, Cuba.

Along with Brooklyn-born Sandy Koufax, Rene Valdes of Cuba was the talk of the Dodgers' 1957 spring training camp. Coming off a 22-win season in the Pacific Coast League in 1956, Valdes held out for a better contract before reporting to Vero Beach. And throughout spring training, Valdes looked as impressive as any new pitcher in camp. Faster than Koufax, with better control and an excellent curveball, Valdes was a member of the Dodger pitching staff when the team opened its final season in Brooklyn.

Known as "El Latigo" (the whip), Valdes got his start in professional ball in Cuba where he played under his given name, Gutierrez (y Valdes). In his first three years in organized ball, from 1952 to 1954, playing under the name Valdes because, as El Latigo said, "the newspaper reporters can say it," he won 19, 19, and 20 games, respectively.

But the promise Valdes showed in the spring waned. After giving up a game-winning hit to the Braves' Ernie Johnson, the opposing pitcher, Valdes was sent back to Montreal. While he never played in the majors again, Valdes teamed with Tommy Lasorda and Sparky Anderson to lead the Royals to the International League pennant in 1958.

Earlier that spring in Dodgertown, a reporter, noticing that Valdes sported an unusually large amount of gray hair for a 29-year-old, asked the pitcher how long he thought he could stand to wait to make the major leagues again. Valdes asked how old Satchel Paige was when he made the majors. "About fifty," answered the reporter.

"Satchel Paige wait," replied Valdes, "I can wait."

He waited.

Statistics: Rene Valdes

Year	Team	W	L	PCT	G	IP	H	BB	SO	ERA	SV
1957	BKN-N	1	1	.500	5	13	13	7	10	5.54	0

1958

Felipe Rojas Alou

Outfield. Batted right. Threw right. 6'1", 195 lbs. Born 5/12/35, Haina, Dominican Republic.

Felipe Alou arrived in the United States with a trunkload of talent but with a slew of roadblocks in his way. To make the majors, Alou would have to deal with racial and ethnic prejudice, learn a new language, and hit the good breaking stuff. He did it all, but unlike his brothers Matty and Jesus, he made some noise along the way.

Alou holds the distinction of kicking off what later became a flood of major league talent from the Dominican Republic. Ozzie Virgil was born there but moved at an early age and was a U.S. citizen by the time he made the majors in 1957. Alou was all Dominican, having been a member of his nation's Olympic sprint team. The Giants were active in scouting Caribbean players in the mid–1950s, and they signed Alou in 1956. He hit .380 to lead the Florida State League that season and was among the beneficiaries of a group of fans that knew how to show their appreciation. They passed the hat for outstanding efforts. Once, Alou hit a game-winning three-run homer with two outs in the bottom of the ninth and was presented with $89 from grateful fans.

But his first problem was the language. He had been sent English books and records before his arrival but said they were not much help, especially in the South. "When I got to the U.S., I found that English is English but that what Americans speak is American," he said. "Nowhere on the records or in the textbooks was there anything similar to, 'Y'all come'n back tumarrah, heah?'"

Less amusing were the constant knockdown pitches on the field and degradation off the field. "Pitchers—even some from my own team—used me for target practice," he said. "Once I overheard several of my teammates instructing pitchers on another team what pitches I had been hitting well and what pitches had been giving me trouble." The situation threatened to unnerve Alou, who by his own admission had a "volcanic" temper. He got help from his manager, former Giants second baseman Buddy Kerr, and teammate

Julio Navarro. "When opposing pitchers would throw at me, Buddy would come out on the field ready to defend me," Alou said. "He would tell me that I was a good prospect and that if I didn't let the race situation bother me I would make it to the majors. . . . He told me of others who had persevered and made it." Navarro coached Alou on being black in the American South. "He counseled me daily, telling me about things I could and could not do, places I could and could not go because my skin was tan, something that supposedly made me inferior to people whose skin was white."

A particularly ugly incident outside a Cocoa Beach restaurant pushed Alou almost over the edge. The restaurant owner called the police after a waitress told Alou and two black teammates that they could eat in their car in the parking lot. The policeman told Alou to get out of the car, then threatened to drag him out. "I wasn't going to get out, no matter what," he said. "Too often I had been made to feel ashamed of the color of my skin. . . . I was willing to die right there rather than make any further concessions." Kerr came out and defused the situation, but Alou said, "That night I knew a loneliness and despair that made me ache all over."

Alou decided to channel his anger into his hitting, and it paid off. He made it to the majors midway through the 1958 season and soon became a regular in one of baseball's first all-black outfields — Willie Mays in center, Willie Kirkland in right, and Alou in left. His breakout season came in 1962, as the Giants beat the Dodgers in a three-game playoff for the NL pennant, then beat the Yankees in a classic seven-game World Series. Alou led a stellar lineup with a .316 average, and had career highs in home runs and RBIs.

After the 1962 season, Alou went to the Dominican Republic to play in a three-game series against a team of Cuban all-stars. The series was arranged by Dominican government officials in hopes of easing the political unrest that reigned that winter. But Commissioner Ford Frick didn't take to the idea, and Alou received word that he and the other major-leaguers who planned to play would be fined unless they pulled out. The nation's president, Dr. Rafael Bonelli, issued a statement: "I am the president of the Dominican Republic, and I say that it is all right to play." That was all Alou needed. He played — and was fined $250 by Frick.

Alou was an outspoken advocate for the rights of Latin American players throughout his career. After the fine, he "voiced the opinion that Latin ballplayers would remain misunderstood until we had some representation in the office of the commissioner." In 1965 Cuban baseball executive Bobby Maduor was hired to handle Latin American affairs by new commissioner William D. Eckert.

Alou was traded away from the Giants and his two brothers before the 1964 season, and a knee injury limited his playing time with Milwaukee. But when the team moved to Atlanta in 1966, Alou was reborn. He led the NL in at-bats, hits, runs scored, and total bases, and his .327 batting average was second in the league to brother Matty. He also had a career-high 31 home runs, and to cap the year off, in July his son Moises was born.

Alou was traded four times in his final six years in the majors. In 1992 he hit the big leagues again, this time as manager of the Montreal Expos. And once again he had family nearby; Moises was the team's starting left fielder.

Statistics: Felipe Alou

Year	Team	Games	AB	Runs	Hits	2B	3B	HR	RBI	BA
1958	SF-N	75	182	21	46	9	2	4	16	.253
1959	SF	95	247	38	68	13	2	10	33	.275
1960	SF	106	322	48	85	17	3	8	44	.264
1961	SF	132	415	59	120	19	0	18	52	.289
1962	SF	154	561	96	177	30	3	25	98	.316
1963	SF	157	565	75	159	31	9	20	82	.281
1964	MIL-N	121	415	60	105	26	3	9	51	.253
1965	MIL	143	555	80	165	29	2	23	78	.297
1966	ATL-N	154	666*	122*	218*	32	6	31	74	.327
1967	ATL	140	574	76	157	26	3	15	43	.274
1968	ATL	160	662*	72	210*	37	5	11	57	.317
1969	ATL	123	476	54	134	13	1	5	32	.282
1970	OAK-A	154	575	70	156	25	3	8	55	.271
1971	OAK/									
	NY-A	133	469	52	135	21	6	8	69	.288
1972	NY-A	120	324	33	90	18	1	6	37	.278
1973	NY-A/									
	MON-N	112	328	29	76	13	0	5	31	.232
1974	MIL-A	3	3	0	0	0	0	0	0	.000
Totals										
17 Years		2082	7339	985	2101	359	49	206	852	.286
League Championship Series										
1969	ATL-N	1	1	0	0	0	0	0	0	.000
World Series										
1962	SF-N	7	26	2	7	1	1	0	1	.269

*League leader.

Ruben Amaro

**Shortstop. Batted right. Threw right. 5'11", 170 lbs.
Born 1/6/36, Veracruz, Mexico.**

Baseball often runs in families, though rarely so strongly as in the Amaro clan.

Ruben was the first to play in the majors, and he played the longest—11 years. He did not hit as well as his father, Santos, or run as well as his son Ruben, Jr., but as manager Johnny Keane put it, "He'll play well anywhere they let him use a glove."

Amaro's father was a hard-hitting outfielder whose playing and managing career spanned 25 years in Mexico and Cuba. Amaro was a light-hitting shortstop whose career was plagued by injuries. But his outstanding glove and versatility kept him in the big leagues longer than his bat alone could have warranted. "It is too bad," Amaro said, "that the son did not inherit more of his [father's] batting ability."

Amaro got his start in professional baseball with Mexicali in 1954 and broke into the majors with the 1958 St. Louis Cardinals. He was traded to the Phillies in 1960 and for half a dozen years played wherever the team needed him. In 1961 manager Gene Mauch said Amaro had "the best year I ever saw a major league shortstop have." In 1964 he played all four infield positions and a game in the outfield and had his best season at the plate. But it was not enough as the Phillies suffered the greatest late-season collapse in baseball history. Amaro's consolation prize was a Gold Glove award at shortstop, even though he played only 79 games at short all season.

When Yankees shortstop Tony Kubek was forced to retire after the 1965 season, they traded for Amaro. But in his fifth game as a Yankee he collided with outfielder Tom Tresh and missed the rest of the season with torn knee ligaments. The following year he solidified the Yankee infield and led American League shortstops in chances per game.

But after spending 1969 as a part-time player with the Angels, Amaro was released. He had played just 41 games that season, but his versatility was intact as he once again played all four infield positions.

Statistics: Ruben Amaro

Year	Team	Games	AB	Runs	Hits	2B	3B	HR	RBI	BA
1958	STL-N	40	76	8	17	2	1	0	0	.224
1960	PHI-N	92	264	25	61	9	1	0	16	.231
1961	PHI	135	381	34	98	14	9	1	32	.257
1962	PHI	79	226	24	55	10	0	0	19	.243
1963	PHI	115	217	25	47	9	2	2	19	.217
1964	PHI	129	299	31	79	11	0	4	34	.264
1965	PHI	118	184	26	39	7	0	0	15	.212
1966	NY-A	14	23	0	5	0	0	0	3	.217
1967	NY	130	417	31	93	12	0	1	17	.223
1968	NY	47	41	3	5	1	0	0	0	.122
1969	CAL-A	41	27	4	6	0	0	0	1	.222
Totals										
11 Years		940	2155	211	505	75	13	8	156	.234

Ellis Narrington Burton

Outfield. Batted both. Threw right. 5'11", 160 lbs.
Born 8/12/36, Los Angeles, California.

Ellis Burton had speed, a fine glove, and could switch-hit. Unfortunately, he never made contact from either side of the plate often enough to satisfy the five major league organizations for whom he played. In 556 lifetime at-bats in the majors, he struck out 117 times.

Burton did have his moments, however. Twice in the majors he hit home runs from both sides of the plate in a single game, a feat at the time matched only by Mickey Mantle and Jim Russell. And on May 3, 1961, Burton did something no player in organized baseball had ever done; he hit home runs from both sides of the plate in a single inning. Playing for Toronto against Jersey City, Burton slammed a two-run shot left-handed, then hit a grand slam right-handed in a 10-run inning.

Burton signed with the Pirates in 1955 but never made it past Class B with Pittsburgh. The Cardinals drafted him in 1957, but in two late-season stints he fanned 22 times in 58 at-bats. He was traded after the 1960 season to the expansion Los Angeles Angels, but never appeared in an Angels uniform. After hitting .286 with 15 homers at Louisville in 1962, he was drafted by another expansion team, the Houston Colt .45s. Burton had played for the minor league Houston Buffs in 1958 and liked it there, so he moved his home to Houston. But although he hit .307 and led Houston in doubles, triples, and home runs in spring training, he was sold to Cleveland before the season started. "I was amazed," Burton said. "I don't know what more I could have done."

Burton started the season as the Indians' regular right fielder, and manager Birdie Tebbetts was excited by his "terrific, usable speed." But Burton did not hit, and he was fined for missing the team flight twice in a matter of days. He was traded again, this time to the Cubs. Chicago gave Burton his first real shot at a starting job, this time in center field, but his 12 home runs could not offset a .230 batting average, and he spent most of his final two years in the majors in the dugout.

After baseball he went into banking and in 1974 became manager of the Bank of America in Burbank, California.

Statistics: Ellis Burton

Year	Team	Games	AB	Runs	Hits	2B	3B	HR	RBI	BA
1958	STL	8	30	5	7	0	1	2	4	.233
1960	STL	29	5	5	6	1	0	0	2	.214
1963	CLE/									
	CHI-N	119	353	51	80	19	1	13	42	.227

Year	Team	Games	AB	Runs	Hits	2B	3B	HR	RBI	BA
1964	CHI-N	42	105	12	20	3	2	2	7	.190
1965	CHI-N	17	40	6	7	1	0	0	4	.175
Totals										
5 Years		215	556	79	120	25	4	17	59	.216

Orlando Manuel Cepeda

**First base. Batted right. Threw right. 6'2", 210 lbs.
Born 9/17/37, Ponce, Puerto Rico.**

When Orlando Cepeda broke into organized baseball, the Giants played in the Polo Grounds, the game was on grass, and pitchers still hit. By the time he was done, the Giants played in Candlestick Park, artificial turf was all the rage, and the letters *DH* had meaning.

In between, Cepeda's career provided a powerful and colorful bridge into baseball's new era. He was the most popular player virtually wherever he played. After his rookie season with the Giants in 1958, the San Francisco *Examiner* conducted a poll asking readers to name their favorite Giant. Cepeda got 18,701 votes. A guy named Mays finished second with 11,510. In January 1959, Santurce Crabber fans passed the hat to pay a $200 fine Cepeda had incurred for throwing a ball into the stands after being pelted with bottles and fruit by hostile Mayaguez fans.

Cepeda was the glue that held together a diverse group of Cardinals long enough to win back-to-back pennants in 1967 and 1968, and upon his arrival in Atlanta in 1969, the Braves won a division title.

But Cepeda's career was not all cheering crowds and clubhouse harmony. He battled nagging knee injuries for years, as well as a reputation as a hothead and a malingerer, a rap many Latin American players faced in the 1950s and 1960s. Umpire Babe Pinelli even went so far as to label Cepeda a "walking powder keg" and a "crybaby" in an article he wrote in 1959. Cepeda's most notorious outburst came as a rookie when he grabbed a bat and went after Pirate manager Danny Murtaugh, who had thrown a punch at Giants pitcher Ruben Gomez. Gomez was a close friend of Cepeda's father and had taken the rookie under his wing. Cepeda had his share of run-ins with umpires, but most came early in his career.

The questions about his work ethic stung, and the evidence suggests it was a bum rap. After knee surgery sidelined him for most of the 1965 season, Cepeda played in at least 142 games for each of the next five seasons. Curt Flood remembered Cepeda playing with a case of the flu that was so severe he could barely hold his head up. "Orlando, goddamnit, you've got to take a couple days off," Flood told him. "You're going to kill yourself." "I don't want them to think I'm faking," Cepeda replied. And after coming out of retirement in 1973 to become the Red Sox's designated hitter, Cepeda rode a stationary bike between at-bats to keep his battered knees loose.

Hitting was Cepeda's birthright. He was the son of Pedro Cepeda, the man known as the "Babe Ruth of Puerto Rico" and as "The Bull," which earned Orlando the nickname "Baby Bull." He swung a 43-ounce bat, and hit some monster home runs. On June 4, 1959, he became the first player ever to clear the left-field bleachers at Milwaukee's County Stadium with a 500-foot blast.

Cepeda signed with the Giants for a $500 bonus and airfare to Florida in 1955. He won batting titles in his first two years in the minors, including a .393 mark at Kokomo in his first season of professional ball. Still, before spring training in 1958, Cepeda did not figure prominently in the Giants' future. "We've got a kid in Minneapolis who might do the job at first base until Bill White gets out of the army, but hanged if I can remember his name," manager Bill Rigney told a reporter. "I think it starts with a C."

Rigney learned Cepeda's name quickly that spring and put it in ink on the Giants' lineup card. Cepeda homered in his first game off Don Drysdale and never looked back, winning Rookie of the Year in a romp. He was so consistent that his batting average never dropped below .305 all year. He hit back-to-back game-winning three-run home runs on June 11 and 12, the first coming in the twelfth inning against Cincinnati, the second beating Hall-of-Famer Warren Spahn. "He is the most relaxed first-year man I ever saw," said Mays. "He's annoying every pitcher in the league."

Cepeda won two-thirds of the Triple Crown in 1961, and the following year hit a sacrifice fly in the ninth inning of the deciding game in the NL playoff against the Dodgers. The Giants went on to win the playoff and the World Series. But knee surgery and the Giants' desire to put Willie McCovey at first base got Cepeda traded to the Cardinals for Ray Sadecki in May 1966.

Cepeda was not too broken up to be leaving the Giants. For several years he had played for manager Alvin Dark, who was at best a difficult man to deal with. Cepeda said Dark forbade Latin players from speaking Spanish on the team bus and in 1964 told a *Newsday* reporter that black and Latin players lacked "mental alertness" and "pride."

Cepeda had a great year in 1967, leading the Cardinals to the pennant with an MVP season. "Cepeda was traded to us after becoming known as a prima donna," wrote Curt Flood in his autobiography. "The fact was that [Cepeda] had been half out of his tree with frustration over the intellectual and spiritual meanness of the Giants and, beyond that, the unforgivable baseball they played. Welcomed into baseball's first genuinely civilized atmosphere, he responded with high spirit, selfless professionalism and tremendous batting power."

Cepeda nicknamed the team "El Birdos" and kept the team loose. Catcher Tim McCarver called him "our spiritual leader," and Flood said he was "our cheerleader, our glue." Cepeda loved the role. "We used to get together after the game," he said. "I've never seen a team like that. We were a team. No superstars."

But after a subpar 1968 season, Cepeda was traded to Atlanta, a very unpopular move with Cardinal fans. He helped the Braves win the inaugural NL West title and hit .455 in a championship series loss to the Mets. He had more knee surgery in 1971 and was released after just three at-bats with Oakland in 1972. He retired but was coaxed off a Puerto Rico beach a year later to experiment with baseball's newest position, designated hitter. All he did was win the AL's first Outstanding Designated Hitter award.

Cepeda retired with numbers good enough for the Hall of Fame, but a conviction for smuggling marijuana may have cost him his spot.

Statistics: Orlando Cepeda

Year	Team	Games	AB	Runs	Hits	2B	3B	HR	RBI	BA
1958	SF-N	148	603	88	188	38*	4	25	96	.312
1959	SF	151	605	92	192	35	4	27	105	.317
1960	SF	151	569	81	169	36	3	24	96	.297
1961	SF	152	585	105	182	28	4	46*	142*	.311
1962	SF	162	625	105	191	26	1	35	114	.306
1963	SF	156	579	100	183	33	4	34	97	.316
1964	SF	142	529	75	161	27	2	31	97	.304
1965	SF	33	34	1	6	1	0	1	5	.176
1966	SF/STL-N	142	501	70	151	26	0	20	73	.301
1967	STL	151	563	91	183	37	0	25	111*	.325
1968	STL	157	600	71	149	26	2	16	73	.248
1969	ATL-N	154	573	74	147	28	2	22	88	.257
1970	ATL	148	567	87	173	33	0	34	111	.305
1971	ATL	71	250	31	69	10	1	14	44	.276
1972	ATL/									
	OAK-A	31	87	6	25	3	0	4	9	.287
1973	BOS-A	142	550	51	159	25	0	20	86	.289
1974	KC-A	33	107	3	23	5	0	1	18	.215
Totals										
17 Years		2124	7927	1131	2351	417	27	379	1365	.297
League Championship Series										
1969	ATL-N	3	11	2	5	2	0	1	3	.455
World Series										
1962	SF-N	5	19	1	3	1	0	0	2	.158
1967	STL	7	29	1	3	2	0	0	1	.103
1968	STL	7	28	2	7	0	0	2	6	.250
Totals										
3 Years		19	76	4	13	3	0	2	9	.171

*League leader.

James Timothy "Mudcat" Grant

Pitcher. Batted right. Threw right. 6'1", 186 lbs. Born 8/13/35, Lacoochee, Florida.

For most of his career, James Timothy "Mudcat" Grant was a delight, a colorful happy-go-lucky ballplayer with a flair for the game. But on September 16, 1960, Grant registered his own quiet form of protest against racism, and it turned into an ugly incident that got him suspended for the last two weeks of the season.

Grant was following his usual custom of singing the national anthem in the Cleveland bull pen. But when he got to the song's final line, he improvised. Instead of singing "the land of the free, and the home of the brave," Grant, with his hand over his heart, crooned, "this land is not free, I can't even go to Mississippi." Pitching coach Jim Wilks, a Texan, asked him what he meant, and Grant replied that he would have no more freedom in Mississippi, or Texas, than he would in Russia. Wilks took offense and shot back, "If I ever catch your black ass in Texas. . ." He stopped there and quickly apologized, but Grant was livid. He went to the clubhouse, got dressed, and left the ballpark. Manager Jimmie Dykes did not realize Grant was gone until he called the bull pen to ask Grant to warm up.

"I got so mad, that I figured if I stayed around I might not be able to control myself," Grant said later. He also called Dykes and general manager Frank Lane later that night to apologize for leaving. The next day, Grant was suspended for the last two weeks of the season. "I don't blame Jimmie for suspending me. He has been good to me and I'm sorry I put him on the spot by walking off. But I'm sick of hearing remarks about colored people. I don't have to stand there and take it."

The rest of Grant's career was marked more by conquests than controversy. A powerful right-hander who could help himself with the bat, Grant spent most of his career as a starter, then became an effective reliever in later years.

Depending on which story you believe, Grant got his colorful nickname for his childhood penchant for fishing for "mudcats" (a kind of catfish) in the swamps around his Lacoochee, Florida, home or at an Indians tryout camp in 1954 when one of his teammates mistakenly thought Grant hailed from Mississippi.

One of seven kids whose father died when he was two, Grant was a high school all-state quarterback in football and all-state forward in basketball. Indians scout Fred Merkle approached Grant after seeing him pitch in a high school tournament, but at the time Grant had plans to go to college. Those plans changed, and he wound up working in a local lumber mill. Merkle found out, tracked him down, and got him to come to Daytona Beach for a tryout.

On the final day of spring training, the Indians offered Grant a contract. No bonus, just a handshake.

He went to Fargo-Moorhead in Class C and was 21-5 with 12 straight wins at one point. His outstanding fastball and better than average curve overpowered minor league hitters. In 1956 he struck out 14 in a 15-inning performance, then came back six days later and fanned 13 more in a complete-game win. By 1957 he had reached Class AAA at San Diego and went 18-7 with a 2.32 ERA and a league-high 178 strikeouts. "I've never seen a young pitcher come along as fast as he has," said San Diego manager Ralph Kiner.

Grant was a solid starter for the Indians for five-plus years, then was traded in June 1964 to Minnesota. The following year Grant was superb, leading the Twins to the AL pennant and pacing the league in wins, winning percentage, and shutouts. The wildness that marked his early career was gone, and he walked an average of just two batters every nine innings. He almost carried the Twins past the Dodgers in the World Series. He outdueled Don Drysdale in the opener, scattering 10 hits in an 8–2 win, then after losing Game 4, came back on two days' rest to win Game 6 singlehandedly. He scattered six hits and hit a three-run homer in a 6–1 win. But Sandy Koufax shut the Twins out in Game 7.

Grant's bat was always a dangerous weapon. He hit .281 with 16 hits in 1960 and had six lifetime homers in the majors. In 1956 he hit .325 for Reading, then spent the winter in Colombia and hit nine home runs, good for second in the league.

He finished his career as a relief pitcher, then went on to a career in broadcasting and show business, performing as lead singer in a band called Mudcat and the Kittens.

Statistics: *Mudcat Grant*

Year	Team	W	L	PCT	G	IP	H	BB	SO	ERA	SV
1958	CLE-A	10	11	.476	44	204	173	104	111	3.84	4
1959	CLE	10	7	.588	38	165.1	140	81	85	4.14	3
1960	CLE	9	8	.529	33	159.2	147	78	75	4.40	0
1961	CLE	15	9	.625	35	244.2	207	109	146	3.86	0
1962	CLE	7	10	.412	26	149.2	128	81	90	4.27	0
1963	CLE	13	14	.481	38	229.1	213	87	157	3.69	1
1964	CLE/										
	MIN-A	14	13	.519	39	228	244	61	118	3.67	1
1965	MIN	21*	7	.750*	41	270.1	252	61	142	3.30	0
1966	MIN	13	13	.500	35	249	248	49	110	3.25	0
1967	MIN	5	6	.455	27	95.1	121	17	50	4.72	0
1968	LA-N	6	4	.600	37	95	77	19	35	2.08	3
1969	MON-N/										
	STL-N	8	11	.421	41	114	126	36	55	4.42	7
1970	OAK-A/										
	PIT-N	8	3	.727	80	135	112	32	58	1.87	24

Year	Team	W	L	PCT	G	IP	H	BB	SO	ERA	SV
1971	PIT/OAK	6	3	.667	57	102	104	34	35	3.18	10
Totals											
14 Years		145	119	.549	571	2441.1	2292	849	1267	3.63	53
League Championship Series											
1971	OAK-A	0	0	.000	1	2	3	0	0	0.00	0
World Series											
1965	MIN-A	2	1	.667	3	23	22	2	12	2.74	1

*League leader.

Juan Francisco "Pancho" Herrera

**First base. Batted right. Threw right. 6'4", 220 lbs.
Born 6/16/34, Santiago, Cuba.**

At an imposing 6'4" and 220 pounds, Pancho Herrera was the prototypical 1950s first baseman. In addition to awesome power, Herrera offered a great glove and surprising agility for his size. But for a variety of reasons, his major league career was brief and relatively undistinguished.

First, Herrera was under contract to the Philadelphia Phillies, one of baseball's last teams to integrate. When the Phillies finally took a good look at him, they had found a first baseman they liked better. They wanted to try him at another position, but a broken ankle in winter ball limited his mobility. When he finally got a chance to start, Herrera cut short his career with an unprecedented ability to strike out.

Herrera got his start in his native Cuba with the Havana Giants, a farm team of the Kansas City Monarchs. The Phillies spent $10,000 for his contract after the 1954 season, and after two years in the lower minors, Herrera had a breakout season with Miami of the International League in 1957, hitting .304 with 17 homers and 84 RBIs. The Phillies finally broke their color line that season, and Herrera started the following season in the majors. But after 11 hitless at-bats, he was back in Miami, where he set a team record with 20 home runs.

The Phillies had Ed Bouchee at first base and wanted to find another position for Herrera. They tried him at second and third during spring training in 1959, but a broken ankle suffered in a Cuban winter league game had slowed Herrera down, so he went back to the minors, this time to Buffalo. All Herrera did there was win the Triple Crown and Most Valuable Player award, hitting .327 with 37 homers and 129 RBIs.

Trade rumors circled Herrera in the off-season, but he arrived at spring training in 1960 to find Bouchee in his spot once more. "When you going to retire, Ed?" Herrera jokingly asked Bouchee. "Every spring I come here and you're here. Then I go back to the minors. Why don't they trade you or something?" A month into the season they did, and Herrera got his chance. He hit well, including a 20-game hitting streak, but set a major league record with 136 strikeouts. He struck out 120 more times in 1961, led NL first basemen in assists but also in errors, and at the end of the season the Phillies traded for first baseman Roy Sievers.

After another fine season with Buffalo, Herrera was traded to the Pirates but never played again in the majors.

Statistics: Pancho Herrera

Year	Team	Games	AB	Runs	Hits	2B	3B	HR	RBI	BA
1958	PHI-N	29	63	5	17	3	0	1	6	.270
1960	PHI	145	512	61	144	26	3	17	71	.281
1961	PHI	126	400	56	103	17	2	13	51	.258
Totals										
3 Years		300	975	122	264	46	8	31	128	.271

Willie Charles Kirkland

Outfield. Batted left. Threw right. 6'1", 206 lbs. Born 2/17/34, Siluria, Alabama.

Willie Kirkland did not play baseball in high school because, as he put it, "Nobody asked me to." Big mistake.

Kirkland learned to hit playing a game called "strikeout" with a tennis ball and a boyhood friend. He learned well enough to have four straight 20-plus home-run seasons in the majors and crack one of baseball's most potent lineups. And while Kirkland never fully lived up to what many thought was almost unlimited potential, he had some brilliant moments in the majors, then went on to find happiness in Japanese baseball.

Kirkland signed with the Giants for a $2,500 bonus, a day he said he would "bless as long as I live." He blazed his way through the minors, hitting for power and average at every stop. In 1954 he hit .360 with 27 homers and 105 RBIs for St. Cloud, then went to Sioux City in 1955 where he earned the nickname "Boom Boom" with 40 homers. He homered five times in his first seven games with Louisville in 1956, then was promoted to Class AAA Minneapolis where he got help taming his strike zone from manager Eddie Stanky and help with his outfield play from coach Dave Garcia. Stanky was so impressed with his speed, he said Kirkland "could bunt .300."

After tearing up the American Association with back-to-back 37-homer seasons, and after a slow start and a quick trip to the minors, Kirkland won the starting job in right field in the Giants' inaugural season in San Francisco. Until he reached the majors, Kirkland was rarely without a toothpick in his mouth while on the field. But when he reached the bigs, Giants owner Horace Stoneham told him it was "bush league," so he switched to chewing gum.

Kirkland held the right field job for three years, fighting off challenges from other young power hitters like Leon Wagner and Felipe Alou. The Giants traded Kirkland to Cleveland after the 1960 season, and he responded by making 1961 his best season ever, leading the Tribe in homers and RBIs. It featured Kirkland tying a major league record with four home runs in four straight official at-bats. In the Indians' last game before the All-Star break, Kirkland homered three times in a row off Chicago's Cal McLish, all on two-strike counts, then walked and sacrificed in his last two at-bats. In his first game after the break, he homered his first time up. But Kirkland slumped badly in 1962 and was truly hurt by the boos he received from Cleveland fans.

He finished his major league career with the woeful Washington Senators, but was reborn as a player in Japan. Kirkland hit 126 home runs in six seasons with Hanshin; and unlike most Americans who played there, he adjusted well — so well, in fact, that he learned the language and married a Japanese woman.

Statistics: *Willie Kirkland*

Year	Team	Games	AB	Runs	Hits	2B	3B	HR	RBI	BA
1958	SF-N	122	418	48	108	25	6	14	56	.258
1959	SF	126	463	64	126	22	3	22	68	.272
1960	SF	146	515	59	130	21	10	21	65	.252
1961	CLE-A	146	525	84	136	22	5	27	95	.259
1962	CLE	137	419	56	84	9	1	21	72	.200
1963	CLE	127	427	51	98	13	2	15	47	.230
1964	BAL-A/									
	WAS-A	98	252	22	52	11	0	8	35	.206
1965	WAS	123	312	38	72	9	1	14	54	.231
1966	WAS	124	163	21	31	2	1	6	17	.190
Totals										
9 Years		1149	3494	443	837	134	29	148	509	.240

Orlando Gregory Peña

Pitcher. Threw right. Batted right. 5'11", 170 lbs. Born 11/17/33, Victoria de las Tunas, Cuba.

Orlando Peña was as much a master of persistence as a master of off-speed pitches. In a major league career that spanned three decades, eight teams, four demotions to the minor leagues, and a stint as a batting-practice pitcher, there always seemed to be a place for Orlando Peña in some team's bull pen.

Peña began his professional career in his native Cuba, then compiled a 146-85 record in the minor leagues. Used primarily as a relief pitcher once he reached the majors, Peña lost a league-leading 20 games with the Kansas City A's in 1962. Following 50 games with the Tigers and Indians in 1967, Peña spent the next two full seasons in the minor leagues.

Peña, among others, was convinced his career was over following a disappointing minor league season in 1969. He was a 36-year-old junkballer whose junk no longer fooled even AAA batters. Still, pitching was his livelihood, so he signed on as a batting-practice pitcher with the Kansas City Royals in their second year of existence.

Whatever he was dishing up to Royals hitters must have looked awfully impressive to the Pittsburgh Pirates, who signed him to a roster contract in 1970. Released by the Pirates, Peña signed an Orioles contract in 1971, then spent the 1972 season in two minor leagues, winning 22 games, losing only three, and finishing the season with a 1.25 ERA. Peña completed his major league career by compiling an ERA of 3.00 or less for the next four seasons.

Following his retirement, he scouted for the Detroit Tigers.

Statistics: Orlando Peña

Year	Team	W	L	PCT	G	IP	H	BB	SO	ERA	SV
1958	CIN-N	1	0	1.000	9	15	10	4	11	0.60	3
1959	CIN	5	9	.357	46	136	150	39	76	4.76	5
1960	CIN	0	1	.000	4	9.1	8	3	9	2.89	0
1962	KC-A	6	4	.600	13	89.2	71	27	56	3.01	0
1963	KC	12	20*	.375	35	217	218	53	128	3.69	0
1964	KC	12	14	.462	40	219.1	231	73	184	4.43	0
1965	KC/										
	DET-A	4	12	.250	42	92.2	96	33	79	4.18	4
1966	DET	4	2	.667	54	108	105	35	79	3.08	7
1967	DET/										
	CLE-A	0	4	.000	50	90.1	72	22	74	3.59	8
1970	PIT-N	2	1	.667	23	38	38	7	25	4.74	2
1971	BAL-A	0	1	.000	5	15	16	5	4	3.00	0
1973	BAL/										
	STL-N	5	5	.500	53	107	96	22	61	2.94	7
1974	STL/										
	CAL-A	5	2	.714	46	53	51	21	28	2.21	4
1975	CAL	0	2	.000	7	12.2	13	8	4	2.13	0
Totals											
14 Years		56	77	.421	427	1203	1175	352	818	3.70	40

*League leader.

Vada Pinson

Outfield. Batted left. Threw left. 5'11", 170 lbs. Born 8/8/38, Memphis, Tennessee.

When Vada Pinson came up to the Cincinnati Reds in 1958 he was billed as the next Frank Robinson. And for good reason. Pinson, like Robinson, had played for George Powles at McClymonds High School in Oakland, California. A trumpet player as well as a ballplayer, Pinson was sure his career of choice would involve a horn and not a bat. He felt this way until his senior year, when the Robinson/Reds connection proved too alluring.

In 1957, his first year of organized ball, Pinson hit .367 with 209 hits, 40 doubles, 20 triples, 20 home runs, and 53 stolen bases with Class C Visalia. Two years out of high school, and the word in the Cincinnati organization was that Pinson was good enough to jump straight to the majors. Which is precisely what he did the following year.

Brought to the Reds' spring training camp in 1958, Pinson impressed everyone who saw him play. Timed at 3.3 seconds from home plate to first base, Pinson invited immediate comparison with Mickey Mantle, Hank Aaron, and Willie Mays—he had speed, great wrists, exceptional power, great instincts, and he fielded his position with a reckless hustle. Everything he did that spring was of major league caliber. And he was remarkably level-headed.

"I came to camp with the intention of making the club," he told the *Sporting News* that spring. "But if I don't make it, I won't be too disappointed."

He was not. When the 1958 season opened, Pinson had won a spot on the Cincinnati roster, making him the first player since Mantle to jump directly to the majors from Class C. In his second game with the Reds he hit a grand slam home run that beat the Pirates 4–1.

That grand slam was more than Pinson's first major league homer. It was a lesson.

"Probably the worst thing that happened to me was hitting a homer against Pittsburgh last year in the second game of the season," he said in 1959. "It won the game but didn't do me any good. I started thinking of myself as a slugger."

Optioned to the Pacific Coast League in May, Pinson finished the 1958 season with Seattle, hitting .343 with 11 home runs, 92 runs scored, 78 RBIs and 37 stolen bases. He was recalled to the Reds in September and went eight for 22.

Rooming with McClymonds alumnus Frank Robinson—who did all the cooking—Pinson was the starting center fielder in every game in 1959. In the first eight games of the season, he drove in eight runs on 12 hits, including two doubles, two triples and two home runs. He finished the season batting .316 and leading the league in runs scored and at-bats. In addition, Pinson stole 21 bases and set a Reds team record with a league-leading 47 doubles. Over the final 25 games of the season, Pinson collected 25 hits, making him the first National Leaguer in history to have 200 or more hits in his first full season. However, his 96 at-bats in 1958 disqualified him—by six at-bats—from Rookie of the Year honors, won by Willie McCovey with less than 200 at-bats.

Over the next eight seasons, Pinson never missed more than six games, in building a reputation as one of the best all-around players of the decade.

Statistics: Vada Pinson

Year	Team	Games	AB	Runs	Hits	2B	3B	HR	RBI	BA
1958	CIN-N	27	96	20	26	7	0	1	8	.271
1959	CIN	154	648*	131*	205	47*	9	20	84	.316
1960	CIN	154	652*	107	187	37*	12	20	61	.287
1961	CIN	154	607	101	208*	34	8	16	87	.343
1962	CIN	155	619	107	181	31	7	23	100	.292
1963	CIN	162	652	96	204*	37	14*	22	106	.313
1964	CIN	156	625	99	166	23	11	23	84	.266
1965	CIN	159	669	97	204	34	10	22	94	.305
1966	CIN	156	618	70	178	35	6	16	76	.288
1967	CIN	158	650	90	187	28	13*	18	66	.288
1968	CIN	130	499	60	135	29	6	5	48	.271
1969	STL-N	132	495	58	126	22	6	10	70	.255
1970	CLE-A	148	574	74	164	28	6	24	82	.286
1971	CLE	146	566	60	149	23	4	11	35	.263
1972	CAL-A	136	484	56	133	24	2	7	49	.275
1973	CAL	124	466	56	121	14	6	8	57	.260
1974	KC-A	115	406	46	112	18	2	6	41	.276
1975	KC	103	319	38	71	14	5	4	22	.223
Totals										
18 Years		2469	9645	1366	2757	485	127	256	1170	.286
World Series										
1961	CIN	5	22	0	2	1	0	0	0	.091

*League leader.

R. C. Stevens

First base. Batted right. Threw left. 6'5", 219 lbs. Born 1/12/25, Moultrie, Georgia.

R. C. Stevens was discovered on a construction crew by the Pirates' George Pratt. Pratt liked everything he saw in Stevens. At 6'5" and over 200 pounds,

Stevens *looked* like a ballplayer, and Pratt signed him to a contract without seeing him play.

Stevens caught the Pirates' attention through a brainstorm of team president Branch Rickey, who assigned Harry Roettger to write letters to mostly black high schools around the country asking for the names of all baseball players. While Stevens did not come with a first name, he did have credentials.

He was assigned to Class D Batavia in 1952 and promoted to Class C St. John's, Quebec, in 1953, hitting .313 with 12 homers and 77 RBIs against Provincial League pitching. Coming off a 1954 season in which he hit .293 with 25 home runs and 115 RBIs, Stevens looked like a first baseman of promise when he reported to Pirates spring training in 1955. Unfortunately for Stevens, he showed up 20 pounds overweight, which incited the wrath of Rickey, who no doubt remembered that 10 years earlier Jackie Robinson had reported to camp 30 pounds overweight and that Dodgers manager Charlie Dressen blamed the loss of the pennant on those 30 pounds.

Following two solid seasons with Hollywood (27 home runs and 92 RBIs) in 1956 and a .294 batting average with Columbus in 1957, Stevens made the Pirates in 1958 as a backup first baseman to Ted Kluszewski.

In the 1958 season opener against Milwaukee, Stevens made his major league debut by beating out a single in the tenth inning. Then, in the fourteenth inning, he singled off Gene Conley to win the game. Two weeks later, Stevens's two-out ninth-inning homer slammed the door on the Cincinnati Reds.

Stevens's potential was never given a full season to blossom, however. Replaced at first base by Dick Stuart, Stevens spent the next three years shuttling between the minors and the Pirates and Washington Senators.

Statistics: R.C. Stevens

Year	Team	Games	AB	Runs	Hits	2B	3B	HR	RBI	BA
1958	PIT-N	59	90	16	24	3	1	7	18	.267
1959	PIT	3	7	2	2	0	0	1	1	.286
1960	PIT	9	3	1	0	0	0	0	0	.000
1961	WAS-A	33	62	2	8	2	0	0	2	.129
Totals										
4 Years		104	162	21	34	4	1	8	21	.210

Willie Tasby

Outfield. Batted right. Threw right. 5'11", 180 lbs.
Born 1/8/33, Shreveport, Louisiana.

After seven seasons in organized ball, Willie Tasby had earned himself a reputation as a journeyman minor-leaguer. Then in 1957 he ran into Del

Wilber, manager of the Class AAA Louisville ball club. Echoing the famous words that Leo Durocher had for another center fielder named Willie six years before in New York, Wilber told Tasby, "Willie, I know what you can do. You're my center fielder no matter what happens. Just remember, the job is yours."

This was the reassurance Tasby had been waiting for since he had signed with the St. Louis Browns out of McClymonds High School in Oakland in 1950. Despite an impressive minor league career, including a .304, 27-homer, 121-RBI season with York in 1954, injuries and the difficult transition required of black ballplayers entering organized baseball in the early 1950s took their toll on Tasby. Wilber's confidence in his young outfielder paid immediate dividends. By the end of the 1957 season, Tasby was the American Association's all-star center fielder. He batted .306 for the season with 12 home runs, 61 RBIs, and 14 stolen bases.

Married and the father of three children, Tasby gave up playing winter ball in 1957, returned to his home in Oakland, and went to work as a turret lathe operator at Trans-Pacific Ocean Aircraft Company.

With Louisville in 1958, Tasby hit .322 with 22 homers and 95 runs batted in. The American Association 1958 Rookie of the Year, Tasby was called up to Baltimore that September, collecting five hits in his first eight at-bats.

To make room for the arrival of Tasby, whom the *Washington Post*'s Shirley Povich dubbed "the pale Willie Mays," the Orioles traded Jim Busby to Boston in December 1958. By the end of the 1959 Grapefruit League season, Tasby was hitting .389. Described by Baltimore sportswriter Jim Ellis as "the most exciting rookie in the Baltimore Orioles' training camp . . . a hinge-hipped flyhawk with a natural flair for showmanship," Tasby was the O's starting center fielder on opening day.

Through the first 33 games of the 1959 season, Tasby batted .313 and played in every inning of every game. Displaying speed in the outfield and a rifle arm, Tasby had 13 assists in those 33 games. In one game alone, he threw out two Detroit Tigers at the plate.

Unfortunately for Tasby, the better he played, the more he was compared to Willie Mays. It was a comparison Tasby found difficult to live with or live down. "I'm only trying to be me," he once said. And he proved it during one rainy game when he played the outfield without shoes for fear that the metal cleats would attract lightning.

Statistics: Willie Tasby

Year	Team	Games	AB	Runs	Hits	2B	3B	HR	RBI	BA
1958	BAL-A	18	50	6	10	3	0	1	1	.200
1959	BAL	142	505	69	126	16	5	13	48	.250
1960	BAL/									
	BOS-A	144	470	77	126	19	2	7	40	.268
1961	WAS-A	141	494	54	124	13	2	17	63	.251

Year	Team	Games	AB	Runs	Hits	2B	3B	HR	RBI	BA
1962	WAS/									
	CLE-A	86	233	29	55	7	0	4	17	.236
1963	CLE	52	116	11	26	3	1	4	5	.224
Totals										
6 Years		583	1868	246	467	61	10	46	174	.250

Antonio Sanchez "Tony" Taylor

Second base. Batted right. Threw right. 5'9", 180 lbs.
Born 12/19/35, Central Alara, Cuba.

The Chicago Cubs opened the 1958 season with one of their most promising teams in years. In addition to the powerful bats of Ernie Banks, Walt Moryn, Bobby Thomson, Lee Walls, and Dale Long, the Cubs had rookie Tony Taylor. And it was Taylor's presence as much as that of any other player that brought a rebirth of optimism to Chicago's North Side.

Not since Stan Hack retired in 1947 did the Cubs have a good leadoff batter and a good third baseman in the same lineup. With Taylor as with Hack, they seemed to have both in one player.

Taylor, a Cuban who bore a striking resemblance to professional boxer Kid Gavilan, was drafted by the Cubs from the San Francisco Giants organization where he had earned a reputation for being an excellent fielder and respectable hitter with a disciplined batting eye. He seemed a natural to fill the roll of "table setter" for the big bats behind him in the Cubs lineup. Coming off a .311 Cuban League winter season, Taylor was only 22 and seemed ready to better his minor league numbers. Moreover, Taylor came highly endorsed by Minnie Minoso, who was uncanny in his assessment of players.

On opening day, however, Cubs manager Bob Scheffing decided to shift his leadoff man to second base. While Taylor had never played second in his life, Scheffing called him "a natural" at the position. And by season's end, Taylor with 137 games at second base was named to the National League all-rookie team at that position. But the honor was not without work.

Taylor opened the season in a miserable slump. He kept "stepping in the bucket." Unfortunately, no one on the Cubs was able to communicate the problem to Taylor. He was benched when his average fell to .171, at which point Scheffing had Taylor watch slow-motion films of himself. The movies worked, and when Taylor returned to the lineup, he hit safely in 11 straight games, including a game-winning home run off the Braves' Warren Spahn.

Named the outstanding player in the Cuban League for the 1958-59 winter season, Taylor returned to the Cubs primed for a great 1959 season.

After 60 games, he was hitting .313, the only Cub over .300. In the field, he had made just two errors in 248 chances. Then on June 18 he was struck under the right eye by a Ron Kline pitch and was carried off the field on a stretcher.

Returning to the lineup, Taylor hit safely in 12 straight games. Despite hitting .280 and stealing 23 bases for Chicago in 1959, the Cubs traded Taylor for Ed Bouchee and Don Cardwell in May 1960. He finished the season with a .284 batting average and a career-high 26 stolen bases.

Taylor remained Philadelphia's starting second baseman for the next 10 seasons, filling in as needed at third base, shortstop, first base, and the outfield. In 1970, following a .301 season and still on the Phillies' active roster, Taylor was hired as an instructor for the Phillies' Florida Instructional League team.

Following 2½ years with the Detroit Tigers, Taylor came back to the Phils and led the National League with 17 pinch-hits and a .370 pinch-hitting average.

When he retired after 19 big league seasons, Taylor ranked among the best pinch-hitters of all time. His 2,195 games played ranked sixty-eighth on the all-time list.

Statistics: Tony Taylor

Year	Team	Games	AB	Runs	Hits	2B	3B	HR	RBI	BA
1958	CHI-N	140	497	63	117	15	3	6	27	.235
1959	CHI	150	624	96	175	30	8	8	38	.280
1960	CHI/PHI-N	146	581	80	165	25	7	5	44	.284
1961	PHI	106	400	47	100	17	3	2	26	.250
1962	PHI	152	625	87	162	21	5	7	43	.259
1963	PHI	157	640	102	180	20	10	5	49	.281
1964	PHI	154	570	62	143	13	6	4	46	.251
1965	PHI	106	323	41	74	14	3	3	27	.229
1966	PHI	125	434	47	105	14	8	5	40	.242
1967	PHI	132	462	55	110	16	6	2	34	.238
1968	PHI	145	547	59	137	20	2	3	38	.250
1969	PHI	138	557	68	146	24	5	3	30	.262
1970	PHI	124	439	74	132	26	9	9	55	.301
1971	PHI/DET-A	91	288	36	77	12	3	4	24	.267
1972	DET	78	228	33	69	12	4	1	20	.303
1973	DET	84	275	35	63	9	3	5	24	.229
1974	PHI-N	62	64	5	21	4	0	2	13	.328
1975	PHI	79	103	13	25	5	1	1	17	.243
1976	PHI	26	23	2	6	1	0	0	3	.261
Totals										
19 Years		2195	7680	1005	2007	298	86	75	598	.261
League Championship Series										
1972	DET	4	15	0	2	2	0	0	0	.133

Leon Lamar Wagner

Outfield. Batted left. Threw right. 6'1", 195 lbs. Born
5/13/34, Chattanooga, Tennessee.

Leon Wagner was one of many excellent black ballplayers the New
York–San Francisco Giants signed in the late 1950s. The Class AAA Phoenix
ballclub on which Wagner played for part of the 1958 season may have fielded
the most awesome minor league lineup of all time. In addition to Wagner, the
Phoenix team included (at various times) Andre Rodgers, Dusty Rhodes,
Felipe Alou, Orlando Cepeda, Willie Kirkland, and Willie McCovey. By the
end of the season, Wagner, Cepeda, and Kirkland were playing for the Giants,
and each was named to the National League all-rookie team.

Hitting .315 when he was called up from Phoenix, Wagner actually improved on his numbers once he reached San Francisco. His .317 average was
second on the team only to Willie Mays's .347.

Playing part-time in 1959, Wagner saw his output tail off dramatically,
although equally dramatic was his first major league grand slam home run, a
two-out bottom-of-the-ninth game-winning blast off Dodger Art Fowler.

Following an off-season trade to the Cardinals in 1959, Wagner saw even
less playing time in St. Louis in 1960. But in 1961 he got the break he needed
when the Cards traded him to the American League expansion Los Angeles
Angels in January.

Playing in cozy Wrigley Field (until then, a minor league ballpark known
nationally as the site for a popular winter TV show called "Home Run Derby")
and then Dodger Stadium, Wagner, reunited with his former San Francisco
manager Bill Rigney, led the Angels in home runs in each of his three seasons
with the club. His 107 RBIs in 1962 established an Angels record that stood
until Bobby Bonds drove in 115 runs in 1977. In the second All-Star game that
season (the last of the twice-a-year affairs), Wagner went three for four, including a two-run homer as the American League broke a five-game winless
streak. His 37 home runs in 1962 remained the team record for 20 years
(though Bonds tied it in 1977) before Reggie Jackson hit 39 homers in 1982.

Always a team player, Wagner was appreciated and well liked by his teammates. So the question remains why, given his numbers, the Angels traded
him to Cleveland following the 1963 season. Wagner led the Indians in home
runs and RBIs in 1964, and in homers again in 1965. With Cleveland and the
Chicago White Sox in 1968, he led the American League with 46 pinch-hit appearances.

Affectionately known as "Daddy Wags," Wagner finished his playing
career in San Francisco and remained on the West Coast to pursue a career in
acting. Among the films he appeared in was *Bingo Long's Traveling All Stars*

and Motor Kings, a movie about life in the Negro leagues, starring James Earl Jones.

Statistics: Leon Wagner

Year	Team	Games	AB	Runs	Hits	2B	3B	HR	RBI	BA
1958	SF-N	74	221	31	70	9	0	13	35	.317
1959	SF	87	129	20	29	4	3	5	22	.225
1960	STL-N	39	98	12	21	2	0	0	11	.214
1961	LA-A	133	453	74	127	19	2	28	79	.280
1962	LA	160	612	96	164	21	5	37	107	.268
1963	LA	149	550	73	160	11	1	26	90	.291
1964	CLE-A	163	641	94	162	19	2	31	100	.253
1965	CLE	144	517	91	152	18	1	28	79	.294
1966	CLE	150	549	70	153	20	0	23	66	.279
1967	CLE	135	433	56	105	15	1	15	54	.242
1968	CLE/									
	CHI-A	107	211	19	55	12	0	1	24	.261
1969	SF-N	11	12	0	4	0	0	0	2	.333
Totals										
12 Years		1352	4426	636	1202	150	15	211	669	.272

1959

George Lee Altman

Outfield. Batted left. Threw right. 6'4", 200 lbs. Born 3/20/33, Goldsboro, North Carolina.

A lot of great hitters liked what they saw in George Altman. Ty Cobb liked his ability to hit to all fields and his level swing. Rogers Hornsby liked his speed. And Ernie Banks liked his knowledge of the strike zone. Altman had all the tools, including intelligence, and he was bright enough to begin planning for his future after baseball almost before his career started. His professional path started in the Negro leagues, passed through the majors, went east to Japan, and wound up in a seat on the Chicago Board of Trade.

Altman was a three-sport star in high school and won a scholarship to Tennessee A&I to play basketball, his first love. But he reasoned he had better career opportunities in baseball, and he got a break when the athletic business manager at A&I turned out to be a booking agent for the Kansas City Monarchs. Altman got a tryout, and upon graduating from college, he joined the Monarchs, earning $300 a month. He had an all-star season as a rookie in 1955, but at the end of the season was part of owner Tom Baird's fire sale, going to the Cubs with two other players for $11,000.

After two years in the minors, one in the service, and a spring-training bout with malaria, Altman started the 1959 season in center field for the Cubs. He started slowly at the plate but hit .285 the last two months of the season after switching to a lighter bat like the one Banks used. He almost single-handedly knocked San Francisco out of the pennant race. The Giants had already printed World Series tickets when Altman beat them on September 22 with a two-out two-run homer in the ninth inning. He homered the next day in the eighth to give the Cubs the lead en route to a 9–8 win, and the Dodgers and Braves wound up in a playoff for the pennant.

In 1961 Cubs owner P. K. Wrigley experimented with a committee of managers, and while the team finished seventh, Altman had his finest season, leading the NL in triples and establishing career highs in home runs, doubles, and RBIs.

The Cubs traded Altman to the Cardinals after the 1962 season, and after one year with St. Louis he spent a season in the cellar with the laughable New York Mets before returning to the Cubs. In 1967 he was sent down to Portland as part of manager Leo Durocher's "youth movement," and he was ready for that to be his last season in baseball. But a few of his Portland teammates told him about the financial advantages of playing in Japan, including high salaries and lower taxes, so he signed on with the Lotte Orions.

Altman played in Japan for eight more seasons and became the first player to qualify for both U.S. and Japanese player pension programs. He earned more than $50,000 a season in Japan and hit .309 with 205 home runs, crediting his success to martial-arts training. But it was not all gravy. Altman did not realize he would have to supply his own bats and towels, so he had to borrow a bat and dry off with an undershirt after his first practice. And at 6'4" he stood out, saying he always felt "like 1,000 eyes were watching me."

"I don't say Japanese baseball is perfect," he said. "My wife hates it over there. But it beats being a has-been over here."

Statistics: George Altman

Year	Team	Games	AB	Runs	Hits	2B	3B	HR	RBI	BA
1959	CHI-N	135	420	54	103	14	4	12	47	.245
1960	CHI	119	334	50	89	16	4	13	51	.266
1961	CHI	138	518	77	157	28	12*	27	96	.303
1962	CHI	147	534	74	170	27	5	22	74	.318
1963	STL-N	135	464	62	127	18	7	9	47	.274
1964	NY-N	124	422	48	97	14	1	9	47	.230
1965	CHI-N	90	196	24	46	7	1	4	23	.235
1966	CHI	88	185	19	41	6	0	5	17	.222
1967	CHI	15	18	1	2	2	0	0	1	.111
Totals										
9 Years		991	3091	409	832	132	34	101	403	.269

*League leader.

Marshall Bridges

Pitcher. Batted both. Threw left. 6'1", 165 lbs. Born 6/2/31, Jackson, Mississippi. Died 9/3/90, Jackson, Mississippi.

Marshall Bridges learned the hard way that when a woman says no, she means no. Bridges was in a Fort Lauderdale nightclub during spring training in

1963 when he tried to pick up a young lady at the bar. That he was married with three children made it bad enough, but things got worse when after repeatedly spurning his advances, Carrie Lee Raysor, 21, pulled out a pistol and shot Bridges in the leg.

In a way, Bridges was lucky. He suffered no permanent damage and made a quick recovery. But the Yankees were not used to their players being shot at, and the incident probably cost him his spot as the team's number one relief pitcher. It earned him nicknames like "Lead Leg" and "Bang Bang," and it obscured an otherwise solid, fun-loving career.

Bridges was one of the game's characters, with a great sense of humor and an endless supply of stories, most of them extremely tall—like the time he said he saw a rabbit run so fast it turned blue, or the 250-pound shark he caught while deep-sea fishing, or the time he told teammate Jim Coates that he built his house all by himself. "Are you a mason?" Coates asked. "Let's not bring religion into this," Bridges replied.

Then there was his hitting. It is true that he was a good hitter and played first base for one year in the minors. But he hit .211 that year, not the .350 he claimed. And the three best hitters in baseball were not, as he claimed, "Williams, Bridges, and Musial." He became known as "The Rug" because nothing lies like one.

He was a popular target of Yankees practical jokers, who were among baseball's best. The ringleaders, Mickey Mantle and Whitey Ford, knew Bridges was deathly afraid of snakes and mice. So they refrigerated a rubber snake, planted it in Bridges's pants leg, then stood back and watched as he tore his pants off trying to get away from it. Another time they put dead field mice in his shoes, and he had to wear paper shower shoes home from the ballpark. Once, while he was with the Reds, Bridges fell asleep in the dugout before a game. His teammates plugged the dugout drain and flooded the area before he woke up.

Bridges, a hard thrower, began his career with the Memphis Red Sox of the Negro American League. His minor league career looked like a Greyhound route map with stops in Sioux City, Danville, Beaumont, Amarillo, Austin, Topeka, Sacramento, and Rochester before he hit the majors with the Cardinals in 1959, striking out 76 batters in as many innings. He was sold to the Reds the following season, and in 14 games for the Reds he won four, saved two, and sported a 1.08 ERA.

Cincinnati gave him up a year later, much to the delight of Yankee manager Ralph Houk. Bridges did not allow a run in his first 14 appearances, and he impressed Houk with his grit. "You should see Marshall when he gets into trouble," Houk said. "Some pitchers go all to pieces. He just seems to growl and get tougher and madder." Bridges was hit in the head by a line drive one day at Fenway Park and seemed to be out cold when Houk reached the mound. But as Houk hovered over him, Bridges opened his eyes and smiled, then got up and finished the game. Bridges was the Yankee bull-pen ace that season and was second in the league in saves. In the World Series, he gave up a grand slam to the Giants' Chuck Hiller, the first grand-slam hit by an NL player in a World Series.

The shooting incident cut short Bridges's Yankee career, and he finished his major league playing days with the Washington Senators. He quit for good after playing in Hawaii in 1966, but baseball was never far from his mind. "Hardly a night passes that I don't dream about baseball," he said in an interview two months before his death. "I dream way back to my sandlot days playing with Jackson Cubs. Man, I'd be cussing and raising sand in my sleep, cursing at guys who should have made the plays behind me."

Statistics: Marshall Bridges

Year	Team	W	L	PCT	G	IP	H	BB	SO	ERA	SV
1959	STL-N	6	3	.667	27	76	67	37	76	4.26	1
1960	STL/										
	CIN-N	6	2	.750	34	56.2	47	23	53	2.38	3
1961	CIN	0	1	.000	13	20.2	26	11	17	7.84	0
1962	NY-A	8	4	.667	52	71.2	49	48	66	3.14	18
1963	NY	2	0	1.000	23	33	27	30	35	3.82	1
1964	WAS-A	0	3	.000	17	30	37	17	16	5.70	2
1965	WAS	1	2	.333	40	7.1	62	25	39	2.67	0
Totals											
7 Years		23	15	.605	206	345.1	315	191	302	3.75	25
World Series											
1962	NY-A	0	0	.000	2	3.2	4	2	3	4.91	0

Joseph O'Neal "Joe" Christopher

**Outfield. Batted right. Threw right. 5'10", 175 lbs.
Born Frederiksted, Virgin Islands.**

Not many players ever expressed gratitude for being a member of the New York Mets in the 1960s, but for Joe Christopher, the Mets finally gave him what he had always wanted—a chance to play. When Christopher was traded to Boston after the 1965 season, he wrote a letter of thanks to Mets president George Weiss. "I want to thank you for having confidence in me. It made me have confidence within myself." He added a P.S. "It still hurts not to be a Met."

It took seven frustrating seasons in the Pirate organization to crack Christopher's confidence. He signed with the Pirates for a $250 bonus and brought a boatload of confidence with him from his native Virgin Islands. "We signed Joe on his native ability," said Pirates general manager Joe L. Brown. "He's loaded with it."

But when he landed with Phoenix in 1955, he was immediately told to forget everything he knew about the game. He was moved from shortstop to the outfield and told to quit swinging for the fences. "I was pretty nervous and upset," Christopher said of the changes. The Pirates wanted to turn him into a line-drive hitter, taking advantage of his speed and the spacious power alleys at Forbes Field, so Christopher went along. "I turned down a fine civil service job in the post office back home to come into baseball," he said. "I don't intend to make it a mistake."

Christopher hit well in the minors — .327 in 1958 with Salt Lake City — and terrorized catchers with his base running. The *Sporting News* called him "a flashing Pepper Martin type who steals bases head first and will take an extra sack at the drop of an enemy outfielder's eyelash." But after three seasons of limited duty with the Pirates, the Mets grabbed him in the 1961 expansion draft for $75,000. It looked like the chance he had been waiting for. "I know I can hit in this league," he said. "I could be a good player, all I need is a chance."

Christopher was a big part of the Mets' first moral victory of the season as he tripled and scored the winning run in the first Mets-Yankees exhibition game in 1962. He finally became an everyday player in 1964 and made the most of it, becoming the first Met ever to hit .300 with more than 500 at-bats. He established career highs in every offensive category. He even got a measure of revenge against the Pirates when he bashed them for four extra-base hits on August 16. "I guess they see now they made a mistake," he said.

But Christopher's erratic outfield play kept his critics busy. Even teammate Tracy Stallard knocked him, saying Christopher was "the only .300 hitter in baseball who hurts a team." The criticism stung, but Christopher's mantra remained "I can hit. I can run. I can field. I can throw." He also took a shot at the press: "I'm a better player than you noodnicks think I am." Amid all the criticism, Christopher got a boost in the form of a letter from Jackie Robinson. "He told me not to let it bother me, but go out and play my game as if nothing had happened."

But 1965 saw Christopher's average drop 51 points, and that was his last full season in the majors.

Statistics: Joe Christopher

Year	Team	Games	AB	Runs	Hits	2B	3B	HR	RBI	BA
1959	PIT-N	15	12	6	0	0	0	0	0	.000
1960	PIT	50	56	21	13	2	0	1	3	.232
1961	PIT	76	186	25	49	7	3	0	14	.263
1962	NY-N	119	271	36	66	10	2	6	32	.244

Year	Team	Games	AB	Runs	Hits	2B	3B	HR	RBI	BA
1963	NY	64	149	19	33	5	1	1	8	.221
1964	NY	154	543	78	163	26	8	16	76	.300
1965	NY	148	437	38	109	18	3	5	40	.249
1966	BOS-A	12	13	1	1	0	0	0	0	.077
Totals										
8 Years		638	1667	224	434	68	17	29	173	.260
World Series										
1960	PIT-N	3	0	2	0	0	0	0	0	.000

Herman Thomas "Tommy" Davis

Outfield. Batted right. Threw right. 6'2", 195 lbs. Born
3/21/39, Brooklyn, New York.

Tommy Davis was born to be a Brooklyn Dodger. He grew up in Brooklyn. He went to Brooklyn Boys High School. "Ever since I was old enough to know what time it is, I've wanted to play for the Dodgers in Brooklyn," he said. But he was born a few years too late. By the time he became a Dodger, the team had left Brooklyn behind.

But Davis did not waste any time once he made the majors. Before he was through, he became the first NL player to win back-to-back batting titles since Stan Musial, posted a single-season RBI total that has not been matched since, and finished his career as the best pinch-hitter in baseball history.

Davis hit .480 as a senior at Brooklyn Boys and was all-state in basketball, playing alongside future NBA great Lenny Wilkens. The Yankees offered him more money to sign, but hometown loyalty plus a chat with Jackie Robinson convinced him to sign with Brooklyn in 1956. He blazed a trail through the minors, winning two batting titles in four years, including a monster season at Kokomo when he hit .357 with 115 runs scored and 104 RBIs. He also stole 68 bases, apparently on speed alone, and was known to sportswriters as the "chocolate lightning streak." After he stole his sixty-sixth base, manager Pete Reiser told him, "Tom, you're the worst base runner I ever saw." "He was right too," Davis said.

Dodger brass could hardly contain themselves when describing Davis's abilities. "He's probably the best prospect I've seen in many years," said Roy Campanella. "He runs like the wind and has a tremendously powerful arm." "His potential is practically unlimited," said Montreal manager Clay Kirby.

Davis grew up watching Duke Snider play center field for the Dodgers. In 1960 he took over center field and played alongside Snider. By 1962, Snider was gone, Willie Davis was in center, and Tommy had the kind of year players dream about. He had 230 hits, the most since Musial had the same total in 1948. His 153 RBIs were the most since Joe Medwick's 154 in 1937, and no one since has matched Davis's total. "Every time Tommy came up with a man on second, he drove him in with a single," said teammate Sandy Koufax. "When he came up with a man on first, he drove him in with a double." In Game 3 of the NL playoff against the Giants, Davis hit a two-run homer in the sixth to give the Dodgers a 3–2 lead. But the Giants scored three in the ninth to steal the pennant.

The following year Davis won another batting title, and this time the Dodgers left the Giants in their dust. Davis hit .400 as the Dodgers swept the Yankees in the World Series; his RBI single produced the only run in Game 3. In 1965 Davis missed most of the season with a broken ankle, and despite a strong comeback and another Dodger pennant in 1966, he was traded after the season to the Mets. The rest of Davis's career was spent switching uniforms, as he played for eight teams in 10 years, including two stints each with the A's and Cubs. His clutch hitting helped the A's win the AL West in 1971—he was 13 for 28 as a pinch-hitter—and as designated hitter was a key part of the Orioles' AL East titles in 1973 and 1974.

He finished his career as the highest-average pinch-hitter in history at .320. He had six career grand slams, and was an All-Star twice. But he never shook his reputation as a lackadaisical player. "Tommy didn't really wake up until after his first time or two at bat," said teammate Maury Wills. "Then the third time—it could be Bob Gibson out there, it didn't matter—boy, Tommy was ready. I wondered what he would have hit if he woke up before the game started."

Davis said it worked for him. "They used to call me lazy, but the lazier I felt, the better I'd hit."

Statistics: Tommy Davis

Year	Team	Games	AB	Runs	Hits	2B	3B	HR	RBI	BA
1959	LA-N	1	1	0	0	0	0	0	0	.000
1960	LA	110	352	43	97	18	1	11	44	.276
1961	LA	132	460	60	128	13	2	15	58	.278
1962	LA	163	665	120	230*	27	9	27	153*	.346*
1963	LA	146	556	69	181	19	3	16	88	.326*
1964	LA	152	592	70	163	20	5	14	86	.275
1965	LA	17	60	3	15	1	1	0	9	.250
1966	LA	100	313	27	98	11	1	3	27	.313
1967	NY-N	154	577	72	174	32	0	16	73	.302
1968	CHI-A	132	456	30	122	5	3	8	50	.268
1969	SEA-A/									
	HOU-N	147	533	54	142	32	1	7	89	.266
1970	HOU/OAK-A/									
	CHI-N	134	455	45	129	23	3	6	65	.284

Year	Team	Games	AB	Runs	Hits	2B	3B	HR	RBI	BA
1971	OAK	79	219	26	71	8	1	3	42	.324
1972	CHI-N/									
	BAL-A	41	108	12	28	4	0	0	12	.259
1973	BAL	137	552	53	169	20	3	7	89	.306
1974	BAL	158	626	67	181	20	1	11	84	.289
1975	BAL	116	460	43	130	14	1	6	57	.283
1976	CAL-A/									
	KC-N	80	238	17	63	5	0	3	26	.265
Totals										
18 Years		1999	7223	811	2212	272	35	153	1052	.294
League Championship Series										
1971	OAK-A	3	8	1	3	1	0	0	0	.375
1973	BAL-A	5	21	1	6	1	0	0	2	.286
1974	BAL	4	15	0	4	0	0	0	1	.267
Totals										
3 Years		12	44	2	13	2	0	0	3	.295
World Series										
1963	LA-N	4	15	0	6	0	2	0	2	.400
1966	LA	4	8	0	2	0	0	0	0	.250
Totals										
2 Years		8	23	0	8	0	2	0	2	.348

League leader.

Donald Johnson "Don" Eaddy

**Third base. Batted right. Threw right. 5'11", 165 lbs.
Born 2/16/34, Grand Rapids, Michigan.**

Don Eaddy struck out in his only at-bat in the major leagues. Still, by the time he made it to the majors, he had had enough triumphs for several careers.

Eaddy was a brilliant athlete at Ottawa Hills High School in Grand Rapids, Michigan, captaining the baseball, football, and basketball teams and lettering in each four times. He barely slowed down at the University of Michigan, where as a third baseman he was named All–Big Ten four times and All-American once, and helped lead the Wolverines to the 1953 College World Series title. He was also named All–Big Ten in basketball his senior year and earned his B.S. degree in four years.

He was signed after graduation by Cubs scout Tony Lucadello and made quite an impression on the Cubs in spring training before being assigned to Des Moines of the Western League, where in his first game he started a triple play. Eaddy spent most of the season with Burlington in the Three-I League and hit .302. But early in 1956 he was called into the air force, where he spent the next three years and rose to the rank of second lieutenant.

Back in baseball in 1959, Eaddy split his season between Lancaster in the Eastern League, Fort Worth of the American Association, and a 15-game stint in the National League. The Cubs used him primarily as a pinch-runner. Eaddy had another fine season with Lancaster in 1960, hitting .304, leading the league in fielding percentage, and being named to the all-star team. In 1961 he led Texas League third basemen in fielding percentage and in 1962 paced them in assists, chances, and double plays, and again was an all-star.

And his career featured one more championship. In the 1963-64 winter season, Eaddy hit .345 for Cinco Estrellas in the Nicaraguan League and drove in the winning run in the final game of the league championship series.

Statistics: Don Eaddy

Year	Team	Games	AB	Runs	Hits	2B	3B	HR	RBI	BA
1959	CHI-N	15	1	0	0	0	0	0	0	.000

Robert "Bob" Gibson

Pitcher. Batted right. Threw right. 6'1", 189 lbs. Hall of Fame, 1981. Born 11/9/35, Omaha, Nebraska.

Bob Gibson kept a mental notebook containing every hitter he ever faced and every injustice he ever suffered. There were plenty of both.

Gibson poured his fury out from the mound, and was the most dominant and intimidating pitcher of his era. He was loyal to his family and his teammates, and even his teammates knew enough to steer clear on the days he pitched, and even the day before. Catcher Tim McCarver dreaded going out to the mound when Gibson was on it. "Keep your ass away from me while I'm working," Gibson would yell at him. "The only thing you know about pitching is that you can't hit it."

And once you were no longer his teammate, all bets were off. Bill White was Gibson's roommate when they were with the Cardinals, but the first time White faced him after being traded to the Phillies, Gibson hit him in the arm with a pitch.

He was one of the fiercest competitors who ever played the game. Never in his career did he ask to be taken out of a game, and he once went 59 games without being taken out of a game except for a pinch-hitter. He did not ask to be adored by fans, or even liked. But he did demand — and command — respect. "I owe the fans 100 percent on the field and I give them exactly that," he said. "Anything else I give is completely up to me."

Gibson's 100 percent was simply awesome. And it was made even more remarkable by the fact that this tremendous athlete spent his boyhood sick and poverty-stricken. As a child, Gibson suffered from rickets, asthma, and a rheumatic heart. "He was born sick," said his mother, "and got sicker." At 3½ he was taken to the hospital with pneumonia. He looked up at his older brother Josh and asked if he was going to die. "You'll make it," Josh replied. "And when you come home I'll get you a baseball glove and bat."

Gibson grew up in a segregated housing project in the slums of Omaha, Nebraska, and his tough childhood stayed with him. "He was pushed around as a kid, and he vowed to himself that he wouldn't be pushed around again," said teammate Mike Shannon. He survived all his illnesses and grew into an outstanding athlete, winning a basketball scholarship to Creighton University, and later playing a season with the Harlem Globetrotters. After graduating he signed with the Cardinals for $4,000, and was off to St. Petersburg for his first spring training camp. But when he got to the Cardinals' team hotel, he got a rude welcome. He was hustled out the side door, put in a cab and driven to a house where the other black players stayed. "It was a shame . . . and a terrible disappointment," he wrote in his autobiography. "I had traveled 2,000 miles and I still had not escaped the ghetto. 'So this,' I said to myself, 'is the major leagues.'"

Gibson struggled his first two years in the minors, but he was a favorite of Omaha manager Johnny Keane's. His struggle continued his first two years in the majors under manager Solly Hemus. Once, Hemus patted Gibson on the back in the clubhouse, called him Julio — mistaking him for Cardinal teammate Julio Gotay — and told him what a good job he was doing at shortstop. He nearly destroyed his locker. But he got a break when Keane replaced Hemus midway through the 1961 season, and soon everyone in baseball knew his name. He threw everything hard: two fastballs — one that sailed and one that sank — a nearly unhittable slider, and a hard curve. Perhaps his most effective pitch was his brushback, a pitch thrown not to scare a hitter or to hit him, Gibson said, but rather "to make him think."

And he did more than just pitch. He won nine Gold Gloves for his fielding, and hit 24 career home runs, including five in 1972.

In 1964 Gibson showed for the first time that he could get even better when the games got bigger. After losing Game 1 of the World Series, he struck out 13 in 10 innings to win Game 5, and came back on two days' rest to pitch Game 7. The Cardinals led 7–3 in the ninth when a tiring Gibson gave up two solo home runs. Keane stayed in the dugout. "I had a commitment to his heart," he said. Gibson got the next batter, and the Cardinals were world champions.

Despite missing two months of the 1967 season with a broken leg, Gibson came back and put on one of the most dominating World Series performances ever, allowing one earned run in three complete games, including a three-hitter — and a home run — in Game 7. In 1968 Gibson had the greatest season for a pitcher since the dead-ball era — a 1.12 ERA, 13 shutouts, 28 complete games in 34 starts, and nearly five strikeouts for every walk. He won only 22 games because of poor run support. Had the Cardinals scored just four runs in each of his starts, he would have gone 30-2. He performed in the shadow of Detroit's 31-game winner Denny McLain that season, but showed who was the better pitcher when the pair faced off in the World Series opener. Gibson threw a five-hit shutout, walked just one and set a Series record with 17 strikeouts. Future Hall of Famer Al Kaline, in his sixteenth year in the majors, said, "I've never seen such overpowering pitching." And if Curt Flood had not misjudged a fly ball, Gibson probably would have won his third World Series Game 7.

But the hero's welcome Gibson received back in Omaha, and the tolerance of his new neighbors in their previously all-white neighborhood hardly warmed his heart. "I wasn't particularly touched [by the homecoming celebration]," he said. "All they're saying is I'm a 'special' Negro. That's the only reason some neighbors accept me. It makes me want to vomit."

Gibson was not all bitterness. When he was not pitching he was a leading jokester in the clubhouse, and he worked to foster team spirit on a racially and ethnically diverse group of Cardinals. According to Flood, Gibson would often ask white teammates — many of whom had never been to a bar with a black man — out for a drink after a game. He was close with McCarver, and with Shannon, who echoed the thoughts of many when he said that if he had one game he wanted to win, he would pick Gibson to pitch it.

But he lived by his own rules, and had no time for duplicity. "It doesn't excite me when I go into a restaurant and they give me the glad hand because I'm Bob Gibson the ballplayer," he wrote. "They might throw the next Negro out."

"I'm kind of sensitive about things, and I might sound as if I have a chip on my shoulder. I do. But I didn't put it there. Somebody else did."

Statistics: Bob Gibson

Year	Team	W	L	PCT	G	IP	H	BB	SO	ERA	SV
1959	STL-N	3	5	.375	13	75.2	77	39	48	3.33	0
1960	STL	3	6	.333	27	86.2	97	48	69	5.61	0
1961	STL	13	12	.520	35	211.1	186	119*	166	3.24	1
1962	STL	15	13	.536	32	233.2	174	95	208	2.85	1
1963	STL	18	9	.667	36	254.2	224	96	204	3.39	0
1964	STL	19	12	.613	40	287.1	250	86	245	3.01	1
1965	STL	20	12	.625	38	299	243	103	270	3.07	0
1966	STL	21	12	.636	35	280.1	210	78	225	2.44	0

Year	Team	W	L	PCT	G	IP	H	BB	SO	ERA	SV
1967	STL	13	7	.650	24	175.1	151	40	147	2.98	0
1968	STL	22	9	.710	34	304.2	198	62	268*	1.12*	0
1969	STL	20	13	.606	35	314	251	95	269	2.18	0
1970	STL	23*	7	.767*	34	294	262	88	274	3.12	0
1971	STL	16	13	.552	31	246	215	76	185	3.04	0
1972	STL	19	11	.633	34	278	226	88	208	2.46	0
1973	STL	12	10	.545	25	195	159	57	142	3.83	0
1974	STL	3	10	.231	22	109	120	62	60	5.04	2
Totals											
17 yrs.		251	174	.591	528	3884.2	3279	1336	3117	2.91	6
World Series											
1964	STL-N	2	1	.667	3	27	23	8	31	3.00	0
1967	STL	3	0	1.000	3	27	14	5	26	1.00	0
1968	STL	2	1	.667	3	27	18	4	35	1.67	0
Totals											
3 Years		7	2	.778	9	81	55	17	92	1.89	0

*League leader.

Elijah Jerry "Pumpsie" Green

Infield. Batted both. Threw right. 6', 175 lbs. Born 10/27/33, Oakland, California.

All Pumpsie Green wanted to be was a ballplayer. By the time he got to the majors, he said he felt "like an exhibit."

Green had the distinction, though he might have called it something else, to be the first black to play for the Boston Red Sox, the last major league team to break the color line. It came 12 years after Jackie Robinson became the first black major-leaguer and at the end of an arduous road that included an investigation of the Red Sox by the Massachusetts Commission Against Discrimination, pickets at Fenway Park, and a slew of allegations and controversy. In the middle of all this was a light-hitting infielder with a great glove and a desire just to play ball. "To me, baseball was a tough enough game to play itself," Green said. "I can't think about racial things and try to get a jump on a curveball."

His given name is Elijah, and he said he doesn't know how or why he got tagged "Pumpsie." "I've had the name as long as I can remember," he said. "They started calling me that when I was a foot high and it was the first name I ever knew I had." As a youngster growing up in the San Francisco Bay area, Green's ambition was to play for the Oakland Oaks of the Pacific Coast League.

He called the integration of the PCL "the greatest thing I'd ever seen" and was a big fan of Oaks star and former Negro league star Piper Davis, who was signed by the Red Sox in 1950 but never made it to the majors. Green signed with Oakland in 1953 out of West Contra Costa Junior College but was assigned to a Class B affiliate. Green's contract was sold to the Red Sox before he had a chance to play for the Oaks, and he moved up through the minors, reaching Class AAA Minneapolis in 1958.

Green hit .253 at shortstop for the Millers and was invited to spring training with the Red Sox in 1959, whereupon his life became more complicated. He was barred from staying at the team hotel in Scottsdale, Arizona. Team officials initially claimed there just was not enough room for Green, but when he was discovered staying 15 miles away in Phoenix, the real reason became clear. "[Oriole pitcher] Charlie Beamon warned me about Scottsdale," Green said. "Nobody likes to be told that he's restricted from the same hotel where his teammates are staying. But I know how things are in certain places. As long as I am in baseball, traveling around the way I do, I just have to accept it."

The housing controversy did not hurt Green's performance, and he was the talk of the Sox camp, hitting .444 with three homers. Boston sportswriters voted him the top rookie in camp, and most expected Green to make the team, especially since teams were allowed to carry 30 players for the first month of the season. But when the Red Sox went east to Texas for a barnstorming tour with the Chicago Cubs, Green's hitting went south. Manager Mike Higgins announced he was sending Green back to Minneapolis for "more seasoning." This was the same Mike Higgins who once told a reporter, "There'll be no niggers on this ballclub as long as I have anything to say about it."

Green later agreed that he "wasn't ready to play big-league ball last spring." He said he played poorly in the field, and admitted he "was in a daze all the time I was in spring training." But 12 years of waiting had left Boston's black leaders with little faith in Red Sox management. "The mealy-mouthed words of the Red Sox management notwithstanding, it is rather easy to conclude that the club has no desire to employ a colored ballplayer," wrote Sam Lacy of the Baltimore *Afro-American*. The Boston chapter of the NAACP, the American Veterans Committee, and the Ministerial Alliance filed discrimination charges against the club. Former Boston manager Joe Cronin, then president of the American League, defended team owner Tom Yawkey, noting that Yawkey "has colored help on his plantation in South Carolina, takes excellent care of them, pays good salaries and they are all very happy."

Jackie Robinson weighed in, saying that there was no doubt that the Red Sox discriminated against blacks but that he was equally sure that Green did need more time in the minors. Meanwhile, the Red Sox were playing poorly, and their shortstop, Don Buddin, a lifetime .241 hitter, was being booed. Pickets carried signs around Fenway: *Race Hate Is Killing Baseball in Boston* and *We Want a Pennant, Not a White Team*.

The commission cleared the Red Sox of all charges after the team promised to "make every effort " to end segregation. But the team was guilty of playing lousy baseball and languished in the American League cellar. Green was having his finest season ever, hitting .320 for Minneapolis, so on July 21 he was called up and pinch-ran and played shortstop for an inning at Comiskey Park.

When the team came back to Boston, Green was not prepared for all the attention. "We were stepping off the plane, and I saw bright lights and cameras. I thought that was the way it is in the majors. But I found out different, because I never saw it again. I didn't know they were there to see me.... The next day, 20,000 people showed up who hadn't been there all year. They roped off center field, and I was the primary reason. The ones who stood out behind the ropes were predominantly black." Green rose to the occasion, tripling off the Green Monster in his first at-bat in Fenway Park.

Green was the starting second baseman for three weeks, but then his season was cut short when he fractured his right hand tagging Mickey Mantle. For the rest of his career he was a utility infielder, gaining notoriety again only when he and teammate Gene Conley disappeared from the team bus on the way from Yankee Stadium to Newark Airport in July 1962. The team bus was stuck in traffic in the Bronx, and Conley needed to find a bathroom. Green went with him, and the pair reportedly went on a Manhattan spending spree that ended with Conley deciding to fly to Israel to visit Bethlehem. Green caught up with the team the next day in Washington, and was fined $1,000. Conley was fined and suspended for three days.

But Green said the bizarre newspaper reports, including the one in the *Sporting News*, that called it "the most fantastic disappearance in the game's history," were pure fiction. "We went into a restaurant, hung around for a while in New York, had a few beers," he said. "For the record, it was really no big deal. Afterwards, I heard things that were amazing to me. The guys asked me, 'Were you and Conley going to Israel?' ... I said, 'I don't know,' and I didn't know. I still don't know."

Green ended his big-league career quietly with the frighteningly bad 1963 New York Mets. "Being the center of attention isn't really my style," he said.

Statistics: Pumpsie Green

Year	Team	Games	AB	Runs	Hits	2B	3B	HR	RBI	BA
1959	BOS-A	50	172	30	40	6	3	1	10	.233
1960	BOS	133	260	36	63	10	3	3	21	.242
1961	BOS	88	219	33	57	12	3	6	27	.260
1962	BOS	56	91	12	21	2	1	2	11	.231
1963	NY-N	17	54	8	15	1	2	1	5	.278
Totals										
5 Years		344	796	119	196	31	12	13	74	.246

Alvin Neil "Al" Jackson

Pitcher. Batted left. Threw left. 5'10", 169 lbs. Born 12/25/35, Waco, Texas.

Al Jackson had the heart of a winner. Unfortunately, he too often wore a loser's uniform.

A smallish left-hander, Jackson did not have an overpowering fastball, so he changed speeds, picked his spots, and tried to stay one step ahead of the hitters. "You can have all the stuff in the world," he said. "You still gotta have a thought in your head or it don't mean anything."

What he did not have was luck. In 1962 he was third in the league with four shutouts — the Mets' only four shutouts — and yet went 8-20. In 1966, probably his finest season, Jackson's ERA was 2.44, just 0.07 higher than teammate Bob Gibson's. Gibson went 21-12, Jackson 13-15.

Jackson once pitched a six-hitter over 15 innings, throwing 215 pitches, only to lose to the Phillies 3–1 on a Marv Throneberry error. Still, his attitude never changed. "It wasn't a job well done because I lost," he said. "I'd rather give up ten runs and win." Phillie manager Gene Mauch knew how tough Jackson was. "I used to try to get on him, but he didn't react, and I said, 'Aw, the hell with it.' He's a gentleman and a great competitor." Giants scout Dutch Ruether agreed. "He's a bulldog. He'll fight you all the way."

The youngest of 13 children, Jackson was born on Christmas Day. One of nine boys, he recalled his mother always saying that she was bringing up a baseball team. "I heard her say it so often it was only natural for me to gravitate toward the sport." But in high school he was more famous for his play on the gridiron, and as quarterback at Waco's Moore High School in 1954 he was named Player of the Year in Texas.

He spent three semesters at Wiley College but then convinced his father he could make a better living in baseball and signed with the Pirates. Despite an outstanding minor league record — 18-9 with a 2.07 ERA, with Lincoln in 1958 and 15-4, 2.33, with Columbus in 1959 — Jackson never got a real shot with the Pirates. At one point he seriously considered quitting but was talked out of it by general manager Branch Rickey, Jr. Still, in seven years in the Pittsburgh organization he pitched in just 11 major league games. "Every fall they would say to me that I had the makings, but that I needed more seasoning," Jackson said.

He hoped to be taken by Houston in the 1961 expansion draft but was not too disappointed when the Mets took him. "I was delighted to go anywhere just to get away from Pittsburgh," he said. Jackson learned quickly how tough it would be to win with the worst team in the twentieth century. But his season included a one-hitter, and he was happy to be pitching. In 1962 he set a Mets record with 13 wins, and it was the second of five straight seasons in which he started at least 30 games a season.

Perhaps his greatest disappointment came in 1967 with the Cardinals. Jackson was a valuable spot starter and reliever but was the only regular member of the staff who did not pitch in the World Series against Boston.

When his playing days were over, Jackson became a pitching coach in the Mets minor league system before being promoted to jobs as pitching coach for the Red Sox and Orioles. He was not on Boston manager Don Zimmer's list of candidates for the job in 1976, but he got a strong recommendation from a reputable source, manager Whitey Herzog. "Take Al," Herzog said. "You'll never go wrong."

Statistics: Al Jackson

Year	Team	W	L	PCT	G	IP	H	BB	SO	ERA	SV
1959	PIT-N	0	0	.000	8	18	30	8	13	6.50	0
1961	PIT	1	0	1.000	3	23.2	20	4	15	3.42	0
1962	NY-N	8	20	.286	36	231.1	244	78	118	4.40	0
1963	NY	13	17	.433	37	227	237	84	142	3.96	1
1964	NY	11	16	.407	40	213.1	229	60	112	4.26	1
1965	NY	8	20	.286	37	205.1	217	61	120	4.34	1
1966	STL- N	13	15	.464	36	232.2	222	45	90	2.51	0
1967	STL	9	4	.692	38	107	117	29	43	3.95	1
1968	NY-N	3	7	.300	25	92.2	88	17	59	3.69	3
1969	NY/CIN-N	1	0	1.000	42	38.1	45	21	26	6.81	3
Totals											
10 Years		67	99	.404	302	1389.1	1449	407	738	3.98	10

Willie Lee McCovey

First base. Batted left. Threw left. 6'4", 215 lbs. Born 1/10/38, Mobile, Alabama. Hall of Fame, 1986.

One year after their "Baby Bull" first baseman Orlando Cepeda won the National League Rookie of the Year award, the Giants called down to the Pacific Coast League for another first baseman, who turned out to be even more awesome than Cepeda—Willie "Stretch" McCovey.

Hitting .349 with 20 home runs in half a season with Phoenix, McCovey was just as impressive with the Giants, who came within three games of overtaking Los Angeles and Milwaukee for the 1959 National League pennant. McCovey got his call to the majors on July 31 after Carl Hubbell saw McCovey in action in a doubleheader—a triple and a homer in the first game; a single, double, triple, and homer in the second.

In his first game with San Francisco, the 21-year-old rookie went four-for-four with two singles and two triples off Philadelphia's Robin Roberts. In his first six games, McCovey collected eight hits in 12 at-bats, scored nine runs, and drove in eight. He hit in 22 consecutive games, one shy of the major league record for a rookie. (The Phillies' Roberts put an end to the streak on September 11.)

The joke around the National League that season was that the only man who could stop McCovey was Giants manager Bill Rigney. With Cepeda hitting well over .300, Rigney's dilemma was whom to play at first base. To make room for McCovey's bat, Rigney tried last year's rookie sensation in the outfield and at third base, but Cepeda, the better first baseman of the two, grew dejected and began to slump. For a few games Rigney even decided to save McCovey for pinch-hitting duties only, and the rookie delivered, hitting safely in both his pinch-hit at-bats.

When the ballots were counted in the voting for the 1959 National League Rookie of the Year, McCovey was the unanimous choice. Not only had Giants first basemen won back-to-back rookie honors, but they joined Frank Robinson as the only players to win the award unanimously. (Vince Coleman also won by unanimous vote in 1985.)

McCovey came to the Giants by way of the team's famous tryout camp, run by Carl Hubbell, in Melbourne, Florida. He signed for the ridiculously low sum of $175 a month. But McCovey made up for that oversight 21 years later when he joined Reggie Jackson, Don Baylor, and Rollie Fingers, among others, in the first mass-market free-agent signing in history.

McCovey was the first true San Francisco Giants hero. Despite the accomplishments of Mays, Willie the outfielder was a transplant. McCovey was homegrown, having come up through the Giants system. Although his overall statistics do not measure up to those of Mays, few sluggers in history could match McCovey's sheer power or the awesome home-run streaks for which he was known. His 500-foot home run on September 16, 1966, is still believed to be the longest home run in the history of Candlestick Park. On April 27, 1969, McCovey hit three home runs in each game of a doubleheader sweep of the Houston Astros.

McCovey hit more home runs than any left-handed batter in National League history. He hit 18 grand slam homers, a National League record. His three pinch-hit grand slams equal the major league record. In 1969 he became the fourth player in All-Star game history to hit two home runs in a game. His two home runs in a single inning on June 27, 1977, made him the first player ever to accomplish that feat twice. (Andre Dawson was the next, in 1985.)

Despite his 521 home runs, McCovey insists that the hardest ball he ever hit was one that never made it out of the infield. The Yankees took a 1–0 lead into the bottom of the ninth inning of the seventh game of the 1962 World Series. McCovey came to bat with runners on second and third and two out.

McCovey owned Yankees pitcher Ralph Terry in the Series. In Game 2 he had hit a tape measure shot into the light standards off Terry, and in the third inning of Game 7 he had tripled, but the Giants left him stranded. This was the same Ralph Terry who had given up Bill Mazeroski's World Series–winning home run in the same situation two years before. But New York manager Casey Stengel stuck with his 23-game winner.

McCovey hit Terry's first pitch far and deep down the right field line, but foul. He took the next pitch for a strike, then smashed a vicious liner at Yankees second baseman Bobby Richardson to end the Series.

The 1969 National League Most Valuable Player, McCovey was elected to the Hall of Fame on the first ballot.

Statistics: Willie McCovey

Year	Team	Games	AB	Runs	Hits	2B	3B	HR	RBI	BA
1959	SF-N	52	192	32	68	9	5	13	38	.354
1960	SF	101	260	37	62	15	3	13	51	.238
1961	SF	106	328	59	89	12	3	18	50	.271
1962	SF	91	229	41	67	6	1	20	54	.293
1963	SF	152	564	103	158	19	5	44*	102	.280
1964	SF	130	364	55	80	14	1	18	54	.220
1965	SF	160	540	93	149	17	4	39	92	.276
1966	SF	150	502	85	148	26	6	36	96	.295
1967	SF	135	456	73	126	17	4	31	91	.276
1968	SF	148	523	81	153	16	4	36*	105*	.293
1969	SF	149	491	101	157	26	2	45*	126*	.320
1970	SF	152	495	98	143	39	2	39	126	.289
1971	SF	105	329	45	91	13	0	18	70	.277
1972	SF	81	263	30	56	8	0	14	35	.213
1973	SF	130	383	52	102	14	3	29	75	.266
1974	SD-N	128	344	53	87	19	1	22	63	.253
1975	SD	122	413	43	104	17	0	23	68	.252
1976	SD/OAK-A	82	226	20	46	9	0	7	36	.204
1977	SF-N	141	478	54	134	21	0	28	86	.280
1978	SF	108	351	32	80	19	2	12	64	.228
1979	SF	117	353	34	88	9	0	15	57	.249
1980	SF	48	113	8	23	8	0	1	16	.204
Totals										
22 Years		2588	8197	1229	2211	353	46	521	1555	.270
League Championship Series										
1971	SF-N	4	14	2	6	0	0	2	6	.429
World Series										
1962	SF-N	14	15	2	3	0	1	1	1	.200

*League leader.

Arthur Lee Maye

Outfield. Batted left. Threw right. 6'2", 190 lbs. Born 12/11/34, Tuscaloosa, Alabama.

"I've seen what it takes to make the big leagues," Lee Maye once said. "I know I can play there. I wouldn't be playing if I weren't sure."

Baseball had come a long way since Jackie Robinson broke the color barrier 12 years earlier. A black player with Maye's live bat could confidently expect to progress through the minor league ranks and make the major leagues in a reasonable time. This is precisely what Maye did, hitting .330 with 99 RBIs for Evansville in 1956, .264 with Jacksonville in 1957, and .318 with 15 home runs and 78 RBIs for Austin in 1958.

With the Braves and Dodgers locked in a tight pennant race, Maye was called up to Milwaukee with about two months left in the 1959 season. Having hit .340 with 17 home runs and 80 RBIs with Louisville that season, Maye was asked to produce the same late-season lightning that Bob Hazle had when Milwaukee won their its of back-to-back pennants in 1957. Maye filled in for the slumping Wes Covington in left field and hit .300 as the Braves tied the Dodgers for the National League pennant, then lost to Los Angeles in a two-game playoff.

A line-drive hitter, Maye was platooned by the Braves over the next four seasons. By the time he was a regular with Milwaukee, however, hitting .304 and leading the league in doubles in 1964, the Braves had Mack Jones in the wings. Jones was four years younger than Maye and based on his 1965 numbers, had three times the power.

Traded to Houston 15 games into the 1965 season, Maye resumed his platoon work with the Astros in their new indoor baseball palace, the Astrodome. Then, after five seasons with three other clubs, Maye retired and returned full-time to his other love — singing.

Maye was the lead vocalist in his own singing group. Arthur Lee Maye and the Crowns cut more than a dozen records, including the semihit "Truly."

Statistics: Lee Maye

Year	Team	Games	AB	Runs	Hits	2B	3B	HR	RBI	BA
1959	MIL-N	51	140	17	42	5	1	4	16	.300
1960	MIL	41	83	14	25	6	0	0	2	.301
1961	MIL	110	373	68	101	11	5	14	41	.271
1962	MIL	99	349	40	85	10	0	10	41	.244
1963	MIL	124	442	67	120	22	7	11	34	.271
1964	MIL	153	588	96	179	44*	5	10	74	.304
1965	MIL/									
	HOU-N	123	468	46	120	19	7	5	43	.256

Year	Team	Games	AB	Runs	Hits	2B	3B	HR	RBI	BA
1966	HOU	115	358	38	103	12	4	9	36	.288
1967	CLE-A	115	297	43	77	20	4	9	27	.259
1968	CLE	109	299	20	84	13	2	4	26	.281
1969	CLE/									
	WAS-A	114	346	50	96	14	3	10	41	.277
1970	WAS/CHI-A/									
	WAS	102	261	28	68	12	1	7	31	.261
1971	CHI	32	44	6	9	2	0	1	7	.205
Totals										
13 Years		1288	4048	533	1109	190	39	94	419	.274

*League leader.

Jose Antonio Pagan

**Shortstop, third base. Batted right. Threw right. 5'9",
170 lbs. Born 5/5/35, Barceloneta, Puerto Rico.**

Jose Pagan began his professional baseball career in his native Puerto Rico. Heralded as a slick-fielding shortstop, he was signed to a Giants minor league contract, then moved up through the system, joining San Francisco late in the 1959 season. After splitting the 1960 season between the Giants and the minors, Pagan became the Giants' regular shortstop in 1961, a position he held for the next four years.

The Giants' starting shortstop in every game in 1962, Pagan led all National League shortstops in fielding that year. His .368 batting average in the 1962 seven-game World Series was the highest among both Yankees and Giants regulars. When Pagan dropped a surprise bunt in the second inning of Game 1, Willie Mays scored, ending Whitey Ford's Series-record scoreless-innings streak at 33⅓.

Traded to the Pittsburgh Pirates for Dick Schofield in May 1965, Pagan turned his career in a different direction, becoming one of the most valuable utility players in the major leagues for the next nine years. When he retired in 1973, Pagan had played every position except pitcher.

In addition to his fielding versatility, Pagan became known as a productive pinch-hitter. His league-leading 19 pinch-hits in 1969 came within one of the National League record. His .452 pinch-hitting batting average that season included pinch-hit home runs on consecutive at-bats, tying a major league record.

Pagan drove in the winning run in the eighth inning of Game 7 of the 1971 World Series.

Statistics: Jose Pagan

Year	Team	Games	AB	Runs	Hits	2B	3B	HR	RBI	BA
1959	SF-N	31	46	7	8	1	0	0	1	.174
1960	SF	18	49	8	14	2	2	0	2	.286
1961	SF	134	434	38	110	15	2	5	46	.253
1962	SF	164	580	73	150	25	6	7	57	.259
1963	SF	148	483	46	113	12	1	6	39	.234
1964	SF	134	367	33	82	10	1	1	28	.223
1965	SF/PIT-N	68	121	16	26	5	0	0	6	.215
1966	PIT	109	368	44	97	15	6	4	54	.264
1967	PIT	81	211	17	61	6	2	1	19	.289
1968	PIT	80	163	24	36	7	1	4	21	.221
1969	PIT	108	274	29	78	11	4	9	42	.285
1970	PIT	95	230	21	61	14	1	7	29	.265
1971	PIT	57	158	16	38	1	0	5	15	.241
1972	PIT	53	127	11	32	9	0	3	8	.252
1973	PHI-N	46	78	4	16	5	0	0	5	.205
Totals										
15 Years		1326	3689	387	922	138	26	52	372	.250
League Championship Series										
1970	PIT-N	1	3	0	1	0	0	0	0	.333
1971	PIT	1	1	0	0	0	0	0	0	.000
Totals										
2 Years		2	4	0	1	0	0	0	0	.250
World Series										
1962	SF-N	7	19	2	7	0	0	1	2	.368
1971	PIT-N	4	15	0	4	2	0	0	2	.267
Totals										
2 Years		11	34	2	11	2	0	1	4	.324

James Arthur "Jim" Proctor

Pitcher. Threw right. Batted right. 6', 165 lbs. Born 9/9/35, Brandywine, Maryland.

After leading his Maryland State College baseball team to a CIAA championship in 1954, Jim Proctor signed with the Indianapolis Clowns of the Negro American League in 1955. Over the next five seasons Proctor pitched for various teams in the Detroit Tigers' minor league system.

Proctor was 15-5 with a league-leading 2.19 ERA with Class AA Knoxville of the Southern League when he was called up to the Tigers in September 1959.

He started his only major league game on the final Saturday of the season against Early Wynn and the American League champion White Sox. The veteran Wynn won his twenty-second game of the year that afternoon, while rookie Proctor gave up four runs on four hits and two walks in ⅔ of an inning and never pitched in the majors again.

Statistics: Jim Proctor

Year	Team	W	L	PCT	G	IP	H	BB	SO	ERA	SV
1959	DET-A	0	1	.000	2	2.2	8	3	0	16.88	0

Richard James "Dick" Ricketts

Pitcher. Threw left. Batted right. 6'7", 215 lbs. Born 12/4/33, Pottstown, Pennsylvania.

A two-time All-American basketball player at Duquesne University, Dick Ricketts was one of the first two-sport professionals of the postintegration era. At 6'7", Ricketts once scored 23 points in the second half of a Holiday Festival Tournament in Madison Square Garden.

Drafted by the St. Louis Hawks of the National Basketball Association in 1955, Ricketts later played for the Rochester (later Cincinnati) Royals.

As a baseball player, Ricketts made a name for himself pitching to his brother Dave (who caught with the Cardinals and Pirates from 1963 to 1970) in American Legion ball. A Pennsylvania Legion Player of the Year, Ricketts once struck out 21 batters in one game.

Ricketts fulfilled the baseball half of his dual career by pitching in the lower minors and earning a tryout with the Class AAA Rochester Red Wings in 1957. In his first month of International League play, Ricketts posted a 4-1 record, including two shutouts and a 2.03 ERA. He won 15 games and lost 13 with Rochester in 1958, leading Richmond manager Eddie Lopat to say, "Ricketts has the best fastball in the International League."

Ricketts reported to the St. Louis Cardinals spring-training camp in 1959 but was optioned back to Rochester. Then, on June 5, after giving up the longest home run in the history of Havana's Gran Stadium, a 532-foot shot by one Rogelio Alvarez, Ricketts was called up to St. Louis where he went 1-6 and left the domain of baseball to his brother.

Statistics: Dick Ricketts

Year	Team	W	L	PCT	G	IP	H	BB	SO	ERA	SV
1959	STL-N	1	6	.143	12	55.2	68	30	25	5.82	0

Billy Leo Williams

Outfield. Batted left. Threw right. 6'1", 175 lbs. Born 6/15/38, Whistler, Alabama. Hall of Fame, 1987.

Billy Williams was one of the great transitional black ballplayers. His career in organized baseball spanned the end of the Jackie Robinson–Larry Doby era and carried into Reggie Jackson's prime and Dave Winfield's first impressions.

Like Satchel Paige, Monte Irvin, Willie Mays, Henry Aaron, and Willie McCovey before him, Billy Williams came out of Alabama in the 1950s and wound up enshrined in the Baseball Hall of Fame in Cooperstown, New York.

Unlike his fellow Alabamans, however, Williams never played on a pennant-winning team. In fact, Williams had to change leagues in his seventeenth major league season before he was able to appreciate post-season competition firsthand. Prior to 1975 with Oakland, Williams labored 16 years for the terminally woebegone Chicago Cubs, who, when they were not playing their characteristic sub-.500 ball, reaped the benefits of the early expansion years, finishing a distant second with noticeable frequency. In their only dogfight pennant race, the Cubs blew a lead of 9½ games in August to the Miracle Mets of 1969.

It was as if the manna that had fallen upon Leo Durocher in 1951 amid one of those other New York miracles, had gone rancid, and Leo was up to his ears in it. But that was not Billy Williams's fault. He hit .304 in the month of September, 11 points above his season average. But Williams could not do it alone — not even with Ernie Banks and Ron Santo in the same lineup. In 1965 each of the three drove in 101 or more runs, and the Cubs still finished eighth.

The first of a new generation of power hitters, Williams's fluid swing produced some memorable hitting feats. Over back-to-back games against the Mets in 1968, Williams hit five home runs to tie a major league record. The next year he tied another major league record by hitting four straight doubles in an 11–3 win over the Phillies. In 1972, when he was named Major League Player of the Year by the *Sporting News*, Williams collected eight straight hits in a doubleheader against the Houston Astros.

But most impressive in Williams's career was his consistency. From his Rookie-of-the-Year season in 1961 until he retired in 1976, Williams averaged 168 hits, 27 home runs, and 92 RBIs. He set a National League record (since broken by Pete Rose) with 600 or more plate appearances for nine straight seasons. In compiling such numbers, Williams set a National League record by playing in 1,117 consecutive games, surpassing Ernie Banks and Stan Musial, among others. (Williams's record was broken by Steve Garvey, whose string of 1,207 games was snapped in 1983.)

Perhaps even more remarkable about Williams's streak, however, was that he ended it voluntarily. On September 3, 1970, Williams needed a rest and took a day off. And he no doubt needed it, having led the National League that year with 205 hits, including 42 homers, good for a .322 average.

A six-time National League All-Star, Williams was given his unconditional release by the Oakland Athletics in November 1976. He later coached with the Athletics and the Cubs.

Statistics: Billy Williams

Year	Team	Games	AB	Runs	Hits	2B	3B	HR	RBI	BA
1959	CHI-N	18	33	0	5	0	1	0	2	.152
1960	CHI	12	47	4	13	0	2	2	7	.277
1961	CHI	146	529	75	147	20	7	25	86	.278
1962	CHI	159	618	94	184	22	8	22	91	.298
1963	CHI	161	612	87	175	36	9	25	95	.286
1964	CHI	162	645	100	201	39	2	33	98	.312
1965	CHI	164	645	115	203	39	6	34	108	.315
1966	CHI	162	648	100	179	23	5	29	91	.276
1967	CHI	162	634	92	176	21	12	28	84	.278
1968	CHI	163	642	91	185	30	8	30	98	.288
1969	CHI	163	642	103	188	33	10	21	95	.293
1970	CHI	161	636	137*	205*	34	4	42	129	.322
1971	CHI	157	594	86	179	27	5	28	93	.301
1972	CHI	150	574	95	191	34	6	37	122	.333*
1973	CHI	156	576	72	166	22	2	20	86	.288
1974	CHI	117	404	55	113	22	0	16	68	.280
1975	OAK-A	155	520	68	127	20	1	23	81	.244
1976	OAK	120	351	36	74	12	0	11	41	.211
Totals										
18 Years		2488	9350	1410	2711	434	88	426	1475	.290

League Championship Series

Year	Team	Games	AB	Runs	Hits	2B	3B	HR	RBI	BA
1975	OAK-A	3	8	0	0	0	0	0	0	.000

*League leader.

Maurice Morning "Maury" Wills

Shortstop. Batted both. Threw right. 5'11", 170 lbs.
Born 10/2/32, Washington, D.C.

"Base-stealing has fallen into limbo," said Ty Cobb shortly before his death in 1961, "and the thrills that go with it are no more. But it'll return."

In 1915, Cobb had stolen 96 bases, a major league record that stood for nearly half a century. Understandably, Cobb was nostalgic for the running game he had so ruthlessly perfected. America was caught up in the power game, particularly the assault on Babe Ruth's record 60 homers in one season by Yankee sluggers Roger Maris and Mickey Mantle. Meanwhile, Maury Wills was quietly moving in on his second straight National League stolen base title with a modest 35 thefts, 15 fewer than in 1960.

"It's impossible to steal more than sixty bases in a season without running foolishly," said Wills in 1962. But by the end of the season, he had swiped a major league record 104 bases. Not only had Wills brought back the "thrills that go with" the stolen base; he was packing stadiums throughout the National League the way only sluggers had. Wills's running was anything but foolish as he led the Dodgers to a dead-heat finish with the Giants, collecting his 103rd and 104th steals in a 6–4 playoff-finale loss to San Francisco on October 3. The Dodgers set a major league attendance record of 2,766,184 in 1962, with Wills the league's Most Valuable Player.

Wills took Robinson's daring on the bases and turned it into a science. He studied and learned about pitchers, their pickoff moves, and their moves to the plate. "When I make a move on the bases," he said, "I think I'm going to be safe every time. It takes a perfect throw to get me." At 5'11" and 170 pounds, Wills was not a burly former football player like Robinson, and he was not the maniacal slasher that Cobb was. He was simply unstoppable.

In 1962 Wills was caught stealing just 10 times, establishing a major league record .889 stolen-base percentage. He led the National League in stolen bases for six straight years, 1960–1965.

On September 7, 1962, he stole a record four bases in one game against the Pirates. That same season, in his hometown, in the first All-Star game, his running astounded a capacity crowd, including President John F. Kennedy, in brand-new D.C. Stadium. Pinch-running for 41-year-old Stan Musial, Wills promptly stole second, then scored on Dick Groat's single. Two innings later he singled, moved to third on Jim Davenport's weak single to short left as Rocky Colavito threw behind him into second, then scored on a foul out to right.

Some teams resorted to watering down the infield to slow Wills down. It did not work. Joe Torre of the Braves actually fell on first base on pickoff plays to prevent Wills from returning safely to the base. But when Wills came in spike-high, Torre gave up the illegal tack.

Wills was such an intimidating force on the bases that he was effective even when he did not steal. Against the Yankees in the 1963 World Series, for example, Wills stole only one base, but that led to all the runs in Game 2 and was possibly the turning point of the series. Leading off against Al Downing, Wills singled, then, taking an outrageously long lead from first base, took off for second before Al Downing even began his motion to the plate. Downing made his move to first, but first baseman Joe Pepitone's throw pulled shortstop Tony Kubek off the bag. Junior Gilliam then followed with a single to right. Wills took a long turn around third, drawing a throw, which allowed Gilliam to advance to second. A threat to steal home, Wills danced off third. Downing, fearful of what Wills could do, threw a fastball to Willie Davis, who doubled off the right-field fence. The Dodgers had all the runs they needed. The Yanks were rattled and never recovered.

That Wills made it to the majors is almost as remarkable as what he accomplished once he got there. He started his career in organized ball in 1951, making $150 a month. He then kicked around the minors for eight seasons, apparently content to play without learning or improving. Wills played every position in the minors, including pitcher and catcher.

Wills's career turned around in 1958. Bobby Bragan, managing the Dodgers' Spokane farm team, turned Wills into a switch-hitter. A natural right-handed hitter, Wills finished the season at .253, then went to Venezuela to work on hitting from the left side. He started out the 1959 season on a tear and was hitting .313 when he was called up to the Dodgers in June.

Still, Wills was basically a nobody. (The Topps Baseball Card Company would not sign him to a contract, the first — and only — time the company passed on anyone.) In 1960, when he could not seem to find his batting eye, the Dodgers assigned Pete Reiser to work with Wills. Reiser, a .295 lifetime hitter and a two-time NL base-stealing champ with the Dodgers in the 1940s, completed what Bragan had started two years before. According to Wills, Reiser "gave me the inner conceit every athlete needs if he hopes to be great."

Wills was a spirited competitor who excelled in the clutch. In the 1966 All-Star game at Busch Stadium in St. Louis, he drove in the winning run in the bottom of the tenth inning. In Sandy Koufax's 7–0 shutout of the Twins in Game 5 of the 1965 World Series, Wills tied a Series record by hitting four doubles. And while it took him 1,167 at-bats to hit his first home run in the majors, on May 30, 1962, he became the seventh player in history to homer from both sides of the plate in one game. Twice a Gold Glove shortstop, he led National League shortstops in assists in 1965.

While he did not physically resemble Jackie Robinson, his independence was cut from the same cloth. On June 10, 1968, Wills, in mourning over the death of Robert Kennedy, refused to play in a game for the Pirates.

"I don't *play* baseball," he once said. "I *work* baseball. This is a business, and I'm in it for the money and so are the other players."

The father of Bump Wills, an infielder for the Texas Rangers and Chicago Cubs from 1977 to 1982, Wills became the third black manager in major league history when he replaced Darrell Evans as skipper of the Seattle Mariners in 1980. He managed Seattle for 24 games in 1981 and later managed in the Mexican League and worked as a television baseball analyst.

Statistics: Maury Wills

Year	Team	Games	AB	Runs	Hits	2B	3B	HR	RBI	BA
1959	LA-N	83	242	27	63	5	2	0	7	.260
1960	LA	148	516	75	152	15	2	0	27	.295
1961	LA	148	613*	105	173	12	10	1	31	.282
1962	LA	165	695*	130	208	13	10*	6	48	.299
1963	LA	134	527	83	159	19	3	0	34	.302
1964	LA	158	630	81	173	15	5	2	34	.275
1965	LA	158	650	92	186	14	7	0	33	.286
1966	LA	143	594	60	162	14	2	1	39	.273
1967	PIT-N	149	616	92	186	12	9	3	45	.302
1968	PIT	153	627	76	174	12	6	0	31	.278
1969	MON-N/									
	LA-N	151	623	80	171	10	8	4	47	.274
1970	LA	132	522	77	141	19	3	0	34	.270
1971	LA	149	601	73	169	14	3	3	44	.281
1972	LA	71	132	16	17	3	1	0	4	.129
Totals										
14 Years		1942	7588	1067	2134	177	71	20	458	.281
World Series										
1959	LA-N	6	20	2	5	0	0	0	1	.250
1963	LA	4	15	1	2	0	0	0	0	.133
1965	LA	7	30	3	11	3	0	0	3	.367
1966	LA	4	13	0	1	0	0	0	0	.077
Totals										
4 Years		21	78	6	19	3	0	0	4	.244

*League leader.

Earl Lawrence Wilson

Pitcher. Threw right. Batted right. 6'3", 216 lbs. Born 10/2/34, Ponchatoula, Louisiana.

Scouted and signed by Boston scout Tom Downey in 1953, Earl Wilson was the first black player in the Red Sox farm system since Piper Davis. Described by Downey as "a well-mannered colored boy, not too black, pleasant to talk to" with a "very good appearance" who "conducts himself as a gentleman," Wilson entered organized ball as a power-hitting catcher. In his first year in the Boston chain, however, he was spiked in his left hand while playing for the Class D Brisbee-Douglas club in the Arizona-Texas League. The gash was severe enough to prevent him from catching, but not from throwing.

When the team needed extra pitching, Wilson volunteered and won his first start 4–3, taking a three-hitter into the ninth inning. He kept pitching for the next 18 years.

Drafted into the marines in 1957, Wilson won 49 games and lost two pitching for his San Diego team during his two years of active duty. He was one of seven black players under contract with Red Sox minor league affiliates during spring training in 1959. But the team that broke camp was as white as it had ever been. When protestors marching outside Fenway Park and a commission on discrimination questioned the team's racial policies, management answered that Wilson, a better major league prospect than Pumpsie Green, would have made the club had he not lost two years to the marines.

Wilson opened the 1959 season with the Class AAA Minneapolis Millers, where he won nine straight games after losing his first decision. When he was called up to the Red Sox in midseason, Wilson had struck out 76 batters in 65 innings, given up just 16 earned runs, and was batting .371.

In his first major league start on August 31, Wilson gave up no hits to the Detroit Tigers in three innings, leaving with a 4–0 lead after giving up nine walks. Wilson spent the next two seasons shuttling between Boston and Minneapolis, finally making the Sox rotation in 1962. That year, on June 26, he became the first black pitcher to pitch a no-hitter in the American League, beating the Angels 2–0. That game was also the first shutout of his career. To sweeten the day, Wilson homered off Bo Belinsky, who had pitched a no-hitter of his own just six weeks earlier.

Plagued by wildness throughout his stay with the Red Sox, Wilson appeared to have mastered his control problems in the spring of 1966 when a racial incident all but ended his career in Boston. One evening Wilson and two white Red Sox pitchers, Dennis Bennett and Dave Morehead, visited a Lakeland, Florida, bar, the Cloud 9. The bartender refused to serve Wilson, telling him, "We don't serve niggers here." The three players left without further incident. Bennett later told reporters, "I don't think they knew we were ballplayers. To them we were just two white guys and a nigger."

Wilson chose not to make an issue of the occasion. He wanted to avoid any adverse publicity, but the press did not comply. Worse, in reporting the incident, newspapers emphasized the fact that Wilson and his teammates were drinking, as if they had no business doing so. Through the first two months of the season, Wilson could not shake the side effects of the publicity. When the Red Sox acquired two black players, pitcher John Wyatt and outfielder Jose Tartabull, on June 6, Wilson told his black roommate, Lenny Green, that there were now too many black players on the ball club. Although the remark was made half in jest, the next day Wilson and Joe Christopher were traded to the Tigers for Don Demeter, who in his brief career in Boston never equaled the number of home runs that Wilson hit for the Sox.

Wilson had reason to be bitter and he expressed it on the mound, winning